THE BEGINNING CONDUCTOR

McGRAW-HILL SERIES IN MUSIC

Atkisson   Basic Counterpoint
Chase   America's Music
Crocker   A History of Musical Style
Crocker and Basart   Listening to Music
Hood   The Ethnomusicologist
Lerner   Study Scores of Musical Styles
Marple   The Beginning Conductor
Ratner   Harmony: Structure and Style
Ratner   Music: The Listener's Art
Salzer and Schachter   Counterpoint in Composition
Sherman and Knight   Aural-Visual Perception of Music
Wagner   Band Scoring
Wagner   Orchestration: A Practical Handbook

The Beginning Conductor

HUGO D. MARPLE
Professor of Music
Texas Tech University

McGraw-Hill Book Company

New York   St. Louis   San Francisco   Düsseldorf   Johannesburg   Kuala Lumpur
London   Mexico   Montreal   New Delhi   Panama   Rio de Janeiro   Singapore
Sydney   Toronto

The Beginning Conductor

Library of Congress Catalog Card Number 73-174620

07-040456-9

1234567890EBEB798765432

This book was set in Theme by Allen-Wayne Technical
Corp., and printed and bound by Edwards Brothers, In-
corporated. The designer was Merrill Haber; the draw-
ings were done by Graphic Services, Inc. The editors
were Robert P. Rainier and Helen Greenberg. John A.
Sabella supervised production.

For my students
who were beginning conductors

Contents

Preface

This book is not intended to train the professional conductor. It does aim to assist the serious student of music who realizes that much of his professional career will consist of conducting amateurs, whether in public schools or church choirs, city choirs, city bands, or community orchestras. In addition, this book offers some assistance to the working conductor who has not felt confident with his baton technique or has lost some of the technique that he once possessed.

The material is presented in a format that will assist the student in rapid skill development. It proceeds step by step. Thus, the more subtle aspects of conducting (for example, in Chapters 14 and 15) are discussed only when the student can comprehend their usefulness and is technically capable of practicing them. Furthermore, the problems dealt with are similar to those a conductor might find in his early years of conducting. Illustrative pieces of music are drawn from repertoires nonprofessional groups are likely to perform. This practice serves two purposes: (1) it conveys points of technique to the student more effectively than would more advanced selections, and (2) it allows the student to study types of scores that he will be using when he begins work as an amateur conductor. Scores are presented in a variety of physical formats to give the student practice in dealing with different sizes of printed material.

The text is written for the general conductor, not for the specialist in choral or instrumental fields. As a music educator, I firmly believe that it is important to train young people to conduct both vocal and instrumental groups.

In today's high schools and communities, most amateur conductors will be expected to direct a choir with instrumental accompaniment; produce and conduct a stage production with instrumental accompaniment; conduct a band with vocal assistance; or conduct an orchestra with choral accompaniment. This text considers the student's broadest needs and approaches conducting as a skill that will help him meet all these challenges. I believe that a course in general conducting is most valuable for the beginning student. He can take special courses in band, choir, or orchestral conducting later.

Unlike many texts on conducting, this one helps the young conductor in learning to read and study a score in preparation for his conducting duties. To teach this skill at the same time that a baton technique is being developed is important. For this reason, score study is developed throughout the text, but particularly in Chapters 9 and 14.

I wish to thank those who have read the text and offered comments. Most of these have been students in my classes who, wishing to develop their own abilities to the fullest, have been sympathetic to my goal of trying to write a text that is most obviously directed to them. They have been understanding of my omissions, helpful with suggestions, and argumentative to the point of provoking changes.

HUGO D. MARPLE

THE BEGINNING CONDUCTOR

Introduction

Not many of us will be professional conductors. Yet, if we remain in the field of music, we will be conducting off and on for the remainder of our lives. I guess it is the realization of this, plus the hope of attaining a position before a respectable group, that spurs most amateurs and young people to approach the study of conducting with such vigor and enthusiasm.

Conducting is a field where great men have proved themselves so proficient that many stories are told about the memorizing ability of certain conductors, their capacity to study a new score, or their musical idiosyncrasies. Even though the field of conducting seems secure to us today, the podium, the stick, and the gesture are comparatively recent additions.

True, there was recorded some type of conducting as early as the thirteenth century, along with unison singing of plain chant to assist the singers in reading the pitches of the notes and, at the same time, to bring a sense of unanimity to the rhythm. Later, when the figured bass concept was prevalent (1600–1750), the master at the harpsichord led the group by nods of the head, a momentary use of one hand, or playing repeated bass notes. So that the musicians could feel and understand the tempo, it is recorded that there were times when even Bach played several measures of loud chords on the harpsichord. When larger groups were making their way upon the musical scene (1740–1775), musicians who had been trained to perform in small groups, using figured bass and a leader seated at the harpsichord, were most reluctant to give up the independence of this system for what appeared to them to be the more rigid system of the conductor.

But the master at the keyboard did not disappear at once. For about two hundred years the keyboard had been the directional position, and once the keyboard lost its primary place it took about fifty years to move from the master seated at the keyboard to the standing conductor. Generally during this time a standing conductor was not used; instead a first violinist directed as he played. For some of these years and for special occasions, the custom was to use double direction: a man at the keyboard along with the first violinist. Even as late as 1829, when Mendelssohn made his first trip to London to conduct his C major Symphony, he assisted the concert master by sitting at the piano and "conducting," although no piano is called for in the score. It was quite common to permit the concert master to set the tempi and indicate cues for the violins as best he could while still playing from the first desk. It is from this history that we still give considerable honor and consideration to the concert master.

History tells of one performance of Beethoven's Ninth Symphony where the concert master, Schuppanzigh, led the strings, Michael Umpauf directed from the piano, and Beethoven was present to set the correct tempi. What a situation, considering today's role for the single conductor! The piano's presence did not mean that it was even played. There was a time when the violinists were most scornful of the keyboard director because he had nothing to play, yet was expected to sit at the instrument and conduct when the concert master was not leading. Little by little the music had changed; no longer was the ensemble dependent upon the person at the keyboard to furnish the chordal bond of holding the harmony and rhythm together, yet he continued to retain some authority.

Obviously, the man at the keyboard either had to change his status or get out of the business. It was at this point that the baton came into prominence. Because the first violinist had his bow, which he could wave about and with which he could set tempi or attract attention, one can imagine that the keyboard musician accepted the baton somewhat in self-defense. Compared to this, the hand surely did not seem adequate, particularly if the person were seated.

Earlier there had been times when even the seated keyboard player and conductor had resorted to a baton in order to direct the music. You are probably familiar with the often-told story of the large baton used by Lully and how he pounded the floor with it to set the tempo. One time (1687), hitting his foot, he contracted blood poisoning which was responsible for his death. Other keyboard men also used batons in the early days of the eighteenth century. One story tells of a large baton that was narrowed in the center so that the conductor could more easily put his hand around it. Surely the noise of floor pounding and the size of these large wooden sticks must have led to a demand on the part of musicians and listeners for something more subtle and discreet.

The baton was destined to become smaller, and by 1820 Spohr tells in his autobiography how amazed the men of the London Philharmonic were when he first pulled a "little stick" from his pocket and began to move it before them. At first they refused to play, for there was apparently a stigma to playing under a baton. But he persuaded them to try it, and he relates

that they were soon convinced that it was a most useful and successful tool. Another early baton was made of hide and filled with hair. The player at the first desk of violins or at the harpsichord had been known from time to time as a master, director, or leader, but when the man finally stood before the group with a baton in his hand he became known as a conductor.

It was the composers of the late 1700s to whom we owe our gratitude for indirectly promoting the art of conducting. They were not only men who wrote music but usually conductors as well. Requiring that all singers and the instrumentalists in the pit follow precisely what was on the printed page, Gluck permitted no improvisation, particularly in his later operas (1761–1787). One can see how this would lead to a request for precision that was not possible from the bench or the first desk. Haydn, in his middle period (ca. 1790), quit writing for harpsichord in the orchestra and, in its place, began using more winds, which tended to force the man off the keyboard bench onto the podium. But it was Weber (1786–1816) who truly led the way to establishing a feeling that the conductor was a man of many talents and one who should know the music in all its aspects. Weber was a virtuoso pianist, a writer, a critic, and a poet. He chose the singers for his operas and the musicians for the pit, changed the seating of the orchestra, held sectional rehearsals, wrote program notes, directed the stage business for the opera, and wrote the music. Why should he not conduct it?

By the middle of the nineteenth century the conductor was on the podium with baton in hand. Famous conductors were often composers. One great conductor of the period was Mendelssohn, who, among other noted accomplishments, helped restore the music of Bach from an almost forgotten status. Berlioz (1803–1869), Liszt (1811–1885), and Wagner (1813–1883) all were noted composers; moreover, they could have been in their own day more noted as conductors, because they were known for conducting a large repertoire as well as their own works. It was in the latter half of the nineteenth century when the conductor who was not a composer came into prominence. Many times these men were players from an orchestra and had earned the respect of the men about them. Only recently have we met the virtuoso conductor who spends most of his time training to become a conductor and not a professional composer or performer.

If we are honest, I suspect we look at the conductor as a man with a sense of power. It is he who tells us, who leads us, to whom we have deferred since we first began to play or sing in school organizations. We too wish for that respect from others. Let us consider the responsibilities that go with the position. We should not be involved with the superficial aspects of conducting. Rather, our primary concern should be only those qualities that will bring to performers and listeners something that they could not obtain for themselves.

When you conduct, you must realize that conducting embraces many areas that will not be studied in a conducting course or be discussed in this book. Such things as sight-reading, orchestration, music theory, and human relations are all part of the conductor's work and his approach to the performance and his performers. But these are not within our bailiwick. Here we deal almost entirely with the manual training and a particular approach to musical problems that is necessary for you in order to make better use of the other skills that you may have learned in other classes. In addition to the text material, you should study the Appendixes. They contain music terms, percussion and instrumental terms, bowings, and tempo indications. Many of these you may recognize, since they are used consistently by conductors. Hence, you should make them a part of your working vocabulary.

Three approaches are open to the conductor: imitation, speech, and gesture. Not often do we find that we can do much with imitation. There are times when you can sing a phrase for the choir or band that will assist in explaining the interpretation to the group, and there are times in the conducting of the amateur group when you may wish to play your instrument for them. But usually this is not the role for the conductor, and it surely is not the role for the conductor during the performance.

Most amateur conductors rely too heavily upon speech. If we have poor techniques in conducting, we overcome them with talking. Many conductors talk too much in rehearsal. For best results, use speech sparingly, since you cannot take this item with you to the performance.

The last approach is truly the one that comes to the conductor most naturally, and from the gesture he should be able to convey most of the information that is necessary for rehearsal and concert. At first, you may feel that the gesture is the weakest of the three, but if you do not provide gesture an opportunity to develop, it will probably remain weak. Given every opportunity to grow, it could become the best technique of the three for all situations. This is the approach we will take in this book.

So you come into conducting class with anticipation and join your teacher and classmates. They should be-come the instrument on which you perform. But they should supply you with very little in the way of music or tonal response. Strange as it may seem at first, you are better off without much musical response in the class. It is too easy for your classmates to play or sing to assist you; too easy to follow the record or the piano, never really leading, never really building a technique to say those things that need be said with conducting; too easy to hear in the room those sounds that should be heard in the head, so that you never learn to imagine the score. Furthermore, good conductors, like good composers, hear within their minds what they see in the score before them.

Your teacher will do several things for you, but some things he cannot do. He cannot demand that you practice enough so that your technique will be secure. Most students do not understand that statement, for they believe that if they can move the hands around in front of them, they are secure. Security comes from experience in learning to use a score, learning to hear with your mind, and being able to express yourself through gesture without giving thought to it at the precise moment it is needed in rehearsal or performance.

Your teacher will be able to:

Assist you with the fundamental motions so that you will avoid some common errors and will not appear clumsy.

Offer suggestions so that the fundamentals will be developed into a style that is meaningful, expressive, and personal.

Help you to understand what your conducting is really asking the players or singers to do. If this is not what you intend, you can develop other approaches so that you do not expect too much from the wrong gestures.

Give you a sense of security with the gesture as being the best means of communication to your performers so that you will rely less upon speech and imitation.

As a conductor, your job will be to:

Establish the tempo, keep it, alter it if required, or correct it.

Assist the performers in hearing the harmony and understanding the form of the composition.

Assist those performers who may need technical or pitch assistance.

Indicate the expressiveness of the composition.

I mentioned that your teacher will assist you with a personal style of conducting. Many young people believe this to mean that they have to do something obviously different, strangely temperamental or erratic. Nothing is further from the truth. You will develop your own style provided you do not purposely set out to imitate some other person. You do not have to do something different with the patterns or the technique. Almost without thinking about it, you will develop a different "look" from that of any other person in your class. This will be because of your height, your weight, your arm size, and your own personality. Do not go out of your way to develop differences. Understand that for the first several weeks you may appear more similar to others than you thought, but your own podium personality will develop almost automatically as you move into the more advanced aspects of your technique in the latter part of the course. The suggestions and corrections made by your teacher will not hinder this in any way.

You probably have seen a number of famous conductors with their ensembles. Do not try to imitate them; be yourself. Many of the conductors with large groups are often very much aware that they are on display before the American audience, and they rely too much upon exhibitionism. Fritz Reiner, conductor at the Metropolitan Opera House and with the Pittsburgh and Chicago Symphonies, had a most in-conspicuous technique. So did Pierre Monteux, long associated with the San Francisco orchestra, and both of these men had the complete respect of their orchestra at all times. Because in the long run it is most respected, aim for a simple and easily understood technique, for you will usually be working with the amateur performer who needs you at your best and least complicated.

This text is designed to serve you in one of two ways. It may be a guide for you while you work with a formal class; or it may be used as a self-instruction manual wherein you teach yourself by reading the written material and practice the patterns, exercises, and music examples. If the latter method is used, check with a teacher of conducting after each series of chapters to gain valuable personal advice. Two items will always assist your development. Practice regularly before a mirror and, if possible, use your school closed-circuit TV. Video tapes are invaluable in the learning process.

Finally, you must understand the music that you are conducting and express yourself in and through it. The rules we establish here can only assist; they cannot be all. You must project your own personality from the podium through the technique you will acquire. The better the technique, the more you will say with the baton, and the easier you will say it for all to comprehend. This, in the end, is what we seek.

1

Auxiliaries

Most conducting books begin immediately with a discussion of beat patterns. Important as these patterns are, two elements of conducting should be presented beforehand. The first of these is the auxiliaries (supplementary but not necessarily subordinate) that a conductor may use to assist his performance and position. Not every person may wish to use each of these at all times, but they warrant attention.

A list of auxiliaries includes the following:

Podium

Risers

Music stand

Conducting chair

Score

Appearance

Stance

Baton (See Chapter 2)

PODIUM

The adequate and well-proportioned podium will considerably aid the amateur conductor. It is important that he feel at home on the podium and with the podium. For this reason many professional conductors have a personal podium and carry it from place to place. Many times the amateur might feel this to be an affectation, considering any podium satisfactory, whether it be that of the conductor in whose school he might visit or that of a conductor who preceded him in a position.

These sentiments, although common and understandable, will not always result in the best performance or the best appearance. A conductor will find as he moves from podium to podium that each one seems to take on different aspects and to bring a different feel to the conductor's performance. On the one hand, if the person is not tall, he should use a podium that will give a little more height to his stance so that he will appear to be a person of average height. If the podium is too short, the players will find that the conductor is tucked between other performers and not easily seen. The balance between the seated performers and the conductor is the guide that should be the controlling element in seeking podium and conductor height.

On the other hand, if the conductor is a tall person, the podium should not be as high as the average podium so that a balance between players and conductor will be maintained; moveover, the conductor who stands too high above his players will find that they will not be able to follow him as carefully as they could if his height were closer to their line of vision. Short or tall, the conductor can lose effectiveness in a situation owing to an inadequate podium.

Other physical aspects of the podium will also affect the performance. If a conductor is used to a well-built podium and works from one that is not well constructed, too much of his attention will be devoted to the podium rather than the music. A conductor used to a large podium will focus his attention upon the inadequate size of a small one. If the podium is too high or higher than one used during rehearsals, the conductor will find that he feels too far removed from his performers to do his best work, and the performers will also react in this manner. Using a podium of a different height from that generally used will cause the conductor to compensate by lifting his arms too high, only to find that his beat seems to become slow and his tempi seem to need urging forward. All these examples show that it is necessary, therefore, that a conductor be "at home" with the podium. This can be accomplished by conducting from a well-built, properly sized podium that has been used for a number of rehearsals.

In order to overcome these problems, the amateur conductor should check the podium available at his school or auditorium, and if it does not seem to satisfy his needs, he should have a podium built. Considering the average person and the typical group that an amateur will conduct, one should use a podium that is 8 inches above the floor with a top surface of 36 by 30 inches. This 8-inch rise will be adequate for the person who is about 5½ to 6 feet tall. Conductors who are taller should use a podium that is 3 inches shorter. This will assure that the conducting pattern area will not be too far above the line of vision for the average performer. If a misproportion occurs, it is common for the conductor to ask the performers to raise the stands to such heights that they often find it tightens the neck or the fingering arm. Unconsciously this will affect the performance.

A conductor shorter than 5½ feet should add 2 or 3 inches to the height of the podium. Here another problem arises. The average height of a step is 8 inches, and almost all of us are used to this height. It is an error to assume that we will become used to a higher step or that we should have to become used to it when mounting a podium. Therefore, if the podium is more than 8 inches from the floor, one should have an additional step with the podium. No step should be cut into the top surface of the podium or set into the podium. This is dangerous for the conductor, making him cautious of his footing while conducting. Any additional step should be to the side of the podium and movable so that it can be placed on any side called for by a particular situation.

Under some circumstances a lady's dress may demand that a 4-inch step be placed beside an 8-inch podium. In each case the step should be as high as the situation demands (4 or 8 inches), as long as the podium is long, and about 11 or 12 inches deep.

Commercial podiums may be purchased that are 8 or 16 inches high. The 16-inch podium is not intended for the unusually short person but rather for the average conductor facing an uncommonly large group or one making use of high risers. This often is the case when choral groups are placed in bleachers or a choir stands on risers behind an accompanying band or orchestra.

The recommended top surface of the podium may seem large to an amateur conductor, for it is likely that he is used to remaining almost motionless while on the podium. However, this text will advise that some foot movement be adopted. It is necessary, then, for the podium to be large enough so that the conductor will be able to move without feeling that his foot has reached the edge of the podium or that he may lose his footing. This is of particular concern when a podium is placed near the edge of a stage. The feeling that one might step off the podium to drop several feet into an orchestra pit or to an auditorium floor is enough to make any conductor remain too close to the front of a podium and much too stationary.

Recently I visited a high school and noticed that the conductor there used a podium that was about 8 inches high but only 15 by 18 inches in top measurement. Since the conductor was a large man with what appeared to be about size 12 shoes, he practically covered the top of the podium when he stood on it. It appeared that he would have difficulty moving the slightest bit and would surely feel uncomfortable on a stage or before an audience with this small surface. A podium with an adequate top surface will tend to overcome problems in the mind of the conductor and will give sufficient surface for what movement is necessary.

Some conductors will add to their security by placing a molding around the sides of the podium. This does not offer any problem when mounting the podium, but acts as a reminder that the foot has reached the edge. Some professional conductors, and usually those who are older, place a metal bar or two at the back of the podium next to the audience. These bars are often just above the waist so that it would be impossible for the conductor to step or fall backward from the podium. These extra safeguards are rarely found with amateur conductors but should be considered.

Lastly, consider the height of the performers in regard to the podium. Many amateur conductors will be conducting elementary school children. These boys and girls are usually not of adult height, and so a conductor should be as proportionately close to them with a conducting pattern as one would be with adults. The podium can easily regulate this situation. A short conductor working with children may find that an 8-inch podium would be correct. However, a taller person may find that a podium of less than normal height may be needed.

One might raise the question, "Is a podium necessary?" There are many amateur conductors who do not use a podium while working with school groups. Unless they are particularly tall, I feel they are at a disadvantage since a podium adds a measure of professional quality to any conducting situation. The decorum and discipline of a podium is obvious even to a beginning student player or singer.

When small children are involved, however, the average height of the group and the informality of the situation may argue in favor of no podium. This may also be true in some churches where the conductor wishes to remain as inconspicuous as possible.

USE OF RISERS

Risers have been a point of some debate with conductors for years. In orchestras, it is standard to use no risers for the violins, violas, cellos, and woodwinds. In some orchestras the brass, percussion, and string basses are placed on small risers usually 6 inches in height in two (or at the most, three) levels. Some professional orchestras do not place the string basses on risers since they are standing and are already above the other players. Recently, some of our famous orchestras have been using small 6-inch risers for back stands of violins and cellos. There is no rule here except that if a rise is used, it should be small.

Risers are standard with most choirs since they

place a premium upon the sound of the back rows of singers equaling the loudness and quality of the front rows. Most choral rooms contain risers that are deep enough to accommodate the chair with the singer standing in front of the chair. Most concert risers for choir are not deep but rise rather steeply. Many church choir stalls have risers built into the floor.

It is with the band and wind ensemble that most controversy occurs concerning risers. Some directors believe that each instrument of the band should be heard with its fullest and most complete sound. To do this, risers are a necessity, and they are built deeply enough to house a chair and stand for the player and high enough so that the instrument will rise above the player immediately below. Other directors believe that, like the orchestra, the sound mix is a most important element; the stronger instruments, such as the brasses, should be placed at the rear of the band so that they can blow through the band and therefore become blended and more mellow as they mix with the woodwinds. For these directors the flat floor is necessary as a performing surface, and the seating arrangement is of utmost importance. It was with a particular kind of balance in mind that some years ago the cornets of the band were moved from the right front to the rear of the ensemble, and instruments with less obvious tone colors were placed in the former position of the cornets.

Some conductors use risers for rehearsals but not for concerts. Their reasoning is that the educational situation demands that the conductor see and hear each person, and the concert situation demands a musical fusion and tonal blend.

Suggestion: Experiment with different riser placements and seating arrangements. This aids the control of sound, betters the hearing of conductor and performers, and may result in better acoustics for the group in a rehearsal or concert room.

Effect of Risers on the Podium

The use of risers could be a controlling factor for the height of the podium. When instrumental and vocal groups sit upon risers, a conductor may use a lower podium than if the risers were not present. One should not use a podium so low that tuba or bass-viol players in the back rows will be forced to lower the stands beyond a comfortable point in order to watch the conductor. However, the conductor should not raise the podium in order to aid those players if it causes difficulty with the players immediately under the baton. A conductor who is working in a rehearsal room with built-in risers will soon be able to estimate and judge this problem and should remedy it by changing to a different podium if necessary. Similarly, during a concert a change of 2 inches in the podium could make a difference in the comfort of the performers and the conductor.

Since choral groups generally use some type of riser during rehearsal as well as performance, vocal teachers believe that the conductor can well afford to stand on the floor. Where such a solution seems satisfactory for the choral group, it is rarely used by instrumental directors. A podium of small height for the choral group will be professionally correct for both the group and the conductor, enabling the group to know just when the conductor is preparing himself for conducting and when he is "off the podium." The podium should be used in rehearsal and not added just for concert appearances. If the conductor is using a music stand, a podium will enable his line of vision between music and singers to be better than if he were standing on the floor looking down at his music and up at performers.

As stated earlier, when conducting a large group, such as a massed choir, band, or orchestra, the conductor will find that he will have to use a higher podium than for a small group since the risers used supersede normal arrangements. Three items should dictate the height of the podium under these circumstances: the height of the top row of risers, the depth of the risers from the front to the rear, and the distance of the conductor from the group.

In regard to this last point, under usual conditions, a conductor will probably wish to stand no less than 6 to 8 feet from the center of his group. In festival situations where a choir may be seated in a section of bleachers with a flat front, the conductor may find it necessary to place his podium quite a distance from the center in order to be seen from the end of each row. Festival wind or string groups might need to be seated on a flat floor with an extra-wide front. In such cases the podium should be farther from the center than with a smaller group. If the podium is not the correct height and at a proper distance, the performers will not be able to see easily. If this situation is not considered carefully the performance may give reason for regret.

THE MUSIC STAND

Another auxiliary is the music stand. Building or welding a stand at a certain height can be satisfactory if the conductor always stands for rehearsal and per-

formance and if the same podium is always the correct one.

Some conductors prefer the large rehearsal stands that are commercially available with storage shelves below the tilt-top rack. Because of their more difficult adjustment or the manner in which they are built, these rehearsal stands are often tilted at the top by a conductor so that they no longer lie in a flat position. Tilting the top of a conductor's stand causes the conductor to lower his eyes further from the performers and to have less eye contact with them. Most conductors, however, prefer an adjustable stand that can service a number of rehearsal and concert situations.

The stand itself should be sturdy and not loose in any of its joints. This looseness is most annoying and is easily corrected. Professional conductors will request a new stand even during a concert if they find that the stand is not correct in every detail. Most amateur conductors will not take the time or deem it necessary to make these changes before an audience even though they may find the stand unsatisfactory. It is not uncommon for the conductor to touch the stand with his baton or finger during a performance. Even touching a stand that is not sturdy could be disastrous. It is best for the amateur conductor to arrive for the concert in ample time to check these items himself to be sure of reliable equipment.

The desk of the conductor's stand should lie flat or practically so. Conductors preferring a rather high, tilted stand appear amateurish. Most experienced conductors will place the desk so that it lies flat. This position enables them to see the score easily, if necessary, without lowering the eyes too far below the contact point of the performers; it also permits a smaller score to sit on the upper portion of the desk without resting on the shelf lip of the stand. Scores that rest on the shelf lip may offer page-turning difficulties; those that lie closer to the center of the stand will be easier to turn.

Stand height is important to the conductor, but repetitious adjustment is distracting. Nervousness or lack of preparation causes many amateur conductors to adjust the stand continuously throughout the concert. Adjustment should be made prior to the concert, and then the stand should not be touched unless a serious problem arises. It is advisable for the conductor to make this adjustment prior to the time of his formal entrance. Likewise, nervousness or unsureness causes some teachers to alter the height of their stand many times during the rehearsal. Adjust the stand before rehearsal begins, and devote your energy to looking at the students and talking directly to them.

Proper stand height will enable one to see the score and at the same time will not interfere with conducting patterns. Since conducting patterns usually bring the right hand to the waist, it is advisable to have the stand slightly below this height. This will seem too low, and first preferences will be to have the stand higher and the music closer to the eyes, resulting in a feeling of greater security. However, the score should not be read while conducting but should be used only as a reminder for certain items and problems. With this in mind, then, it is logical for the stand to be no higher than suggested. The conductor should realize that the most important part he has to play in the concert is that dealing with his hands and their movement, along with other bodily reactions to the music. Therefore, he should not place a stand so high as to interfere in any way with these movements. With a little practice a person will become adjusted to a lower stand.

When the stand is too high, the well-trained or well-disciplined conductor will find that he will be conducting to the side of the stand, ignoring its height and not permitting it to be a guide for his motions. This will create a problem for those performers on the left side of the conductor since the stand will cut off their vision for the point of the downbeat, which is recognized as the most important beat of the pattern. In some cases it could also necessitate an oversize rebound so that the conducting hand can be moved to the left. Do not create these problems for yourself.

THE CONDUCTING CHAIR

As a recent item, the conducting chair has only a few devotees. Since it could lead to problems or may not assist the conductor in forming the best of habits, it probably should not be used by the beginning conductor. For the experienced conductor this tool is invaluable since it permits him to sit down and not use strength for standing that he could use for the intensity of the rehearsal. Most professional conductors use a chair during much of the rehearsal since rehearsals are 2½ to 3 hours in length. School rehearsal periods are usually limited to about one hour, and therefore, the chair may not be needed to the same extent.

The conducting chair is well built so that the seat portion can be adjusted in height. The footstool portion of the chair can be used as a standing podium since it is about 8 inches from the floor and will not tip in any direction no matter where the weight of the conductor may be placed.

THE SCORE

Before a concert a conductor should make sure that the scores are in good condition. During rehearsal well-worked scores are apt to become torn or the edges or corners of pages ripped and sticky. A careful conductor will assure himself of all pages and will mend all scores that need repair before the performance.

Once, conducting from an early printed score of the Brahms Academic Festival Overture, I noticed that an entire corner of one of the pages had worn away through use. When paging from the corner, I actually turned two pages. To avoid problems or concern at the concert, I taped a corner onto the page to facilitate correct turning. Score care is only one of the small items that leads to a good performance through careful work prior to a concert.

Only needed scores should be present on the conductor's stand, and they should be in correct order. Some texts on conducting will promote the idea that a conductor not look at a score during the first ten or twelve measures. This is probably a notable idea, underlining the need for a person's knowing the beginning of the selection so well that all attention could be concentrated on the performance. However, the conductor should be sure that he has the correct score before him in advance of conducting. Occasionally I have witnessed those who, after one or two numbers, began to search for the next score. Creating a sense of uneasiness or uncertainty in the performance, the conductor appears disorganized when he is in a most obvious public position. If the conductor will check scores just before a performance, he will notice if one is misplaced.

Many professional conductors will designate a member of the performing group from one of the first chairs to replace the scores on the stand after each number. While the conductor is responding to the applause, a performer close to the conducting stand will take the preceding score from the conductor's stand and replace it with the score of the number to be performed next. This has the advantage of keeping the conducting stand clear so that the conductor will not have more than one score at a time on the stand. Most amateur conductors, however, prefer to depend upon themselves, rather than ask another person to aid them.

DRESS

Another auxiliary of the conductor is his dress or appearance. This item is of importance to the performers as well as the audience. Conductors should weigh carefully the problem of conducting while being dressed exactly as a member of the performing group. For example, if a person is conducting a choir, should he wear a robe even though no tight-wrist robes are available. What should a young lady wear as a conductor of a male choir? What should a person wear if he is conducting a uniformed band and no conductor's uniform is available? Should a band director wear a uniform during a concert if his band wears one? To answer these questions, first consider good taste and then remember to consider your role as conductor.

Many a conductor has forgotten his role at commencement when he has robed himself so that he would appear as a member of the faculty. How much more efficient he might have been if he had realized that he was a conductor and dressed more in keeping with the group that he was expected to conduct. His presence would have added to the prestige of the group, and at the same time he would be indirectly telling them that he considered performance his first and foremost duty.

A conductor can dress more formally than his group. If a conductor is working with an orchestra when the group is wearing white shirts and blouses with dark skirts and trousers, the conductor would be in good taste to appear at an evening concert in a tuxedo. Here he is more formally dressed than his students. He is wearing black and white, and he informs the students that he considers this an important occasion. It would be an error for him to wear tails, even though they also are black and white. Usually it would be an error for him to appear in a tuxedo or tails if the group were wearing a uniform of school colors. It would appear more in keeping if he were to wear a suit, and if possible, some darker shade of the color that might be represented in the uniform of the group. An inconspicuous tie is preferred.

A young lady might have more of a problem in determining what to wear with a group. If the performers are wearing white shirts or blouses and dark skirts and trousers, it would seem inappropriate for the lady conductor to wear the same unless the performance was extremely informal. In this case she could consider a dark two-piece suit with a white blouse. Most problems for the lady conductor will come when directing an organization that wears a school uniform. Most ladies prefer not to wear a uniform, but they often create some problem if they do not try to dress in keeping with the uniform. Many flowered dresses or multicolored suits clash with a background of the uniform. Taking into consideration the colors of the uniform or choir robe, a dress or suit could be purchased that would make appropriate conducting apparel. The cut of the clothes should be considered when one makes a purchase, since the arms must move easily and without restrictions.

STANCE

Another facet of appearance is stance, which may affect a group psychologically, if in no other way. Too many times the amateur conductor will believe that he is standing erect, but to an audience he will appear to be leaning to one side or hunched forward, or his weight may appear to be centered on one foot. If the latter, the amateur too often will beat time with a foot, and although he is not making much noise, the movement will be most obvious to an audience, whose eyes are often in a direct line with a conductor's feet. The problem of tapping a foot is a musical one since it is an indication of a misplaced rhythmic energy which should be evident in other parts of the body.

Recently in a conducting class a student called our attention to the stance of a demonstrating student. The speaker stated that she was aware that the beginning conductor was standing on two feet on the podium, and yet the manner in which he carried his weight on his feet made it appear as if he were bowed slightly so that his waist had a slight protrusion. She correctly analyzed this as giving the conducted group the impression that the conductor was too relaxed or lethargic about what he expected. After a brief discussion the student conductor corrected his problem.

The conductor who raises one shoulder higher than the other is sure to appear stiff and be stiff, even though he may not recognize it himself. Some conductors, particularly choral conductors, are prone to the lifting of both shoulders when conducting, trying to simulate the energy that they hope the choral group is using to support the tone. It is questionable if this will produce much except psychological tension in the performers.

Some conductors are apt to forget their conducting training and place a hand in a suit pocket. This or other problems will be easily seen by others and quickly recognized as questionable by both the trained and untrained audience. Correct procedures must continually be thought of until a conducting routine is built that exempts poor habits. Watch other amateur conductors in concert and note their bad habits. This will underline conditions that you must look for within yourself.

2

The Baton

Although an auxiliary, the baton warrants a chapter of its own since it is so intimately connected with the conducting process.

TO USE OR NOT TO USE

With many conductors the use of the baton is a questionable point. Some conductors believe that a baton should be used at all times. Others believe that instrumental work is most successful with a baton but choral groups should be conducted without one. In recent years a few conductors have decided that the stick is not always essential and have been working sometimes with and sometimes without one on the theory that they can procure more variety of expression from the orchestra or band with this flexibility. Conductors who do not use a baton are more apt to depend upon the subtle and constant movement of the hands as they try to interpret the music. With choral conductors, the hand motions more often give the performers the feel of the music rather than a primary emphasis on the beat and the musical phrase.

Other conductors, some with major orchestras, have used batons for almost all musical compositions except perhaps the slow movement of a symphony or composition of a similar style.

An example of the reverse of this trend is Robert Shaw conducting his well-known and excellent Chorale. Over the past several years I have observed Shaw conducting rehearsals and performances, all without a baton. No one can complain of any conductor not using a baton who conducts so well and whose results are so musical. Nevertheless, during the last two or three years Shaw has been using a baton. The expressiveness of his conducting and the finesse of the performance have in no way suffered.

A student will have ample opportunity to make this decision about a baton in his conducting future, but during the time he is learning conducting procedures, he should have the experience of working most of the time with a baton. If correctly used, the baton can bring control to the group more easily. This is our goal.

SHAPE AND SIZE

Many shapes and sizes of batons are available. Over a period of years professional conductors may change the style of baton they use. The exact type of baton for a beginner is important, however, and may not be the same style recommended for the experienced. The reasons are obvious. Teaching experience has proved that a baton with an elliptically shaped ball on the end works most satisfactorily for students and young conductors. As an experienced conductor, I still prefer this type. It gives the conductor an open grip and, at the same time, does not call for him to reshape the hand from the position developed when no baton is used.

Those who are small or of average height and are conducting a small or average-sized group should use King David 27B. This baton has a cork ball handle and is 14 inches long. A well-balanced baton, it is excellent for a beginner conducting school groups, either instrumental or choral. If a conductor is over 6 feet tall, or if he is conducting a festival group, he should probably use a longer baton. In the latter case I would recommend the King David 3B. This also has a good ball for the hand but is 22 inches long. Both batons are wood and painted white. Metal batons are not recommended.

To use a baton well is difficult and requires much practice. At first you will undoubtedly feel uneasy with a baton. Actually the baton should be considered an extension of the arm; moreover, it aids the hand and arm in making precise movements. The full or broad motions call for movement with the arm, while the small motions are still a matter of the wrist. It is these wrist movements that the stick interprets so much better than the fingers alone.

Remember that the tip of the baton, and not the hand, should become the center of attention. During

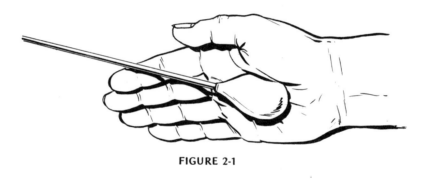

FIGURE 2-1

FIGURE 2-2

the first day of practice, it might be advisable to keep your eye on the tip of the baton in order to call it to your attention. Without this accent on the tip, you are merely conducting with the hand and holding the baton.

HOLDING THE BATON

The ball of the baton should be placed in the center or palm of the hand. With the hand palm upward, let the stick of the baton cross the index finger at the first joint. Bring the thumb over to the baton, holding it in place easily but not pushing it against the first finger. Let the fingers of the hand curve easily around the ball, not clamping it to the hand. When the hand is turned over so that the palm of the hand is parallel to the floor, it is in a correct position for conducting.

At this point the hand should be slightly cupped, the baton should point to the left at a modest angle, and you should recognize that the baton is being held with thumb and index finger alone while other fingers only guide and lightly touch the ball (see Figures 2-1 and 2-2).

During conducting there are times when the baton should have a small vertical motion in the hand. For this movement, the tip of the baton should move upward and downward about 2 inches. At the same time the ball of the baton should move in the palm of the hand, touching the center of the hand at the bottom of the movement and the curved fingers at the top of the movement. If this movement is not evident, then the thumb is pressing too tightly or the fingers are cupped too tightly around the ball of the baton. Excessive movement of the stick indicates that the thumb should be tightened or the fingers of the hand curved slightly more (see Figure 2-3).

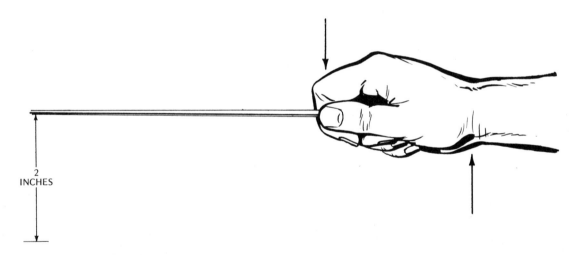

2
INCHES

FIGURE 2-3

PRACTICE EXERCISES

1. Pick up the baton from a stand or table several times to assure yourself of a correct hand position quickly.

2. When moving to or from class, carry the baton correctly in your hand rather than in a book. The hand may be at your side with the baton pointing toward the floor, but you should sense the correct handhold and feel the baton move slightly in the hand.

3. When holding or moving the baton in front of you, keep the wrist flat so that the palm of your hand is toward the floor at all times.

4. Keep the elbow out from the body allowing 7 or 8 inches from rib cage to elbow.

5. Practice moving the wrist with slight motions upward and downward so that the tip of the baton moves about 3 inches. Practice this, holding the baton correctly, (1) directly in front of the body, (2) to the left of center, (3) to the right of center. Practice slowly and quickly with metronome. (M.M. 80 and 120). (Place a yardstick on the outer edge of a music stand with the 15-inch marker directly in front of your nose. Tap the 15-inch marker for the center of the body, tap the 6-inch indicator for the left of the body, and the 23-inch indicator for the right of the body.)

6. With the baton in hand, move the arm up and down a number of times, carefully observing exercise 3. The movement for this exercise is in the arm and not the wrist. For a downward movement, the hand should move on a line just to the right of the body and the tip of the stick should fall just about in a line with the nose or the center of the body. Move the stick from the eyebrows to the waist. Be sure to practice behind a music stand correctly adjusted for height (just below the waist). (See Figures 2-4 and 2-5.)

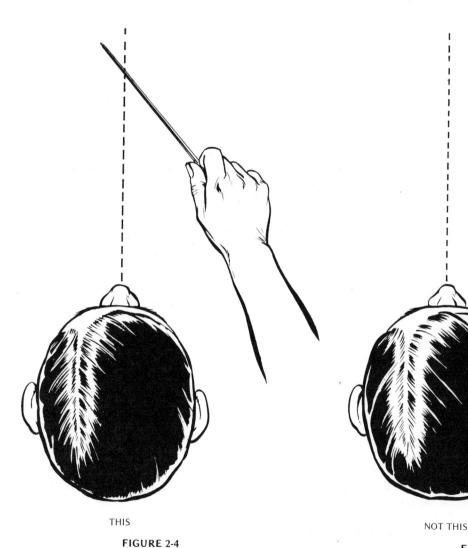

THIS

FIGURE 2-4

NOT THIS

FIGURE 2-5

7. With baton in hand and observing exercise 3, move the arm so that the baton sweeps horizontally parallel to the floor. Do not swing toward the body with the baton. Keep it always in front of you as if writing on the blackboard with the baton tip (see Figure 2-6).

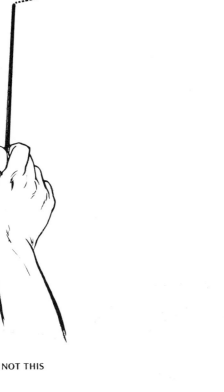

NOT THIS

THIS

FIGURE 2-6

8. Combine both movements: downward, to the left, to the right, upward. This gives a sweep of all conducting directions.

9. Some students will elevate or dip the wrist with early use of the baton. The back of the hand should be level with the immediate lower arm. This student should concentrate on the wrist and hand rather than the stick tip for some minutes of practice (see Figures 2-7 and 2-8, page 16).

10. The tip of the stick may rise above the eye during practice but should not go below the waist. If the tip of the baton goes below the waistline, there is a problem in holding the stick. This will be immediately obvious, since the tip of the stick will strike the stand placed before the novice conductor.

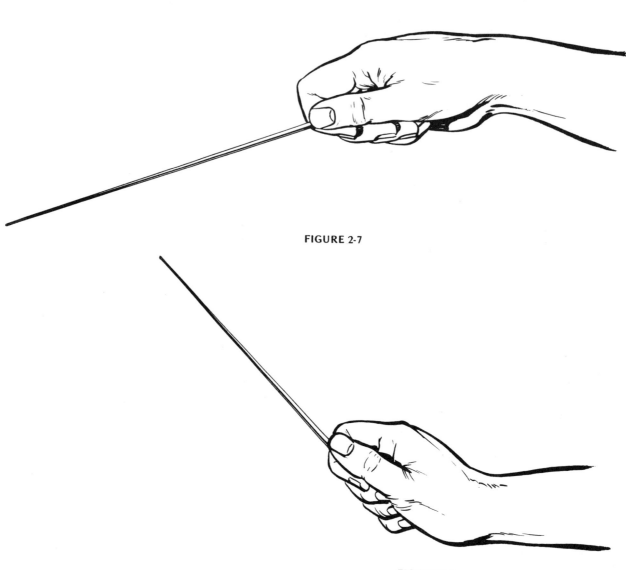

FIGURE 2-7

FIGURE 2-8

3

The Rebound: Three Types

One of the most important arm and hand movements in conducting is the rebound, for it is here that conducting style is first formed. Many young conductors beat the time correctly with a baton but fail to change the impression of this beating as the style of the music changes. All styles of conducting cannot be approached early in our study or without considerable practice, but so important is this aspect of conducting that its introduction should be made at this time before the patterns themselves are discussed and used.

Specifically, it is the movement between beats that is most important. This concerns the quality of the motion through the patterns and the ability of this motion to suggest the nature of the music. For example, if the baton moves as if through air, it would suggest lightness; as if through water, it would suggest heaviness or measured movement. The eye and the psychology of the performer are impressed by the type of motion that the conductor uses between beat points much more than by the beat itself. For this reason the rebound development should begin early.

The rebound is the distance the stick moves immediately after it reaches the most extended point in the pattern. For example, on the downbeat the stick finally reaches a point that each conductor considers the bottom of the beat. When this point is reached, the baton should then move back upward for a short distance as if it were bouncing off a rubbery floor. Each beat has such an outer limit point, and the rebound should follow immediately once that point is reached. Rebounds will vary for different kinds of beats and for different styles of conducting, but the idea of a rebound should be instilled at an early point in our learning process.

THE FOREARM REBOUND: MARCATO

This type of rebound is probably the easiest to master since it makes use of so little wrist movement. In fact, it may be performed with no wrist movement if you believe the style of music warrants it. The arm and stick are moved toward the beat point with considerable force. The speed of the arm increases as you approach the beat point, and the motion is changed with an obvious accent. This accent is caused mainly by the quickness of the rebound but also possibly by the almost imperceptible movement of the wrist. One of the main characteristics of this style is the stop or hesitation at the top of each rebound. Your understanding of this will develop as your skill increases. Consequently, let us begin our practice immediately.

PRACTICE EXERCISES

1. Practice just the downbeat with a rebound. At the top of the rebound stop the baton, then move back to the top of the conducting pattern and proceed again. The rebound should be practiced until it feels natural and looks at ease with the arm, the baton, and the pattern. If the downbeat is about 21 or 22 inches from top to bottom, then an average rebound would be about 7 inches from bottom to top. Make use of the forearm and very little wrist. In fact, the wrist moves only about half an inch at the beat point, whereas the arm is responsible for most of the 7 inches of the rebound (see Figures 3-1 and 3-2).

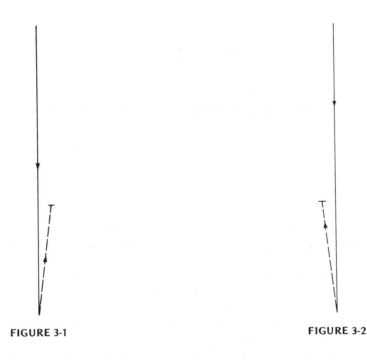

FIGURE 3-1   FIGURE 3-2

   a. The solid line is the beat line, and the dotted line is the rebound line. At the top of each rebound, the horizontal line indicates a stopping point.

   b. Try to retrace the downward line as closely as possible with the returning rebound; however, if you are relaxed, the baton will probably return on one side of the downward line or the other. Plan your patterns so that some of the retracing will be to the left and some to the right of the downward line. This will help you prepare for the correct conducting patterns later, since some patterns need a rebound on the left of the downbeat and others need a rebound on the right.

   c. As you approach the beat point you may wish to increase the speed of the baton slightly, so that the rebound will not appear as if you had to lift the baton back up the downbeat line. The phrase "throw the arm at the beat point" may help an inhibited student obtain more abandon.

2. Practice rebounds to beats given downward and then to the left. Be sure to stop at the top of the

rebound to the downbeat and again after the left motion. Stopping permits you to see exactly where your baton is in relation to where you wish it to be. More importantly, it develops a style of conducting that is difficult for most beginners; this style leads to agitato, marcato, and/or staccato conducting (see Figure 3-3).

If the downbeat is about 22 inches from top to bottom and the rebound is about 7 or 8 inches, then the beat to the left will be about 9 inches to the left. Since the point of the stick is traveling on a diagonal, it will move farther than the 9 inches of the two beat points.

a. Note the diagram below. At the bottom of the sketch are the numbers 6 and 15. These represent inches. Place a yardstick on the far edge of the music stand before you, placing the 15-inch mark at the downbeat point.

b. Be sure that a music stand is always before you in practice. This will enable you to become accustomed to the stand and will help guide the bottom point of your beat. Do not worry if your baton touches the music stand at this point in your progress. If it does, just be sure that the tip of the baton touches the far edge of the stand. For beats to the left, be sure that the baton tip touches the left far corner of the stand. This will assist in keeping the arm in a correct position (see Figures 3-4 and 3-5).

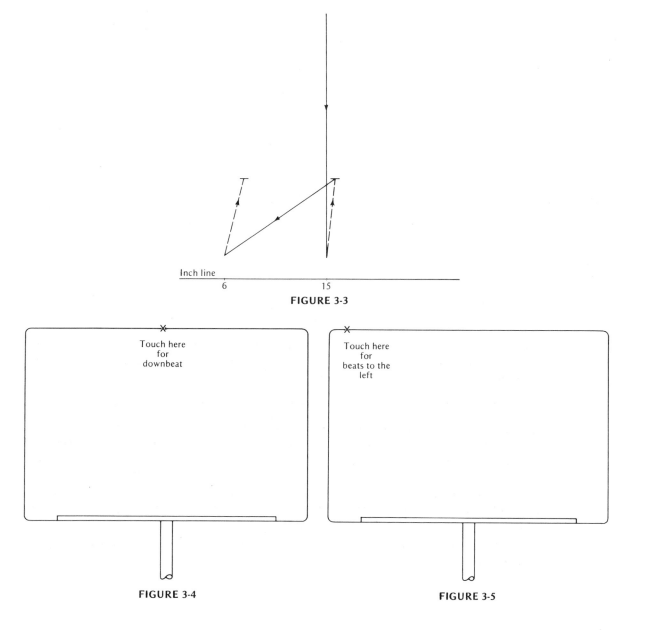

Inch line

6   15

FIGURE 3-3

Touch here
for
downbeat

Touch here
for
beats to the
left

FIGURE 3-4   **FIGURE 3-5**

c. Most beginners want to move into the left stroke without sufficient stop at the top of the rebound for the first beat. To do so only smooths out the pattern (which is the easier pattern for a beginner) and defeats our purpose of introducing a style difference into the baton. Practice exercise 2, stopping at least two seconds at the top of each rebound.

3. Practice rebounds to beats given downward and to the right (see Figure 3-6).

   Remember: Palm to the floor. Do not turn the hand so that the thumb is upward.

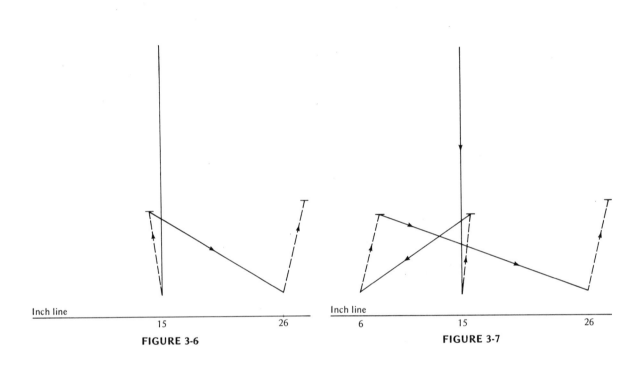

Inch line				Inch line		
	15	26		6	15	26
FIGURE 3-6					**FIGURE 3-7**	

4. Practice rebounds to beats given downward, then to the left, and finally to the right. Be sure to stop at the top of the rebound to each beat as indicated by the small horizontal lines. Keeping the same proportion as before, the stick will move about 20 inches from left to right (see Figure 3-7).

   Note: The rebound is slightly higher for the right beat than for the other two beats.

   Note: The rebound for the downbeat is produced on the opposite side of the beat line to the next direction. If one were to eliminate the beat to the left, then the downbeat rebound would be produced on the left of the beat line.

5. Practice a rebound pattern for an upward beat or last beat in any pattern. This would be for any beat that immediately precedes any measure line. The best practice comes after other beats and rebounds as the examples show. Be sure to stop at each point (see Figures 3-8 and 3-9).

   Note: The beat point for the last beat of any measure is almost at the same place that we found the stick for the rebound to the downbeat.

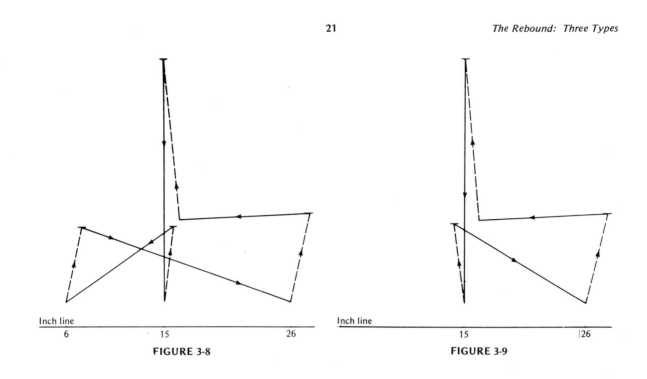

FIGURE 3-8   FIGURE 3-9

REVIEW

1. Making use of the above diagrams, practice the forearm rebound with considerable emphasis upon each beat and with an obvious stop at the rebound point. Exaggerate the energy placed in each beat and each rebound.

2. Making use of the above diagrams, practice the forearm rebound in various sizes from quite small to large, since you will need all sizes of patterns for music in the future. Small patterns will have a smaller downbeat, less movement to the left, to the right, and upward. All motions should be in proportion. Large patterns will be extensive but will move more quickly to cover the larger distance.

Remember: For practice of this style in a small pattern, use the same emphasis and energy in driving the arm toward the beat point and in the rebound as in the large pattern. The style and the size of pattern should be treated as two separate items.

Caution: Do not move to the following sections of the chapter until the forearm rebound is well practiced and satisfactory in execution. Moving ahead too soon will hasten your pace but will not train the arm to feel, learn, and respond to this marcato style. Too many amateur conductors have no concept of style. It is not that the mind does not understand the style but, rather, that in conducting practice, the arm has not come to feel what this style means in execution. Thinking the style does not necessarily mean that the arm has portrayed it to the performer.

THE SMALL WRIST REBOUND: LEGATO

This rebound is almost the complete opposite of the previous detailed work. Here the pattern is smoothed at each corner, and no stop is executed at the rebound. A small rebound accent should be evident to the performer so that he will understand precisely where the beat point is located; then each syllable or note may be correctly placed. To execute a good legato re-

bound, be sure that only the wrist is involved and that the baton tip moves only about 1 or 1½ inches. Do not stop the arm in its overall movement, but superimpose the wrist movement at the beat points.

There are times when one might wish to use a smooth pattern and a beat with no rebound. This type of pattern is not advised at the present stage of development, since the young conductor needs the practice of precise indication with all rebounds.

PRACTICE EXERCISES

1. Practice the small wrist rebound during the downbeat. The wrist should make a barely perceptable motion as the hand reaches the beat point, or the farthest point in the vertical motion. Unlike the preceding rebound, this does not stop at any point in the pattern. The arm must continue the motion toward the next beat, and the pattern indicates this by the continuing line.

2. Note that the diagrams show the downbeat with two types of follow-through: one to the left and one to the right. Practice both types, since they usually have a different feel and you must be equally familiar with each (see Figures 3-10 and 3-11).

FIGURE 3-10   FIGURE 3-11

3. Practice the small wrist rebound during the downbeat and the following beat. Notice that the following beat in each case is to the right and to the left. Keep the arm moving after each wrist rebound so that you understand that no stopping is used in this conducting style (see Figures 3-12 and 3-13).

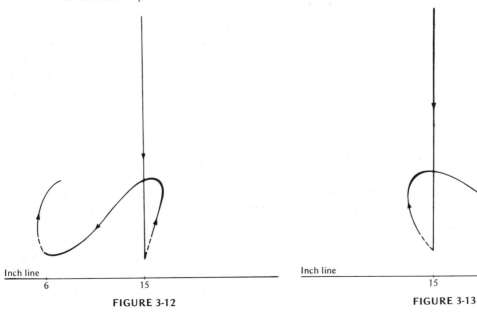

Inch line
 6   15   Inch line   15   26

FIGURE 3-12   FIGURE 3-13

Note: Try to have each rebound the same size. Do not permit a first rebound to be smaller than a second or the reverse.

Note: The rounded lines indicate a legato style; the dotted lines again indicate the rebound (see Figures 3-14 to 3-17).

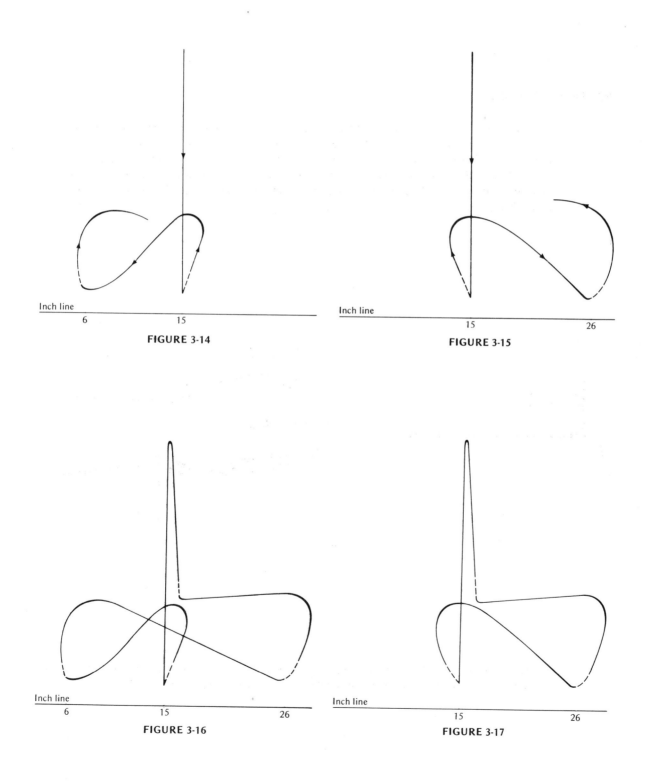

FIGURE 3-14

FIGURE 3-15

FIGURE 3-16

FIGURE 3-17

THE LARGE WRIST REBOUND: STACCATO

At times a larger wrist rebound may be needed in music. This type of rebound may be used with certain staccato passages or certain attacks or emphases. It is executed by a larger movement of the wrist that moves the end of the baton from 4 to 5 inches. The pattern is smoothed between beat points. To secure this, imagine that you are trying to make a Yo-Yo reclimb the string once it has touched the bottom point.

Again the pattern will appear more angular but not as severe as our first style. In the following diagrams the broken line indicates the wrist movement which includes part of the rebound.

PRACTICE EXERCISES

1. Place a horizontal line on a blackboard at the approximate location of the lower extremity of your downbeat pattern. Then place another mark about 5 inches above this line. Take a position before the board so that your arm is comfortable with the baton held correctly before you but not touching the board. Move the baton between the two marks so that you can see and feel how wide this new rebound will be. Move the wrist quickly during this exercise as if it were a rebound (see Figure 3-18).

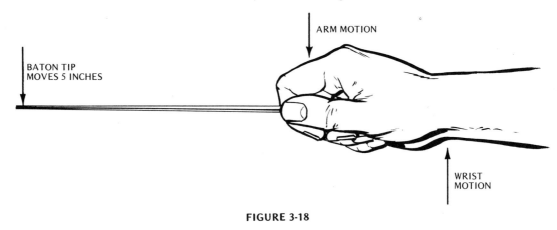

ARM MOTION

BATON TIP MOVES 5 INCHES

WRIST MOTION

FIGURE 3-18

2. Practice a downbeat pattern using the large wrist rebound. Following the pattern below, try to use a 4- or 5-inch wrist movement and a semiangular contour (see Figures 3-19 and 3-20).

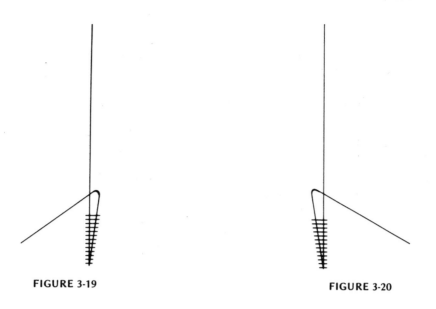

FIGURE 3-19   FIGURE 3-20

3. Following the patterns below, practice the large wrist rebound for the downbeat and for beats to the right, the left, and for the final beat of a measure (see Figures 3-21 and 3-22).

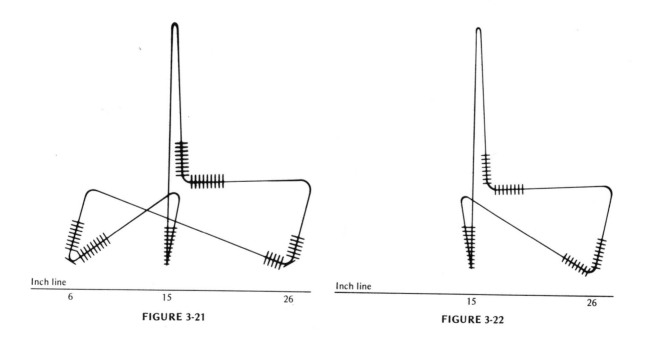

Inch line   Inch line

6   15   26   15   26

FIGURE 3-21   FIGURE 3-22

REVIEW

1. Demonstrate each style of rebound for members of your class without telling them which style you are conducting. They should be able to distinguish each style that you conduct with no hesitation.

2. Relaxation Exercises: If the arm becomes tired or tight during practice, relax the arm by practicing exercises 5, 6, 7, and 9 from Chapter 2.

   Remember: Be sure that you are holding the baton correctly. Do not place so much emphasis upon the rebound that the basic position has become incorrect.

   Remember: Keep the palm of the conducting hand toward the floor at all times. This is particularly true when moving the hand toward and away from the center of your body.

4

Simple Patterns for Conducting

The most obvious activity of a conductor is that of moving his hands in some rhythmic pattern with the music. Of all his activities this would seem the easiest for the beginner. If properly executed, these actions are simple only in appearance. Conducting frequently appears effortless because we see so many conductors who only move their hands and do not conduct the music or the group. The following patterns may appear deceptively easy, but there are many problems that attend even the smallest motions. Some of these are discussed in this chapter before we deal with the patterns.

Be receptive to the idea that moving the right hand in a conducting pattern may be learned through careful practice. Most students who approach the problem without timidity make a decent beginning, overcoming the simple problems with ample preparation to tackle the more complex ones.

CONSIDERATIONS BEFORE PATTERN PRACTICE

Position of the Right Hand

Many newcomers to a conducting class may have conducted at an earlier time. Perhaps they directed the local high school band as student conductor, a high school orchestra as a senior, a church choir, or a drum and bugle corps. These experiences are valuable but many times lead to an ingraining of bad habits in regard to important details. One such bad habit is the wrist being turned so that the thumb points upward. There might be a limited number of times when a conductor will use his hand in this position, but it is poor practice to permit oneself the luxury of following this procedure, since the hand in the correct position has the best appearance, the most grace, and the most subtle authority. If you have difficulty in keeping the wrist in position, try conducting with a 50-cent piece on the wrist. This is only a device to correct this problem or bring it strongly to the student's attention and should not be used for any length of time, for it soon becomes a stunt and will hinder the performing of other more important movements with the right hand.

Looking beyond the Right Hand

Most beginning conductors will watch the right hand as they proceed with the pattern. Of course, a little observation will do no harm, but one should learn early to look out, to look beyond the hand, the podium, and the score to the players or singers. In a conducting class, look directly at your classmates. From time to time try looking around at different parts of the room. Do not always look just at the person immediately in front of the podium.

Importance of Relaxation

Probably the most difficult part of the conducting position is a relaxed hand and arm. If any part of the hand or arm is tight, it will become evident in the practice of different patterns and different styles and in the fatigue that will come in the arm, neck, or back. When you feel tight in any of these areas or if an ache is evident, relax the arm by exercises mentioned in Chapter 2.

Value of the Baton

Since it is much easier to grip the baton correctly and obtain a correct image with it, the beginner will reap obvious benefits by using a baton for the first lessons even if he insists that he will not use one for formal conducting. In this way one has considerable experience before attempting an area that is most difficult to master, that of conducting without a baton. When conducting without a baton, students often will conduct with the fingers of their right hand close together prior to instruction. Others keep their fingers straight, which gives a wooden appearance. Other students, in attempting to relax the hand, will curve the fingers at the middle joint, giving an appearance of a stubby tool. There are many variations of such problems. Often these problems will cure themselves after careful work with a baton over several periods of drill. If by that time some progress is not made, I try to shape the fingers of the hand for the student, although I find this much less desirable than having the student work out the problem naturally. Some assistance can be found by placing the fist of the left hand into the palm of the right hand and lightly closing the right hand over the left.

Use of the Left Hand

Most amateur conductors too often use the left hand to mirror the right-hand pattern. This leads to ineffective conducting, since the left hand has many important tasks besides pattern work. To avoid this, it is best to have the beginner work for a considerable time using only the right hand. The student should feel comfortable with the left hand relaxed at his side.

Chapters 8 and 17 will offer considerable detail regarding the left hand.

Posture

Good posture often means different things to different people. One can place the feet too close together for good appearance. One can also stiffen the back so that the appearance of rigidity results. Most often, however, the beginner will lean backward, thinking that he is now straight and tall. Since the conductor usually works with people who are in front of him and somewhat at a lower level than he, and since he will make some use of a score on a stand or rack, it is best to consider a slightly forward stance rather than one that leans awkwardly backward. This can be overdone, however. Young ladies will appear a little less awkward on the podium if they have their right foot slightly in front of the left. Heels, high heels in particular, are often a detriment to good podium posture.

Practice Fatigue

Early in practicing the conducting patterns one should keep in mind that the average beginner usually tires after three to five minutes. Believing that he has conducted some length of time, he falls quickly into one or more of the problems just discussed. The beginning student of conducting must remember that the practicing of a simple pattern over a long period of time is necessary. In the first place, many a composition is longer than three minutes, and endurance is a problem. In the second place, and most important, the hand patterns must be unthinking habit. The student must be able to look at the score and have his hand fall into the correct pattern without particular thought. This frees the mental capacities for the music and the group conducted. It is extremely difficult to underline this idea strongly enough in the mind of the beginner.

Proportion of the Conducting Pattern to the Body

One of the problems a beginner faces is to make his conducting pattern in proportion to his body. When discussing this proportion, it should be understood to mean the size of pattern that one uses in the average composition. It would not be the atypical pattern for special effects, but the one each person uses a majority of the time. Since it is used so regularly, it must be practiced so as to be predictable as well as consistent. A small person who conducts with a large beat will look as if he were trying too hard, whereas the reverse could appear over-timid. Rules 1, 2, and 6 on page 28 are particularly helpful in obtaining a pattern that is in proportion to the size of the conductor. Many young ladies who are conducting for the first time seem to have particular problems in this area. Unless altered early, a habit will follow that will be more difficult to correct later.

PATTERNS FOR TRIPLE METERS

After working with hundreds of students, I have found the simplest pattern for the beginner to be the one for triple time. The pattern is simply a triangle with elaborations to fit the type of the music conducted.

When considering a triangle as descriptive of the pattern for triple meter, many immediately envisage a true geometric triangle with 90- and 45-degree angles. Adhering too closely to this mental picture and executing the corners of the triangle too acutely gives a squareness to the conducting and also to the performance. In addition, some students often stop the beat momentarily at the corners of the pattern. Usually, if the latter point is corrected, the former will be relieved also.

This pattern moves to the right from the body for a right-handed conductor or to the left for a left-handed conductor. Even if you are a left-handed writer, try conducting right-handed. In almost every class this question arises. The student should be given the option of conducting with the right or left hand but with the explanation that in the field of music there are extremely few who hold the baton in the left hand. Students who insist usually work left-handed for a few sessions only to change as the demands become heavier and the material more complex.

This pattern is used most often for 3/4, 3/2, 3/8, and 9/8 signatures and could be used for 3/16 and 9/16 signatures.

The diagrams here illustrate two styles. The first (4-1) shows a pattern for a forearm rebound. The rebound is indicated by the dotted line, and the point where the baton stops is indicated by the horizontal bars.

The second diagram (4-2) is for a smoother passage or selection using a small wrist rebound. Again the rebound is indicated by dotted lines. Note that they are somewhat shorter than the dotted lines of the first diagram. This difference means much to a change in style that these two patterns represent, and this contrast is most obvious to the observer. The style of the

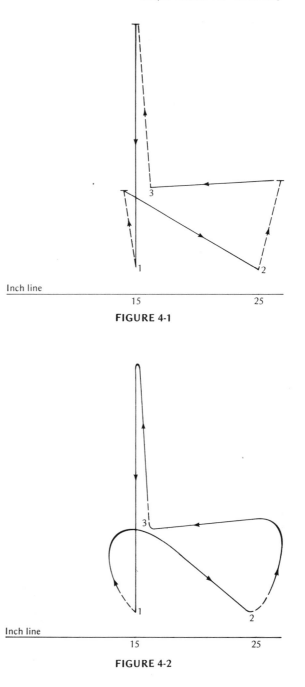

FIGURE 4-1

FIGURE 4-2

music should be reflected in the manner of conducting and the rebound, and these two patterns are indicative of style differences that we need to practice. Note that in the second diagram the hand does not stop at the top of the rebound but is in continuous movement, considerably more smooth and rounded than in the previous style. To execute the rebound, the hand moves slightly downward, pulling the baton with it, at the exact moment of the beat. This downward movement and its return indicates the beat and its rebound.

Note the inch measurement indicated for each pattern. Smaller-sized patterns may be necessary for soft passages, which may be practiced later, and for a small person. Your conducting pattern should fit you. Try the measurements suggested and let your classmates help you decide if they look correct for you. When beginning conducting, aim for this average-sized pattern. This may be likened to playing an instrument: a good tone is developed by practicing forte, not by playing piano or pianissimo.

Some good rules for the beginner would be:

1. Start the conducting pattern with baton tip at eye level.

2. For beat one, lower the hand about to the waist.

3. Keep the arm flat at the wrist, so that the palm is toward the floor.

4. Do not stop the motion at the corners of the pattern; instead, stop at the top of the rebound for the accented pattern.

5. Do not watch your hand, but look beyond it.

6. The elbow should be away from the body, about 9 inches from the rib cage, and just to the front of it.

7. At no time in the conducting pattern should the arm be completely stretched forward.

8. The fingers of the conducting hand should not be closed tightly around the ball of the baton.

9. The movement for the downbeat should be just to the right of the center of the body.

10. Do not use the left hand at the beginning of your progress.

11. Stand with good posture. This means weight on the balls of your feet, feet slightly apart, chin in, back straight, shoulders back. Do not look wooden in your stance.

PRACTICE EXERCISES

1. Stand on a well-built, proper-sized podium, preferably in front of a group. If it is a conducting class, each person should take a turn on the podium while others in the class practice at their chairs. Several podiums would be an asset. Each person should have enough room to allow for unrestricted conducting; because of arm and baton length, 6 feet on all sides of a person should be minimal.

2. Place a stand before the podium at correct height.

3. Practice the triple-meter patterns at least five minutes each before moving to a different style or different pattern. This will seem long at first, but remember that a march is usually about three minutes in length, and this is a short piece of music.

4. To assist the practice of the forearm rebound pattern (Figure 4-1), set your metronome at 66. Count six pulsations between each metronomic indication. Reach the beat point on count one, the rebound on count three, and wait at the top of the rebound during the counting of four, five, and six. This will assure you of proper speed during the rebound and beat pattern and proper stopping at the top of each rebound.

5. To assist the practice of the small wrist rebound pattern (Figure 4-2), set your metronome at 66. Count six pulsations between each metronomic indication. Reach the beat point on count one: at this time the wrist should move, dipping the hand slightly forward and downward, about one inch. On count two, the wrist should have regained its normal position, which in our pattern is the top of the wrist movement. There is no waiting during the counting of three, four, five, or six, but rather the baton and hand are in constant and steady motion.

Remember: The student should make a habit of moving the hand straight downward for the first beat of the measure. In leading to the rebound many bring the hand downward at an angle toward the left of the body. This only makes the conducting much less definite and can lead to confusion with the second beat of the pattern.

PATTERNS FOR QUADRUPLE METERS

The second set of conducting patterns is for quadruple signatures: 4/4, 4/2, 4/8, 12/8, 4/16, and 12/16.

Again, one pattern (Figure 4-3) is for a phrase or selection of staccato and/or agitato music using the forearm rebound. The other pattern (Figure 4-4) is for a more legato passage using the small wrist rebound.

Here the downbeat is similar to the triple meter, but the hand moves to the left for the second beat, across the body to the outside for the third beat, and upward for the fourth beat.

For this pattern one must be alert to two rules besides those stated earlier for triple time:

1. Do not permit the hand to swing toward the body for the second beat. Almost every amateur who conducts quadruple signatures is prone to this problem; the right hand correctly executes the downbeat, but when it leaves the rebound for the second beat point, it travels in an arc or line toward the left elbow or shoulder. If one were to conduct in this manner, it would again reduce the three-dimensional effect for a number of your group. The point of the second beat should be just as far from the midpoint of the body as it would be for beat three. The only difference, of course, is that the beat point is on the opposite side of the body. Aid for this problem can be found at a blackboard where a sample of the beat has been drawn. Trace this sample pattern many times, realizing that the point for the second beat is away from and not toward the body. Do not let the chalk leave the board at any point along the pattern.

2. The horizontal movements for this pattern should be slightly above the waist.

If the horizontal movements of this pattern offer a problem for the beginner, it is usually because he traces the movement too high. Occasionally a person will conduct too low for this pattern, although in the triple pattern this was not evident. Usually a reminder will suffice to correct the problem (see Figures 4-3 and 4-4).

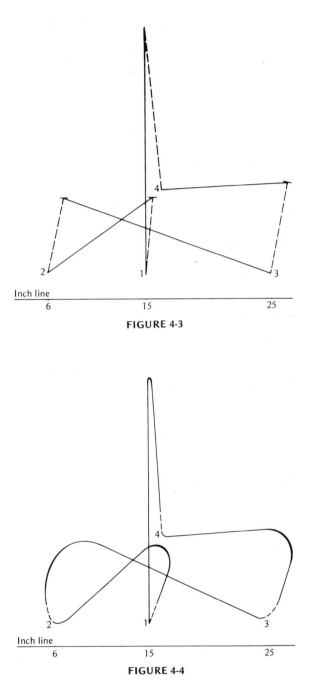

FIGURE 4-3

FIGURE 4-4

PRACTICE EXERCISES

1. Practice the quadruple meter patterns at least five minutes each before moving to a different pattern.

2. Practice the forearm rebound for five minutes at a moderate tempo. Try not to accelerate or slow the tempo during the entire exercise.

3. Practice the small wrist rebound for five minutes at a slow tempo. Try not to accelerate or slow the tempo during the entire exercise.

PATTERNS FOR DUPLE METERS

The next pattern to be studied is that for duple meters. This is used for 2/4, 2/2, 2/8, and 6/8 signatures and could be used for 6/4, 6/2, or 2/16 signatures.

In addition to those general rules from the earlier parts of the chapter, two others should be mentioned that are peculiar to this pattern:

1. Do not permit the crook at the bottom of the pattern to become too large.

2. Be sure that the second beat is placed in the crook.

Although this pattern is simple in appearance, it offers more problems to beginners than any simple pattern used. One problem is that in its simplicity the conductor often fails to practice it, and it fails to carry a definite form. This lack of definiteness leads to an uncertainty, so that it often becomes impossible for the performer to tell which is the downbeat. A broadening of the loop at the bottom of the pattern will lead to an almost circular beat. If this happens, the only recourse for the conductor is then to rely upon a circular motion near the top of the pattern for a second beat. I have seen some conductors with this problem so acute that in intense passages this pattern developed into a counterclockwise figure eight which was completely confusing to performers.

By placing the second beat in the crook of the pattern, one gives a bit of a bounce or definition which often can help the feeling for music played in duple time. Following are the patterns for duple meters (Figures 4-5 and 4-6).

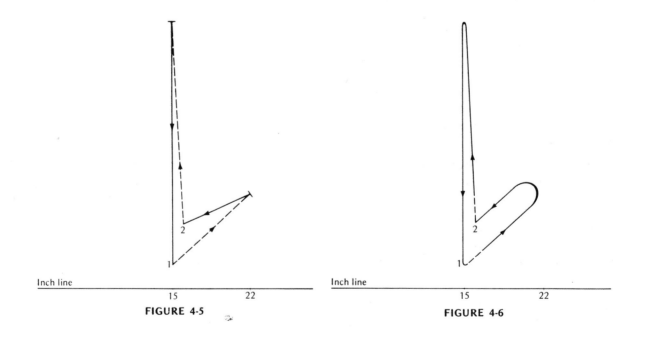

FIGURE 4-5   FIGURE 4-6

PRACTICE EXERCISES

1. Practice each of the patterns for duple meters at least five minutes. Be particularly critical of yourself in regard to the placement of beat two in each pattern.

2. Work with a partner and try to improve

   a. The size of your pattern while working with duple patterns.

   b. The rebounds while working with duple patterns.

3. Practice with energy, since it is usually duple time that is used for many fast and vigorous musical selections. At M.M. 120 it takes a considerable amount of energy to keep an energetic duple pattern going for three to five minutes. Remember that performers sing or play with an energy similar to the conductor's. The energy used or the enthusiasm given will be returned to you in satisfactory style results.

REVIEW

1. After each pattern takes on some smoothness, practice with a metronome. Practice each pattern at three speeds: M.M. 48 to 56, M.M. 72 to 80, M.M. 110 to 120.

2. Practice the three patterns in alternation: 3/4, 4/4, 2/4, 3/4, 4/4, etc. This will tend to bring independence to your right hand.

3. Practice alternating the three patterns using the following different signatures: 2/4, 3/8, (♩ = ♪), 4/4 (♪ = ♩), 2/2, (♩ = 𝅗𝅥), etc. This will enable you to practice independence in your thinking and movement.

4. Practice each pattern before a mirror so that you may compare your efforts to those of other conductors that you have seen.

5. Obtain a partner and a yardstick. Place the yardstick on your music stand before you and ask your partner to check the points of your pattern while you keep your eyes from looking at the measurement. You should come close to the suggested size of pattern.

6. Practice the patterns in front of your class standing on a podium with a stand correctly adjusted before you. Each student should observe your conducting, write a critique of your work, and give these comments to you afterward. This is a learning situation for the writer and the conductor.

5

Tempo

One should realize by this time that there are many intricacies involved in the art of conducting. So far, we have dealt almost entirely with the problem of the right hand and baton and their correct manipulation. This area would be quite enough in itself. However, there are many more facets that have considerable bearing upon the conducting situation. One of these is the matter of tempo.

If you are to be a reasonably good amateur conductor — if you are to carry off your assignments with your performing groups with some degree of skillfulness — then you must be aware of tempo. This is not a new area for any student of music. You have been made aware of tempo from your own solo or ensemble performances. Nevertheless, if you are like most students, the problem of tempo has not been a truly personal one. True, you may have played solos where the tempo was not given you just before the performance began, but you had been helped with the tempo by your teachers, so that you knew approximately the tempo necessary for your performance. In ensembles you have probably accepted a conductor's right to establish the speed of the composition.

SELECTING THE TEMPO: CLARITY OF THE PARTS

As a conductor, you will need to be aware of the total composition so that you can establish tempi for others. This is a difficult job, and it should be approached with care. Wagner stated that "the whole duty of the conductor is comprised in his ability to indicate the right tempo."[1] This may be an oversimplification, but it does emphasize the importance of the problem. As Krueger points out in *The Way of the Conductor*,[2] one should "test the tempo by three criteria: clarity of utterance, fidelity to the rhythmic pattern of a theme, and the effect of the tempo on the overall form."

First, one should be aware of the clarity of the parts. As you conduct, listen to the melody, the countermelody, and rhythmic lines. Rarely will a conductor permit speed to violate the technique of the

[1] Richard Wagner, *On Conducting*, William Reeves, London, 1897, p. 20.

[2] Karl Krueger, *The Way of the Conductor*, Charles Scribner's Sons, New York, 1958, p. 196.

melodic line, but it is possible to violate the melodic line so that this line becomes either tedious or frivolous. Many an amateur will permit the emotion of an athletic or political event to sway his judgment as to the proper tempo of the melodic line of a march or show tune. When this happens, the music becomes frivolous. Over the past several years it has been popular for marching bands to move the marching tempo to 140 M.M. or more. A few contemporary tunes can take this tempo, but most of the standard marches cannot.

Most often the problem of clarity comes in the inner and lower parts. Usually in our amateur groups some of the lesser-skilled performers are in these sections. Then we must decide whether the skills of the inner voices will control the tempo, as Krueger points out, or whether the general effect is more important to us. Perhaps some compromise will be the answer.

An old adage says that "the quickest notes should set your tempo." This is a good rule of thumb. Be sure that you reckon with the rhythm of lines other than the melody as well as the melodic line. So often what makes a march really alive and sparkling is not the speed so much as the clarity of the inner voices and the clarity of the rhythm parts. In an orchestra this quality may be in the middle strings or the brass and woodwinds.

The tempo can affect a composition's overall form in the manner in which the sections fit together and the contrast of the movements with each other. It can, in fact, affect the intent of the original form or type of selection. Once I heard an amateur orchestra play the first movement of Mozart's Symphony No. 40 at about 60 M.M. = the quarter note. This is an allegro movement, and this tempo not only violated the tempo marking but also the classic intent and definition of a first movement of a symphony. To state the problem another way, how slow can a street march be played, assuming technical problems of young players, and still be a march?

PERSONAL BASIS FOR SELECTION

Tempi are personal. If you were to check the recordings of the same composition by several conductors, it is possible you would find that in most cases the sections of a composition may vary from as little as 4 metronomic points to as much as 30. The reason for this is that each conductor has the prerogative to conduct a composition at a tempo at which he believes it "sounds best." This sounding best is a combination of several things.

First, it might depend upon the group. It would be foolish for a conductor of an amateur group to establish a tempo solely because this is the tempo used by professionals. It would be better to slow the tempo somewhat and perform the composition within the reach of the performers than to insist upon a tempo that might produce poor results. Of course, one should not perform the composition at all if the tempo need be so slow that it violates the original intent of the composer and the markings and tempo that he has indicated.

Second, "sounding best" might depend upon the way a conductor felt. Charles Munch in his book on conducting relates a story about Kreisler playing while Brahms conducted. Brahms was leading the group at such a tremendous speed this particular day that Kreisler objected. Brahms answered that the speed was appropriate for the day and the way he felt.[3] There is no denying that our physical well-being has some effect on the tempo and the way we conduct. A good conductor will not permit this to influence him too greatly, particularly if he is conducting amateurs. This is an appropriate point for the amateur conductor to remember, for often he becomes just nervous enough during his early public performances so that he is not aware when he is moving too slowly, or what is more likely, that he has discarded caution and is racing through what could have been a well-executed composition.

Several procedures can help a young conductor avoid violating a rehearsed tempo during performance.

1. Practice conducting any group as often and as much as possible. A church choir is excellent for this purpose since it requires public conducting at least once a week, sometimes under less than ideal conditions.

2. In addition to practicing your score with your group, when many items detract from concentration on the score, also practice alone, when you can concentrate on only the score and your conducting.

3. Rehearse your score completely no more than four hours before a concert and then do not have contact with any other music until the concert. Keep your mind fresh for your work.

4. In your mind, review your tempo for a composition before you step on the podium or before you raise your arms for a preparatory motion.

[3] Charles Munch, *I Am a Conductor*, Oxford University Press, New York, 1955, p. 63.

5. Do not let an error or two even in an important place disturb your general approach. Recognize that you are conducting amateurs and that you must expect the unexpected.

6. Even though the tempo becomes fast and your arm motions fast and vigorous, breathe slowly and deeply. This will assist your control and help eliminate your tendency to nervousness.

7. The sound of your group depends on your attitude or your psychological approach to them. If you feel and act unsure, your group will be uneasy. Be outwardly calm and confident.

Third, individuals have different concepts of what tempo indications really mean. Some conductors may take allegro to mean M.M. 120 in a particular composition, whereas others may feel that M.M. 92 would be much more meaningful. Another conductor may believe it should be played at M.M. 132.

Fourth, one conductor may be more interested in the general effect of the music, whereas another may be interested in the complexity of line during a certain section. If a conductor is more interested in effect, he will subordinate the complexity of line in his mind, selecting a tempo to achieve an overall effect.

Fifth, a conductor must be aware of vitality in the sound of the group. Absence of this life in the tone will result in a less than satisfying effect, so a tempo must be established that will aid the conductor in securing this vitality. The ideal tempo will vary with the group but all these will be within the range of good tempo for the particular composition.

RHYTHM AS A FACTOR

Rhythm is a factor that should help determine tempo. It is indeed foolish to push a tempo to the point where the rhythm becomes lost. Many times the rhythm of a composition will control the tempo for the melodic line: If the rhythmic underpinnings can be played neatly, the melodic line will appear to float and in many cases will appear to be performed at a faster tempo than is the case. Sometimes the amateur conductor will mistake speed for clean rhythm, as in conducting an allegro section. If the allegro section is clean in the under parts so that the melodic lines and countermelodies float above the rhythm, the allegro will appear to be moving at a rapid tempo.

LOUDNESS AS A FACTOR

Passages that are loud can be stated with a slower tempo than if they were performed softer. Many a composition will respond to a slightly broader tempo when the loudness increases or the instrumentation becomes complete. When this slower tempo is executed by the conductor, the listener often will not be aware of it, but he would have been aware of the impending lack of clarity if the fast tempo had been retained.

Amateurs tend to alter the tempo more obviously than professional conductors, and at the same time to use more conspicuous devices to affect the alteration. It is the amateur who will overdo the ritard, the accelerando, or the allargando at the end of a composition, or distort a romantically flowing line until it loses all the subtlety and professional rendering that it could have had.

OTHER CONSIDERATIONS

There are several other items such as the acoustics of the room, the nerves of the performers, and the location of a number on the program which to some extent affect the tempo selected. The amateur conductor will not be in a position to consider all these factors immediately, but through experience he will be able to judge them. Perhaps he will even become more sensitive to these factors at a performance than at a rehearsal. If this occurs, it usually indicates that the pressure of the performance increased the attention to detail. Try to capture this at rehearsals.

The conductor should have some idea for tempi for a composition based on his experience and his rehearsals. Munch in his book quotes Kreisler as summarizing that compositions written in long note values can move along, while short note values can be given a little time.[4] This apparently is a good place to begin.

MUSICAL TERMS

Most scores indicate tempo markings. You are probably familiar with these terms, but now as a conductor you must translate these terms into exact tempi. To assist you, "Appendix 6: Tempo Indications"

[4]*Ibid.*

gives a list of the common terms in metronomic marking sequence. Now is the time to become well acquainted with the meanings of these terms so that you may use them in your musical thinking and as an aid in understanding what a composer means when he uses them in connection with a composition. In each case the tempo markings carry a metronomic range, some of which overlap other terms. Here then lies the problem of the conductor: to understand the limits of the tempo indicated and to select a tempo within those limits that fit the composition and the group that he is conducting.

PRACTICE EXERCISES

1. Conduct simple patterns at a stated metronomic marking without using the metronome. After several measures, begin the metronome at the indicated tempo to see if you are using the requested tempo.

2. Use the metronome to give a tempo. Without looking at the metronome, state the metronomic tempo. Practice this until you are satisfied that you can judge a tempo with considerable accuracy.

3. Set the metronome at a selected marking. Begin conducting, keeping with the metronome. After several measures stop the metronome, but keep conducting the pattern, trying to maintain the same speed or tempo as before. After a dozen or more additional measures, start the metronome again on the same selected marking. You will then know if you have had a tendency to speed or slow the tempo. Most amateurs will rush a tempo, particularly one slower than 72 M.M.

4. Plan a musical terminology quiz for your classmates made up of terms that you yourself can answer correctly.

5. Check your tempo estimation regularly with the telephone busy signal. My telephone registers M.M. 61 when I dial my own number.

6

Preparatory Motion: Two Most-used Patterns

The preparatory motion is given by the right hand (or hand containing the baton) so that the conducted group may correctly begin. The preparatory, if executed correctly, will aid the performers in commencing in unison. This problem is often treated as insignificant by the veteran but is of considerable importance. Experienced conductors who originally never studied the preparatory carefully often are still having difficulty after a number of years. Recently a student of mine reported attending a concert where an experienced band conductor had such difficulty in starting his group that he resorted to foot tapping and counting! Not so ludicrous but much more common are conductors who begin an incomplete measure by counting or conducting an entire measure, excusing themselves by blaming the musicianship of the students.

A careful study of the preparatory is essential. In fact, one teacher of conducting I know believes that all problems come from the preparatory. Consequently, he spends an entire semester on this motion because of its importance.

THE PREPARATORY FOR BEAT ONE

The right hand is truly the conducting hand, and with it lies the responsibility of executing a well-intentioned preparatory. Many conductors use the left hand as well as the right to aid in the execution of the preparatory (see Chapter 8), but a conductor will find that a good right-hand technique will be indispensable. In preparing for a downbeat, the baton hand should be held to the right of the body, the baton pointing slightly upward and inward, the elbow away from the body about 10 to 12 inches depending upon the size of person.

While the baton is held motionless for a moment, the conductor should look over the group that he is to conduct. This is advisable, particularly with school or amateur groups, since too often a problem arises that necessitates adjustment at the last minute just before the downbeat is given. With such groups a conductor is apt to be aware of misplaced music, misplaced personnel, a kicked or out-of-place stand, or other distracting items which students will be adjusting or attempting to reconcile hurriedly before the number begins. There will be those who disclaim these problems as pointing to an undisciplined group. Nevertheless, the unusual will happen, and the good conductor is alert to the bizarre by being sure that all is prepared before the preparatory is underway. I have seen several top-ranking professional conductors raise the arm for the preparatory, note something amiss, and return the arm to the side until the problem has been corrected. Sometimes the problem is just noise in the auditorium rather than a problem on stage with the performers. A beginning conductor should not hesitate to drop the arm slowly and discontinue the preparatory if all is not ready.

One evening Artur Rubinstein was the guest soloist with the Louisville Philharmonic. The preparatory was given, only to be retracted before the music began. Mr. Rubinstein was not settled after all on his piano stool. When he stood a bit to make an adjustment, one of the legs of the stool fell to the floor. It was a few minutes before the concert could continue. This will not happen often, but the unexpected has a way of being present more than we plan.

The pattern for a satisfactory preparatory for music beginning on the downbeat or first beat of any measure could be one of the following. The first pattern (Figure 6-1) is used more often for a larger group or a selection that begins modestly loud or loud. The second pattern (6-2) is used more often for small groups and/or modest or quiet beginnings. Figure 6-3 is a possible but less-used pattern.

When conducting without a baton, many conductors prefer to turn the hand slightly to the right during the preparatory, permitting the hand to take on the appearance of an invitation. Note the half turn that begins the preparatory motion. This will aid the performers in being set for an attack and will give the conducting pattern a bit more style.

By far the most important suggestion to be given a novice in conducting a preparatory motion is Rule 8 (page 40): The speed of the preparatory should be

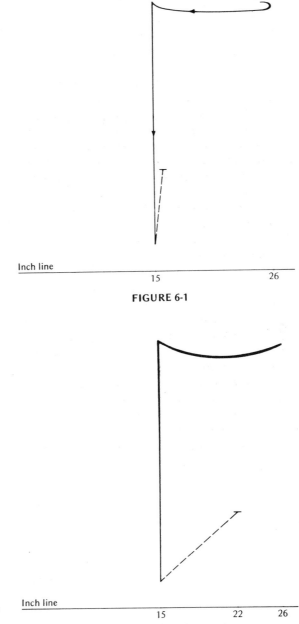

Inch line

15   26

FIGURE 6-1

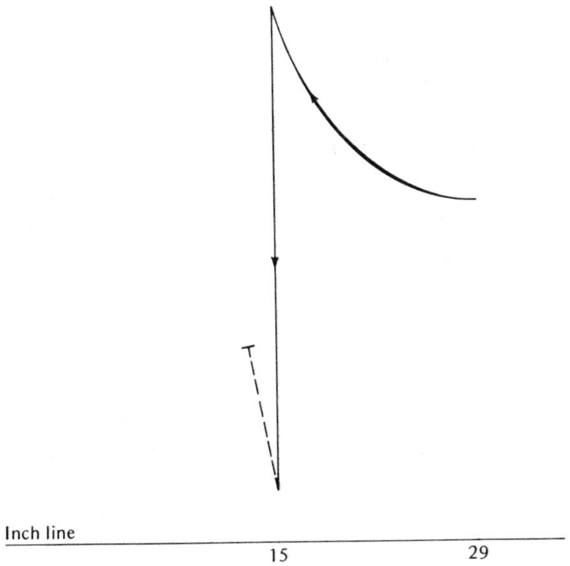

Inch line

15   29

FIGURE 6-2

Inch line

15   22   26

FIGURE 6-3

equal to the speed of the baton on the downbeat. A conductor, while waiting motionless prior to a preparatory, should consider the composition's tempo as well as checking his group. In any composition of more than one section, he should be aware of the changes in tempo that are to be conducted so that he can make a correct first preparatory that will enable the entire selection to maintain its intent. Fast compositions will be begun with poor attack if the preparatory is fast while the downbeat is slowed. The reverse is equally true. Any conductor who executes a preparatory and downbeat in this manner is either inexperienced or has not given enough consideration to the first tempo. This is a common error among new conductors. At times even experienced men become victims of this problem.

Some years ago I was visiting a music camp on the campus of a state university in Michigan. During the concert the guest conductor missed his tempo for a slower section of an overture and changed his conducting speed during the preparatory to this section that featured a trumpet solo with accompaniment. The soloist started quickly and changed while the accompaniment started slower and, after hearing two notes from the soloist, tried to adjust. The section was finished by the soloist two beats ahead of the tubas. Others were at other places.

Some conductors seem to delight in making it difficult for performers to begin. Many prefer to execute a preparatory in a florid manner so that several curls or curves of one or both hands are used before an attack is to be made. Other conductors seem to insist on the delayed attack. In the delayed attack the conductor gives a preparatory and the downbeat and is well into the rebound before the attack is expected. I have seen this type of preparatory and attack used most successfully with professional groups. However, if you watch carefully, even these professional conductors do not use the delayed attack throughout a composition. In fact, many I have observed use it only at the beginning of movements or during unison attacks.

Still other conductors like to impress audience and performers with quick starts. They walk quickly to the podium, give almost no preparatory, then a downbeat, and expect the group to begin. Some years ago at Ft. Wayne, Indiana, I was attending a music convention at which an orchestra from one of the Big Ten schools was to perform. The conductor began as described above, and the orchestra began so poorly that he decided to start the composition over again. Unusual preparatory approaches are full of pitfalls for the amateur and are not recommended until one has considerable experience with himself and as a conductor of a specific group.

RULES PRECEDING THE EXERCISES

1. Most preparatory beats are begun with the right hand and baton held away from the body about eye level.

2. The elbow should be bent slightly and about 11 or 12 inches from the rib cage.

3. The baton should point somewhat inward toward the center plane of the body.

4. The forearm is on a slant toward the right with the wrist about 18 or 19 inches from the nose.

5. The baton should be held motionless for a moment or two before the motion is begun.

6. The motion of preparatory should be upward toward the top of the pattern and then followed by the pattern.

7. The upward motion should be or act as an invitation to begin.

8. The speed of the preparatory should be equal to the speed of the baton on the downbeat.

9. The preparatory should be a simple motion, not tending to portray complications.

PRACTICE EXERCISES

1. Practice each preparatory with and without a baton. When working without a baton, try to turn the hand slightly to the right on the upward motion of the preparatory.

2. Practice each preparatory with a metronome at three suggested speeds: M.M. 120, 88, and 60. A metronome will keep steady rhythm during the preparatory and the following pattern. Note that the preparatory and downbeat are completed during two beats. A common error for a beginner is to execute this motion during one or three beats. This means that if one is to perform this correctly,

he must begin the preparatory immediately after a particular beat, arriving at the top of the pattern on the next beat. Practice by moving the wrist (imperceptibly) on the beat just at the beginning of the preparatory motion, as indicated by the diagrams below; place the next beat at the top of the preparatory and the next beat at the bottom of the pattern. Be sure to rebound. (See Figures 6-4, 6-5, and 6-6.)

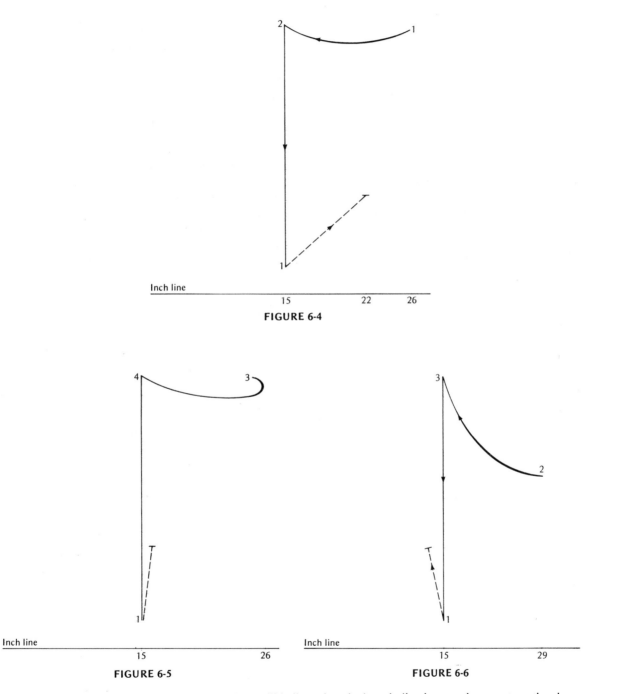

FIGURE 6-4

FIGURE 6-5   FIGURE 6-6

Note: From time to time a student will believe that the beat indications are incorrect on the above diagram. They will be practicing at a slow tempo and can execute the preparatory within the time span of one complete beat from take-off point to attack point. However, when executed at M.M. 120 this will become almost impossible and even if performed will point up the fallacy.

3. Practice the preparatory motion for both the forearm rebound and wrist rebound. Be sure to execute the preparatory in the same style as the following pattern. This will enable the beginner to become acclimated to a preparatory for different styles. Beginners often find that a preparatory for one style is not the aid for another style that it would at first appear.

4. Practice the preparatory beats with a group of players or singers. This is important since amateurs often believe that they have conquered their problems only to find that a performer does not believe that the beat and the preparatory is clear. Example: Have a student begin "America" with a group of four or more singers or instrumentalists. Have the student practice the preparatory at different tempi and styles without telling the group beforehand what the desired requirement might be.

PREPARATORY TO THE UPBEAT

If one feels at ease with the execution of the preparatory for the downbeat, then he can develop the preparatory for the upbeat, or anacrusis. Nothing is more amateurish than having a conductor count aloud the first beat of a measure so that his group may enter on the second. Equally objectionable and more noticeable is having the conductor conduct a complete measure so that a group may enter on the upbeat to the next measure. Such conducting weaknesses may be overcome with a little practice. Again the practice must be most diligent with the right hand, since it is generally that hand that is the true executor of these preparatories. Examine each diagram on the following pages and carefully practice, keeping in mind those points made previously concerning proper conducting form.

Notice that the dotted lines indicate rebounds of three sizes or styles. These wrist or forearm rebounds are of obviously greater speed than other portions of the preparatory and match the style of rebounds dis-

cussed in Chapter 3. When conducting these preparatory patterns, place the rebound in the pattern at the point where the attack is to be made or on the beat where the group is expected to begin. This emphasis executed by the wrist or forearm stresses the point of beginning for the performer and aids him in understanding precisely where an attack is to be made. This emphasis in keeping with the style of the music means a good attack by a group. The more agitated or staccato the music, the larger the snap motion. See Figures 6-7, 6-8, and 6-9 on pages 42 and 43.

GENERAL RULES

1. The preparatory for an upbeat begins immediately after a preceding pulsation.

2. Move the arm at the tempo of the composition to be performed until you reach the loop at the center of the conducting space.

3. The loop is executed a bit faster than other portions of the movement.

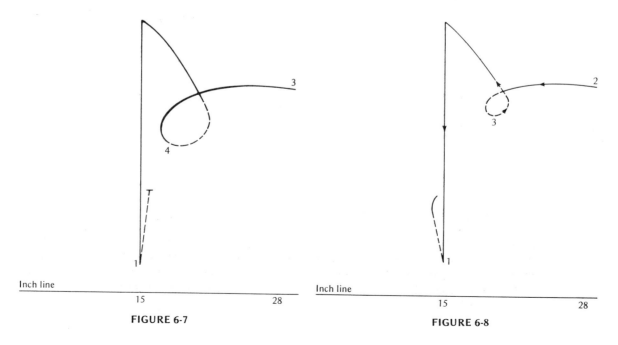

Inch line   15   28   Inch line   15   28

FIGURE 6-7   **FIGURE 6-8**

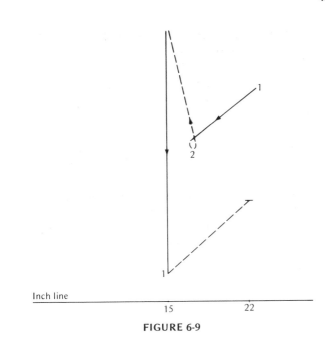

Inch line

FIGURE 6-9

4. The size of loop depends on the tempo: the slower the composition, the larger the loop.

5. The bottom of the loop is exactly on the pickup pulsation. (Figure 6-7, beat 4)

6. The only hesitation comes at the top of the pattern; the quicker the tempo, the more wait at the top of the pattern before the downbeat.

7. When the tempo is on the slow side, performers will begin to play or sing almost immediately after the bottom of the loop has been indicated. During faster tempos, performers will not begin until the top of the rebound for the upbeat has been attained. The conductor who hesitates before the top of the rebound is reached will bring unevenness to the attack and uncertainty to the first several measures (see Figures 6-7, 6-8, and 6-9).

PRACTICE EXERCISES

1. Practice preparatory patterns for upbeats with and without a baton. Practice each style for at least five minutes.

2. Practice the forearm rebound using a triple-meter pattern. Watch carefully what happens to your arm, hand, and baton as you approach beat three after the stop of the rebound for the second beat. After watching the approach and rebound to beat three for three complete measures, stop your pattern and return to the preparatory position for beat three and begin your pattern at this point. The preparatory motion should look the same both times (see Figures 6-10 and 6-11).

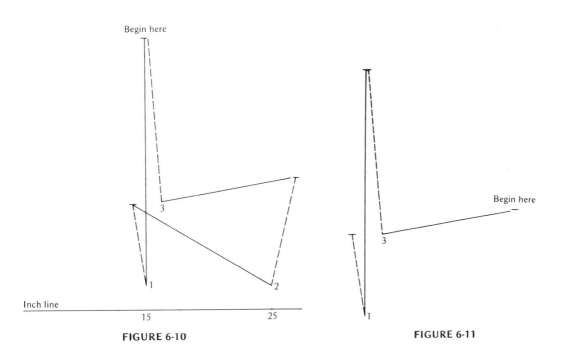

FIGURE 6-10   FIGURE 6-11

3. Practice preparatory motions with a metronome at three suggested speeds: M.M. 60, 84, and 120. Be sure the metronomic pulsation is exactly on the bottom of the loop.

4. In working with a metronome be sure that your beat points are exactly on the pulsations of the metronome. Then conduct several measures beyond the pickup so that you may feel the tempo of the pattern in relation to the tempo of the preparatory.

5. During early practice, feel the pulsation in the fingers immediately before the movement into the preparatory by the arm and baton.

6. Practice the following patterns with a group of singers or instrumental performers. Assign the various members of the C, F, or G major chord to the performers asking that they sing on the neutral syllable "loo," one syllable to the quarter note. Begin on either the downbeat (first beat of the measure) or on the upbeat. Do not tell the group of your choice nor of the choice of tempo.

Remember: The slower the tempo, the larger the loop, and the less the wrist movement at the rebound; the faster the tempo, the smaller the loop, and the more wrist movement on the rebound.

7. Conduct "The Star-spangled Banner." Note the tempo, the style, and the preparatory stance.

THE STAR-SPANGLED BANNER

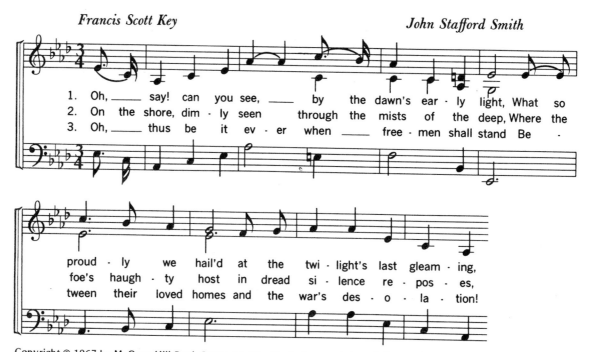

Francis Scott Key   *John Stafford Smith*

8. Conduct "May Day Carol." Note the tempo, style, and preparatory stance. Compare to tempo and style for "The Star-spangled Banner." What differences do you notice? What additional differences are suggested?

MAY DAY CAROL

English Folk Song from Essex County

9. Conduct the several measures of each of the following examples. Note differences and similarities in tempo and style.

GOD REST YOU MERRY, GENTLEMEN

Traditional   *English Carol*

AMERICA, THE BEAUTIFUL

Katharine Lee Bates   *Samuel A. Ward*

The next example has no upbeat preparatory but is included to offer style contrast and an opportunity to practice accents. A review of the forearm rebound (Chapter 3, particularly page 24) might be advisable.

Remember: One type of accent is created by (1) using the forearm rebound immediately before the accent, (2) using a larger rebound immediately before the accent, (3) driving the baton into the beat point, thus stressing the accent. Of these, the larger rebound is probably of prime importance.

The Stars and Stripes Forever
March

Conductor

JOHN PHILIP SOUSA

BATTLE HYMN OF THE REPUBLIC

Julia Ward Howe   *William Steffe*

WE GATHER TOGETHER

Traditional Dutch Tune

1. We gath-er to-geth-er to ask the Lord's bless-ing;
2. Be-side us to guide us, our God with us join-ing,

WHEN JOHNNY COMES MARCHING HOME

Louis Lambert

1. When John-ny comes march-ing home a-gain, Hur-rah, hur-rah! We'll give him a heart-y
2. Get rea-dy for the Ju-bi-lee, Hur-rah, hur-rah! We'll give the he-ro

wel-come then, Hur-rah, hur-rah!
three times three, Hur-rah, hur-rah!

7

Releases

The release is as important as the preparatory. Many an amateur conductor has practiced his preparatory motions so that a group could begin satisfactorily, but the release at the end of the composition showed his lack of attention to this detail.

The release of a composition, phrase, or section may come on any beat or part of any beat. In order that he may not be obligated to bring his hand to a particular position before being able to indicate a stop, the conductor must be at ease with the release in all places in the pattern. When a new attack follows a release, a conductor will be more apt to execute the next preparatory more satisfactorily if the preceding release has been well done, with a correct rhythmic flow. Poor releases often cause enough perturbance to bring about a poor following preparatory.

USE OF THE LEFT HAND

Although we have not yet studied the use of the left hand in detail (Chapter 8), some practice during the release is advisable as a preliminary.

To do so, indicate the release along with the right hand. Although this is not necessary if the right-hand technique is satisfactory, many conductors feel that it is an aid at a time when all must surely be correct. If the left hand is used in this manner, it almost always will move in an opposite direction to the right arm, mirroring it, and will execute the motion with palm downward. Parallel motions on releases tend to be weak and ineffective. If the right arm moves to the right for a release, the left hand will move to the left; if the right arm moves to the left, the left hand will almost always move to the right or upward over the head. This latter type of release will usually be used during a fortissimo passage.

During a soft passage, the left hand may merely close by bringing the first two fingers of the hand down to meet the thumb. The hand is turned so that the palm is down. As the fingers meet the thumb, the hand usually accents the release with a slight movement from the wrist. This accent becomes a small motion of the hand to the right or left, as if it were outlining a comma. Although not as advisable a technique as the one discussed in the paragraph above, it is used by choral more often than instrumental conductors and believed to assist vocalists in realizing final consonants in unison.

Recently I observed a prominent choral conductor, Weston Nobel, and was particularly interested in his release patterns. Most were as described in later portions of the chapter. However, one release on the word "shoes," which came at the end of a selection, was given as the reverse of the description in the preceding paragraph. In Nobel's motion a circle was formed with the thumb and third finger of the left hand and then quickly opened at the point of release. Coupled with a slight wrist motion, this made a most effective release on the vocalized "z" sound of the word.

In extremely loud passages you will often notice that professional conductors will release with both hands over their heads. This is quite effective if the dynamic of the selection calls for so dramatic an ending. For other dynamic levels you will find that the release will be in proportion to the size of beat pattern immediately prior to the release.

RELEASE ON THE DOWNBEAT

In the figures on pages 51–52, three different notations are used to indicate releases properly given on the downbeat or first beat of a measure. The figures include three meter signatures. With slight changes each of these examples could be written with any of the three signatures. In other words, what is written for the quadruple measure could easily be written for triple or duple measures. The signatures are only used to satisfy the example and are not meant to be all-inclusive.

In Figure 7-1a, the composer wishes a full measure for the last note of his composition and, in order to remind the conductor what a full measure might be, he ties the note across the bar line to an eighth. If we follow the music exactly, the correct release would be given on the downbeat of the last measure.

In Figure 7-2a, only one note is written to indicate a duration for the complete measure. If we are to be exact in our counting, this note will also be held until the downbeat of the next measure, since technically this note concludes only as the first beat of the next measure begins. This would mean the beat point of the next measure or until the downbeat is completed.

In Figure 7-3a, the music runs quickly to its ending note without the benefit of any long note or held note. Many times this kind of release comes even during a composition where the performers play or sing a series of quick notes leading up to a rest or general

pause. In this case the release would be performed as indicated below and without ritard.

In thinking of these examples, we must understand that almost any ending with a sustained note or longish resolution may be lengthened or shortened at the discretion of the conductor. There are times when the composer's indications should be followed exactly. Figure 7-3a is such a time. There are also times when the conductor requests his performers to follow his feelings for the release rather than the symbols on the printed page. This means that there could be a number of releases on the downbeat that are not printed so. Much music that may not appear to be ending on the downbeat may carry a release at this point in the conducting pattern because of the prerogative of the conductor.

Note the following points before you practice from the examples:

1. The dotted lines indicate a normal conducting pattern prior to the period of release.

2. The release motion is indicated by the solid line.

3. The solid line area of the pattern is executed with greater speed than the regular tempo of the pattern in order to assist the point of release. Without this change of speed the release will not be clean in all parts.

4. A wrist flick or rebound motion is executed at the lowest point (nearest the inch line) in the release pattern. This is used to indicate the exact place in time for the release. The quicker and/or more staccato the style the larger the rebound.

5. Each of the release patterns are shown with a possible movement counterclockwise and movement clockwise. Releases may be performed correctly in either direction. The student should practice patterns in both directions. After half a dozen trials in each direction some patterns may seem more comfortable in one direction rather than the other. Often the choice of release will be determined by the ensuing attack.

6. If a choice can be made, many conductors will release above the horizontal beat line in order to assure a sight line for all performers.

7. Each release pattern has a rebound, and like the rebound for the beat indications, its size is in proportion to the release pattern.

8. Too high a rebound on a release can offer a problem. The rebound for the release should be approximately as high as the rebound to beat one for the preceding measure.

PRACTICE EXERCISES

1. Figure 7-1*a* should be practiced with a quadruple meter pattern. Practice both clockwise and counter clockwise release patterns for five minutes each.

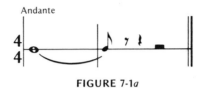

FIGURE 7-1*a*

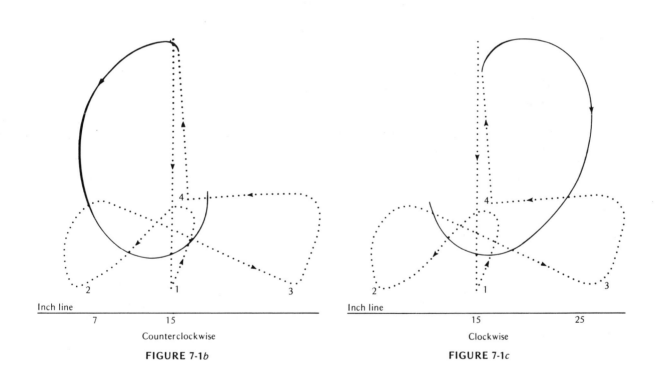

Counterclockwise

FIGURE 7-1*b*

Clockwise

FIGURE 7-1*c*

2. Extend the above example so that it contains four measures of quadruple meter. Conduct the four measures with a release on the downbeat. If you prefer one of the release patterns to the other, then use your preferred one.

3. Practice Figure 7-2*a*, using both patterns *b* and *c*. Do not alternate, but practice each separately for five minutes.

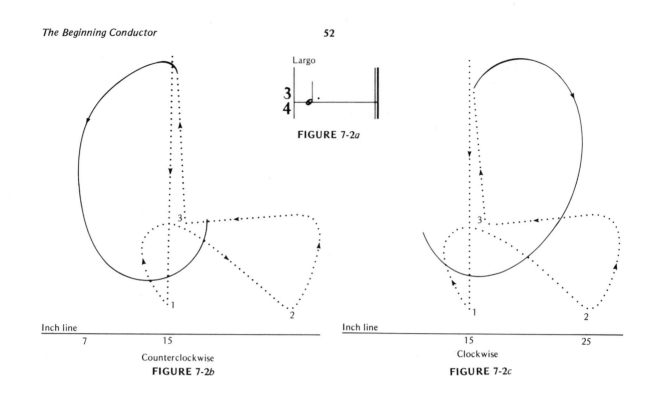

FIGURE 7-2a

Counterclockwise
FIGURE 7-2b

Clockwise
FIGURE 7-2c

4. Practice Figure 7-3*a* using both patterns *b* and *c*. Do not alternate, but practice each separately for five minutes.

    Note: Do not ritard, and do not conduct with a small pattern. The release should be vigorous but in proportion.

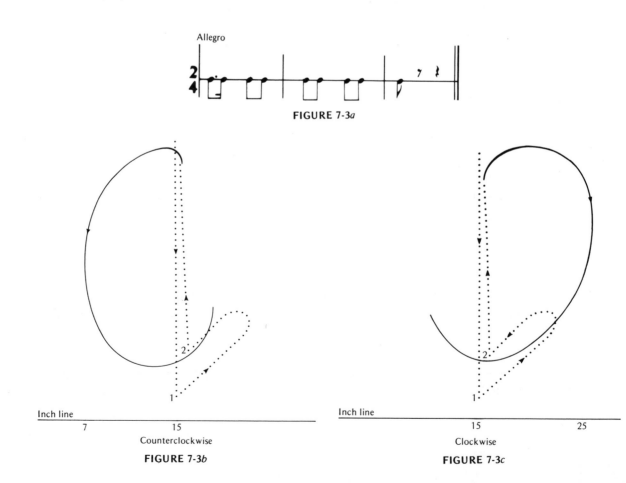

FIGURE 7-3a

Counterclockwise
FIGURE 7-3b

Clockwise
FIGURE 7-3c

RELEASE ON THE LEFT SIDE OF A PATTERN

The examples on pages 53–54 contain no 3/4 and no 2/4 signatures. The reason of course is that in these two signatures, and all other signatures of triple and duple meters, we do not conduct to the left of the downbeat line. Consequently, it would not be desirable to release on the left side of the pattern when the pattern contains no left beats.

Both of the examples are for quadruple meters but with different types of endings. The first example shows music that comes to a rather abrupt finish. If we attempt to be exact with this ending as written, we would hold the final note until the beginning of the second beat. This means that the release must be made at the second beat point. A release pattern to the left should be used.

The second example with a sustained note calls for the release to come at the end of the first beat, i.e., exactly at the beat point for the second beat of the last measure. Again a release pattern to the left should be used.

PRACTICE EXERCISES

1. Practice Figure 7-4a using each of the suggested release patterns. After choosing the pattern you believe fits you best and is most comfortable, practice with concentration until secure.

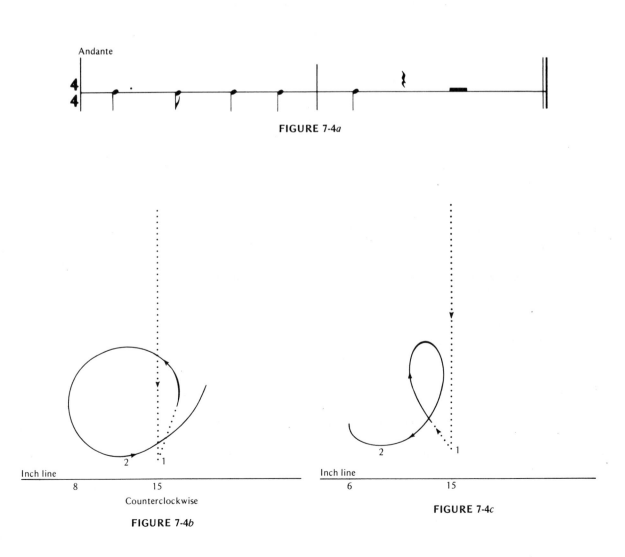

FIGURE 7-4a

Counterclockwise

FIGURE 7-4b

FIGURE 7-4c

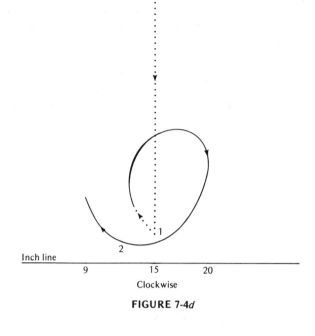

Inch line

9   15   20

Clockwise

FIGURE 7-4d

2. Practice Figure 7-5 using each of the suggested release patterns. Usually the pattern that seemed best for you in 7-4a will also be most comfortable for Figure 7-5.

Moderato

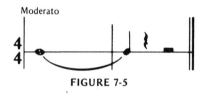

FIGURE 7-5

3. Conduct these releases from a podium for your classmates. They will be able to assist you in deciding which releases appear most effective.

RELEASES ON THE RIGHT SIDE OF PATTERN

In the examples on pages 55–56, none contains duple meters, since this release is on the right side of the conducting pattern. Only examples of quadruple or triple meters would be appropriate.

The 4/4 examples have sustained note endings. The second example of quadruple meter carries the added difference of the ritard. But this would in no way be reflected in a different cutoff point but rather just a slowing of the pattern.

These examples are only samples of the kind of endings that one might find. They are not a complete listing, and the student may find other examples that require this type of release.

PRACTICE EXERCISES

1. No fewer than ten times each, conduct through the diagrams for a release on the right of the pattern. This practice is valuable, since you will probably need different releases under different conditions. You should not be limited to only one.

2. Practice each of the music examples below, trying to ascertain your most effective release pattern.

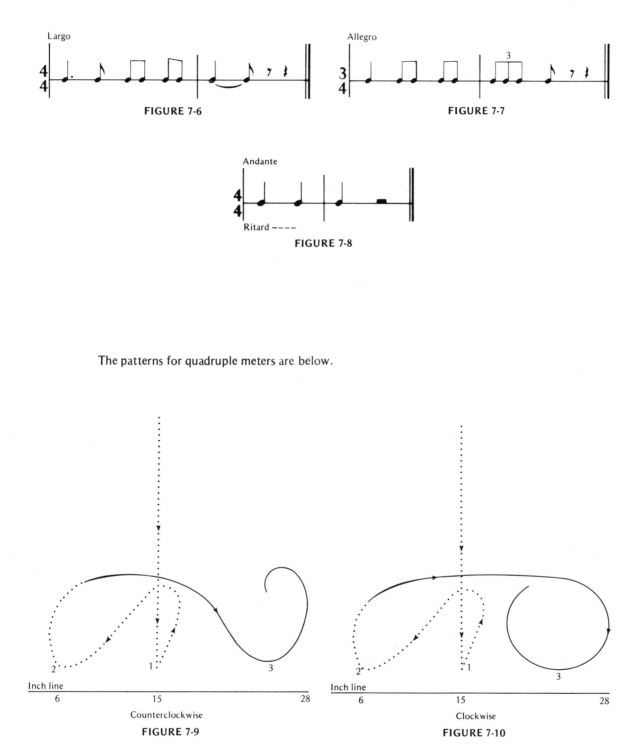

FIGURE 7-6

FIGURE 7-7

FIGURE 7-8

The patterns for quadruple meters are below.

FIGURE 7-9

FIGURE 7-10

The patterns for triple meters are shown on page 56.

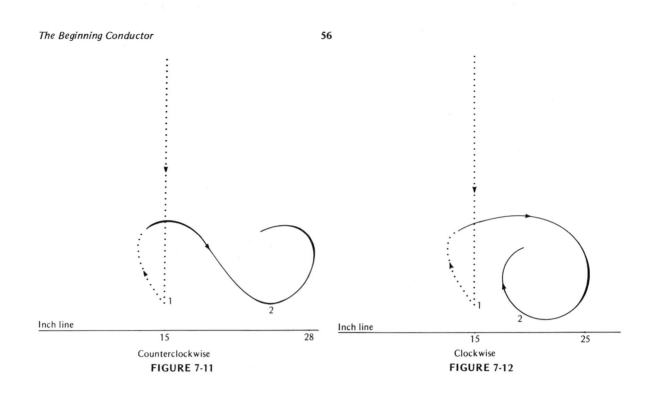

Counterclockwise
FIGURE 7-11

Clockwise
FIGURE 7-12

RELEASE ON THE FINAL BEAT OF THE MEASURE

In the patterns for this release, we have all meters represented. Because of a misunderstanding as to a correct method of execution of these patterns, many directors will continue the sound until the next downbeat. This is possible only if the music is sustained.

Although often practiced, this is not an acceptable method of procedure and points up a lack of technique. The band director approaching the last note of a march which ends on a final beat of a measure cannot prolong the sound, and if he cannot conduct correctly usually will execute two consecutive downbeats. A conductor may get by with this procedure, but it is not correct, and his inadequate execution may cause unnecessary mistakes.

PRACTICE EXERCISES

1. Practice each pattern on pages 57–58 for the release on the final beat of a measure. Quadruple, triple, and duple meter releases should feel equally comfortable.

2. Practice each example with an appropriate release.

3. Compose ending phrases for your classmates to conduct. Be sure they exemplify the release on the final beat of a measure (see Figures 7-13 to 7-15).

FIGURE 7-13   FIGURE 7-14

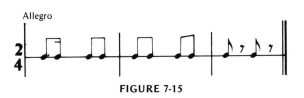

FIGURE 7-15

The patterns for quadruple meters are below.

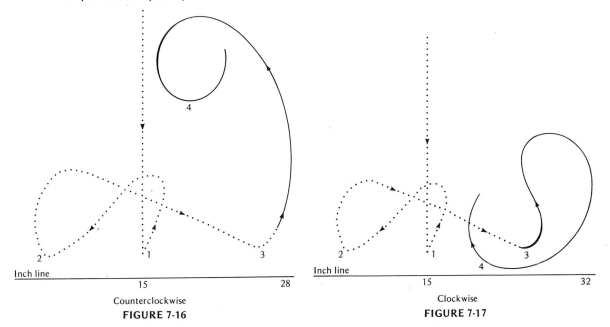

Counterclockwise
FIGURE 7-16

Clockwise
FIGURE 7-17

The patterns for triple meters are below.

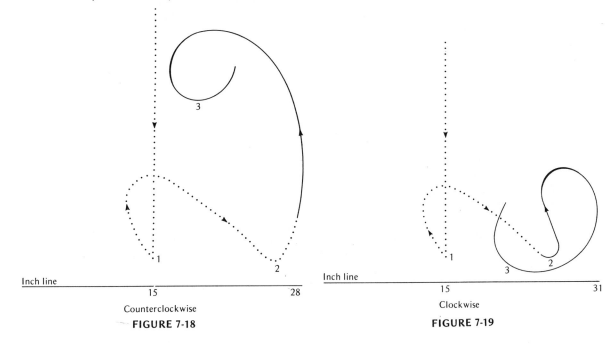

Counterclockwise
FIGURE 7-18

Clockwise
FIGURE 7-19

The patterns for duple meters are below.

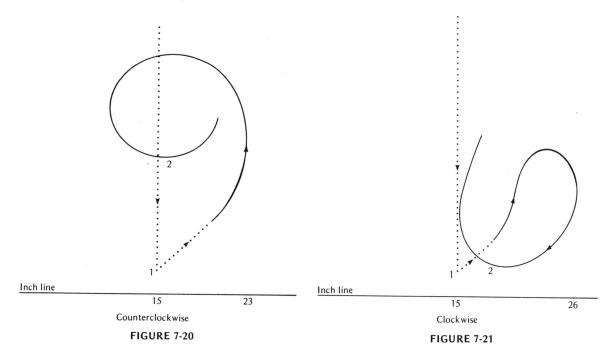

Counterclockwise

FIGURE 7-20

Clockwise

FIGURE 7-21

Some conductors prefer that all releases occur with a down-sweep of the arm and that final note releases finish inward or downward or both so that one appears compact rather than spread. However, there are occasions when this will not seem comfortable to the conductor, and/or when the ensuing attack would demand otherwise. Thus he should be at home with patterns that will enable him to interpret the music as well as possible.

In executing these releases, the right hand will accentuate that beat or part of the beat where the con-

ductor wishes the exact release to be made. A group will watch for this accentuation and will release automatically without problem if the conductor will make this definition. In execution one should realize that this also is a wrist movement, and as the hand leads into this point of the pattern, the arm will pick up speed and the wrist will move in the direction of the overall pattern. Because of these two elements the baton is moving faster than at other points along the pattern. This will accomplish the release.

REVIEW

1. Without the use of the left hand, review each release pattern to be sure the direction of each pattern you have chosen seems most natural for you.

2. Practice release patterns for all signatures in differing tempi. Use a metronome to help you release in rhythm.

3. Stand on the podium before your conducting classmates and have them sing the following short melodies: (a) "Row, Row, Row Your Boat," 6/8; (b) "America," 3/4; (c) "Marines' Hymn," 4/4. Practice varying the exact length of the last note for effect, and in doing so offer yourself the opportunity to practice different ending patterns. Do not use this as an excuse to end most phrases or selections with one or two favorite release positions.

4. Conduct a fortissimo phrase that ends on each of the beat patterns, and practice the left-hand release in opposite direction. The left-hand release should be in size and style with the right.

5. Conduct a pianissimo phrase that ends on each of the beat patterns, and practice the left-hand release in opposite direction. The left-hand release should be in size and style with the right.

6. Practice releases as found in the following musical examples. Disregard the fermata for the time being and practice releases on beats four and one in the following example.

Praise God, from Whom All Blessings Flow
Chorale for Mixed Voices, A Cappella
(S. A. T. B.)

THOMAS KEN

Maestoso

Genevan Psalter
Harmonization by
JOHANN SEBASTIAN BACH
Edited by WALTER E. BUSZIN

From *Choral Music Through the Centuries*, Compiled and Edited by Walter E. Buszin. Copyright © 1948 by Schmitt, Hall and McCreary Company. Reprinted by permission of the publishers.

The "Star-spangled Banner" is often released on beats two or three.

The verse to "Battle Hymn of the Republic" should release on beat two or three.

BATTLE HYMN OF THE REPUBLIC

Julia Ward Howe   *William Steffe*

Release the final note of "When Johnny Comes Marching Home" on beat two or one.

In addition, releases may be practiced with the following examples: "Largo" from *Celebres Sonatas* (p. 82), "Colossus of Columbia" (p. 83), "Locus Iste" (p. 109), First Movement of *St. Paul's Suite* (p. 149), and Adagio and Courrente from *Sonata IV* (pp. 259–260).

8

The Left Hand : Five Functions

Conductors with little or poor training invariably use the left hand too much for the wrong purposes. This incorrect use is the result of a poor technique in the right hand which builds insecurity in the conductor. He then demands more and more from the left hand and feels secure only with it in motion, even though it may not be in motion for the correct purposes.

Those amateurs who have had little or no training before becoming conductors often use the left hand as a pattern-conducting hand along with the right. This usually is not a good use of the left hand. This text emphasizes that delay in use of the left hand during the early practice periods will only emphasize its correct use when the appropriate time comes. The right hand should be so accustomed to the appropriate conducting patterns that it will be almost automatic in its duties when the left hand is practicing.

There should be no feeling of incompleteness on the part of a conductor if he does not use the left hand at all times. During the early chapters of the book it was best to have your left hand at your side so that you would become comfortable in this position. This does not mean that a polished conductor will leave his left hand at his side for great lengths of time, but it does mean that he is capable of doing this without feeling that it is incorrect to do so. If this incorrect feeling develops, or if a young conductor feels as if he were being watched from behind, then what he is doing will not be adequate. The conductor will then become tense, rigid, or so self-conscious that he conducts poorly. This discomfort could affect the patterns but more often is likely to bring a rigidity that creeps from the arm throughout the body and will lend a sense of unsureness to the performers.

POSITIONS WHEN NOT IN USE

When not in use, the left hand usually will be found near the center of the body, about waist high, with the wrist toward the body. From this position you will find that the conductor is able to move the hand most easily and quickly for its various uses. During the conducting of most music the left hand will be used to a great extent, and for this reason it is necessary that the left hand be ready for its responsibilities. Holding the left hand in this position for any length of time can lead to its being tensed, however, and it is at this point that the trained conductor will lower his arm to his side, bringing it to waist position just before using it again.

The difficulty of these actions for the beginner comes in making them a subconscious part of his conducting technique rather than a conscious effort. He should never have to think about lowering his arm, returning it to waist position, or controlling it. At first, the mind must think about the body's actions and must consciously control them. After practice, the left hand should move unconsciously. Only then are we sufficiently acquainted with these motions so that they are a true part of our technique.

This process can be compared to the use of a new word. If we wish to add it to our vocabulary, we must hear or read it. Many wish to spell the word over a few times and syllabify it to make sure that the pronounciation and spelling are set in the mind. Then for the first few times a conscious effort will be made to use the word correctly. After that, it will become an easier word to use until it will be a part of the vocabulary that will slip into place without conscious effort on our part.

So it is with our conducting motions. It must be assumed that we learn a certain amount of skill in each case before we attempt the newer part of the technique. This is true now with the addition of the left hand to our conducting vocabulary.

Some general rules to consider before practicing with the left hand:

1. When not in use, the left hand will be at the side of the body or at the waist.

2. For its various functions the left hand usually moves from the waist into the conducting space. Rarely does it move from the side of the body into the conducting space to execute a movement. After it has completed its movement, it returns to the waist.

3. The left hand always returns to the waist and, if it is not needed for several beats or measures, moves to the side of the body.

4. The left hand rarely moves from the side of the body into a function.

5. When at the waist, the wrist is toward the body, and the hand is to the left of the center of the body. The hand should look and feel relaxed.

PRACTICE EXERCISES

1. Move the left hand from the side of the body to the waist and back to the side of the body. Maintain the correct hand position in both instances. Perform this at least ten times, making use of a different amount of time between each movement.

2. Move the left hand from the side position to the waist position while the right hand is conducting each type of pattern (duple, triple, and quadruple meters).
   Move the left hand as indicated by the letters: w=waist and S=side. (See Figures 8-1, 8-2, and 8-3).

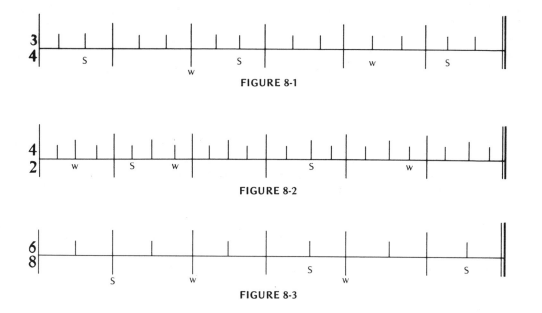

FIGURE 8-1

FIGURE 8-2

FIGURE 8-3

3. Follow the same procedure as in exercise 2, making sure that time signatures change during the example. In this type of exercise, pay attention to the signature and the right-hand execution of the signature. At the marked places raise the left hand to the waist or lower to the side as indicated (see Figure 8-4).

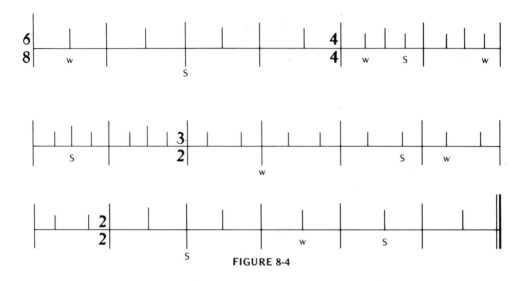

FIGURE 8-4

This type of drill may seem too simple at first, but it will tend to aid the student in a freedom that is basic toward further correct use of the left hand.

USE DURING PREPARATORIES

With most preparatory motions it is usually acceptable and desirable to use the left hand as an aid. More important, this gives the performer the impression that you are inviting him to join with you and the others. It also makes for a larger and more obvious motion which attracts the complete attention of the entire group.

During the preparatory the left hand is outstretched to the left of the body, the elbow is out from the body and slightly bent, the wrist and palm are at a 45-degree angle with the floor, and the hand is arched slightly. The left-hand position is almost identical to that of the right hand if the latter were not using a baton.

As the right hand begins the preparatory motion, the left hand moves on an angle toward the waist. When the right hand has reached the top of the preparatory and has started on the downbeat, the left hand is approximately half the distance toward the waist. Just before the right hand reaches the bottom of the downbeat, the left hand has reached the normal waist position, having the wrist toward the body and the hand immediately to left of center. Other left hand uses during preparatory are explained in appropriate subheadings in this chapter.

PRACTICE EXERCISES

1. Practice the preparatory motion for the downbeat (as in Chapter 6). This time use the left hand as an aid in the preparatory, returning it to the waist as directed above. This is not a difficult problem for the left hand, and yet it is quite important because the left hand must develop a habit of moving toward the waist as soon as the downbeat is begun. Furthermore, it should appear to move smoothly and not in any way be connected with the activity of the right hand. When you are beginning a measure on the left section of the pattern, the left hand must move more quickly to the waist so that it will not interfere with the motion of the right hand; which is to say, the hands should not cross in any way. When beginning a preparatory for a pattern to right or left, the left hand may be higher for the preparatory than the right hand. (See Chapter 16 for additional explanation.)

2. Practice the preparatory motion for the last beat of any measure. Use the left hand to assist with the preparatory. As soon as the right-hand motion is begun, move the left hand to the waist position.

   Note: Whether the right hand is smooth or obviously accented, do not always imitate it with the left hand. Our goal at this time is to develop independent hand movements in style and direction.

3. Hold both hands in a preparatory position for each of the above patterns, checking each finger of each hand to see that they do not look stiff or tight. It is important that the conductor look naturally comfortable during a preparatory.

USE DURING RELEASE

As stated in the chapter on release, most conductors believe that this problem is important enough to demand the use of the left hand.

In the preceding chapter we discussed in some detail the use of the left hand for releases. A summary of additional points is now appropriate.

1. The left hand may imitate the beat pattern for release. If so, it will mirror the pattern, moving in the opposite direction.

2. To be most effective, the left hand will not be used for a beat pattern during the immediately preceding measures but will be used only during the release motions. (In diagrams for Chapter 7, the left hand will be used for only those portions indicated by solid lines.)

3. The left hand need not imitate the right-hand release pattern but may be used in an upward motion. This is most effective during loud passages and when the right hand is moving downward; it is less effective for soft endings or releases that must be executed on other than a downbeat. To execute this motion, the left hand will leave a position near the waist and rise almost straight upward. During the motion the palm of the hand will be toward the conductor, and the forearm will be perpendicular to the floor with the hand rising to just a bit above the top of the head. At the instance of release the wrist and hand will turn further toward the conductor. The rebound of the right hand and the turn of the wrist of the left hand will be executed together and in similar style.

PRACTICE EXERCISES

1. Review the release patterns as explained in Chapter 7 using the left hand along with the right. The left hand should mirror the pattern.

2. Practice the releases in the examples below using the left hand in an upward motion. (See direction 3 above, as well as Figures 8-5 and 8-6).

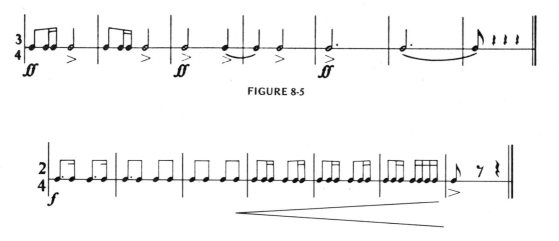

FIGURE 8-5

FIGURE 8-6

USE FOR DYNAMICS

Probably the most common inclination for the left hand in conducting is to use it to indicate dynamics and shadings of expression. The beginning conductor often believes that he is making a difference in dynamics when he uses the left hand for patterns. Actually, however, he is usually so engrossed with the problems of conducting that he is not aware that what began as an intent for a simple indication of dynamics became double-hand conducting. For this reason it is important that each beginning conductor work the left hand carefully step by step until he feels that he can move the left hand independently for each new development of technique.

Using the left hand to indicate dynamic level involves moving it from waist position to a position at least at eye level and returning it. This should not be taken to mean that all dynamic levels will involve this one motion, but rather that within this space limitation, the dynamic levels for the left hand will be most often indicated.

When the hand is near the waist with the palm away from the body and toward the performers, a soft performance is indicated. When the hand is as high as the forehead with the palm toward the conductor, a loud performance is indicated. Intermediate positions indicate corresponding levels and nuances.

If the hand is at the waist in correct position, the palm will be toward the body. In beginning a crescendo, turn the wrist over and slowly move the hand on a 45-degree angle from the center of the body. Pace your movements so that your request for dynamic increase will terminate about at the height of the body. Never end with a straight elbow; it should be bent a bit.

When requesting a decrescendo, move the hand quickly and unobtrusively from the waist to a position about as high as the head. In this move the palm of the hand is toward the performers. At the peak of the motion the hand will pause momentarily, then begin its descent toward the waist. The speed of the descent will depend upon the length of the decrescendo in the music.

Many dynamic movements will be combinations of these two. If the dynamic level does not go beyond a modest volume, the left hand may use only modest movements — not rising too high or moving too low. The nature of the music and the length of the dynamic usually controls the motion.

If one is conducting a crescendo followed by a decrescendo, the hand moves from the waist toward the higher position; at the top of the motion the wrist turns so that the hand moves from the palm inward to palm toward the performers. This movement should not occur hurriedly but rather should be executed smoothly in the time allotted for maximum volume. When the hand is in its outermost position, it will be about two feet from the forehead with the elbow slightly bent, the hand to the left from the body at about the same location as for a preparatory.

It is also possible to indicate a constant dynamic with the left hand. If one wishes a constant fortissimo, one should retain the left hand at the high position. Normally, however, a conductor will not hold the hand stationary. This stationary position, although at a hand level which would be considered an indication of maximum volume, will only tend to deaden the tone color and lessen the volume. In other words, the opposite of what is wished for could happen in this case. In order to overcome this problem most conductors will move the left hand in a vibrating manner, as if trying to imitate a slow vibrato on a stringed instrument. This movement, which indicates a feeling of emotion, usually will tell the performers that the conductor wishes the volume not to diminish and perhaps even to increase a bit.

Another method of obtaining the same result is to move the left hand slightly higher, or in some cases, a bit farther to the left. This movement will have the same effect upon the performing group; they will maintain the volume level or even increase it if the hand moves obviously to the left. It is best to remember that in a case such as this the left hand should not be moved with suddenness or in a jerky manner. This will only give the performers the impression that an accent or a sudden increase in volume is desired.

On the other hand, if one wishes to maintain a soft volume level, a conductor will be able to ask this by keeping the left hand near the waist, the elbow somewhat closer to the body than usual, and the hand turned so that the palm will be toward the performers. If the hand is kept in this position, it will not cause the deadening results in tone color that would be experienced with a stationary hand in a forte position. It is not uncommon for conductors to keep the left hand quite stationary when indicating a sustained soft passage. In other instances the left hand will move slowly in a small circle in front of and to the left of the body. This movement has a tendency to call attention to the left hand and the dynamic level desired and, at the same time, to indicate to the performers that a quiet is requested for the entire group and not just a few performers at the left of the conductor. Here again, the hand should not move fast or in a jerky manner.

The space limits of waist to forehead and from the center of the body to about 2 feet left of the body are average for the left hand. A professional conductor often will use more space. Many times a professional will indicate an extraordinary dynamic level by having the left hand extended as high above his head as possible, or lowered dramatically below the waist. These actions for the experienced conductor are not to be condemned. The beginner will find that as he gains confidence in his own ability, he will use more conducting space as he deems it necessary. It is important to remember, however, that these motions

are still the exception, and it is best that he learn first the most common areas of performance and feel confident with them.

The left hand should be given a great deal of opportunity to work in areas of dynamic indication, since this will be its most important use. Therefore, it becomes necessary to practice the left hand under different conditions until it becomes quite independent in action.

PRACTICE EXERCISES

1. Conduct the following using the dynamics indicated:

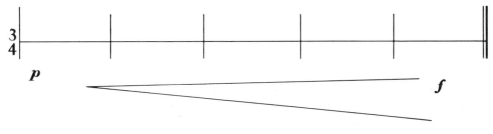

FIGURE 8-7

The left hand should be used to assist with the preparatory. This means that during the preparatory the left hand will be about at the same level as the right hand, with arms outstretched. When the right hand begins to move toward the downbeat, the left hand should also move to the position at the waist which has been practiced before: palm inward, hand just left of center. After two beats with the left hand in the position at the waist, the left hand begins to move away from the body and extend itself. The wrist should turn over as it moves away from the body. The exercise should end with the left hand in about the same position in which it began the preparatory. At no time should the left hand move unsteadily or indicate the beat.

It is a common problem for beginners to accent the beat with the left hand as they conduct it in pattern with the right hand. The left hand becomes continually higher, as it should, but the beats are emphasized so that the left hand does not contain a smooth incline from the waist to the upward position. This indicates that the left hand is still too connected with the performance of the right and that the conductor is reacting too much to the beat and the pulse of the right hand.

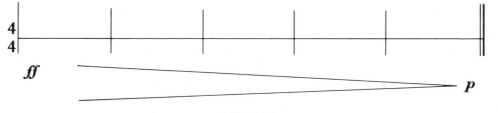

FIGURE 8-8

2. In the above exercise (Figure 8-8) the left hand should be extended for the preparatory.
Remember: for a preparatory the left hand fingers are slightly curved and the wrist is on a 45-degree angle with the floor.
As soon as the downbeat is begun, the left hand should be turned slightly (the wrist is now parallel to the floor and the palm completely facing the performers) so as to indicate to the performers that a lessening of volume is desired. The left hand will then begin to move toward the body and the waist position. The beginner will find this difficult. He will move the left hand too fast, arriving at

the waist before the last beat of the fifth measure. As a result, the performers would be playing with a soft dynamic before the desired time. The student must learn to move the hand and arm in so controlled a manner that he arrives precisely on the last beat of the measure. Again, there should be no unevenness or beat indication with the left hand.

3. In the exercise below the left hand combines the first two exercises while the right hand conducts another simple pattern. We should mention at this point that usually the right hand will aid in the conducting of dynamic levels by conducting a smaller pattern for soft passages, a larger one for loud dynamic levels. This, accompanied by the left-hand technique, is a true indicator of the level desired.

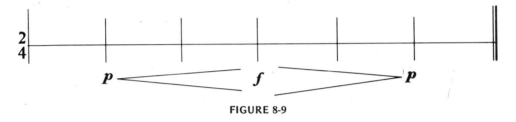

FIGURE 8-9

4. Of the better-known and more often used meter signatures, the duple meter measure offers the beginners the most problems, so let us practice it again. In this exercise, notice that there are two measures where the left hand can be at waist position waiting for the next crescendo. A second possibility would be to use the left hand in a pianissimo position of constant movement, as discussed on page 66. Near the end of the exercise below, the volume indicated is less loud than at the beginning and less soft than near the center. Appropriate differences in the left-hand position should be apparent.

FIGURE 8-10

5. Other combinations and demands for the left hand can be practiced. Write some exercises for your classmates that could be typical of the material you find in literature that high school students perform.

USE WITH PATTERNS

After considerable discussion of the problems involving the left hand for conducting of patterns and much practice in avoiding its use, it now seems almost ironic that we must consider when and how the left hand conducts, making use of patterns.

Note: This section should not be practiced if the student is having any difficulty in smoothly executing any of the previous exercises.

Two situations present themselves to the conductor when left-hand conducting might be warranted.

Directing for Emphasis

There are times that an extreme dynamic or marked feeling is called for. Examples of this could be found during the beginning of a selection, a specific measure, or two, and most often near the end of a composition when a particular climax is desired. At these special times the conductor's use of the left hand as well as the right for the conducting of patterns acts as an emphasis.

The sample scores illustrate this point: The ending of, first, Osterling's arrangement of Wagner's *Die Meistersinger* for band, and, second, Handel's "Halleujah Chorus."

Overture to *Die Meistersinger,*
Richard Wagner, arr. Osterling

Nọ 44 – CHORUS
"HALLELUJAH!"

G. F. Händel
Edited by T. Tertius Noble
Revised by Max Spicker

Rev. xix: 6; xi: 15; xix: 16

Change of Tempo

Whenever the tempo is being changed, the conductor may make sure of his communication with the two-hand technique. Again, you will note the urgency of change or a conductor's desire for definite communication. He will use his left hand only long enough to carry the desired effect to the performers.

Even if used appropriately, there are times when the left hand does not conduct the entire measure along with the right hand. This is particularly true if the conducting pattern is complicated. When this occurs, the left hand is used to emphasize the downbeat and such beats as can be simply executed, and/or it may wait until the upbeat and execute this with the right hand.

In some of the simpler patterns, for example, 2/4 and 3/4, it is possible to conduct these completely with both hands using the pattern. When this occurs, the left hand reverses the pattern so that it conducts away from the body as the right conducts also away from the body. It is during these simple meters that most amateurs make the mistake of unnecessary left-hand conducting.

Concerning the 4/4 meter: When this pattern is used for double-hand conducting, neither hand will cross each other on the second beat. The hands come toward each other, but the second beat is shortened so that the hands do not cross or touch.

Two examples illustrate the advisability of left-hand use with tempo changes, nineteen measures from Merle Isaac's arrangement of the overture to *Hansel and Gretel* and eight measures of McBeth's *Masque*.

Overture to *Hansel and Gretel*
Engelbert Humperdinck, arr. Isaac

Piano - Conductor

Masque
W. Francis McBeth

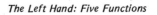

PRACTICE EXERCISES

1. Practice the simple conducting patterns (duple, triple, and quadruple meters) with both hands being sure that emphasis is placed on the pattern as if the music were fortissimo and marcato.

2. Practice double-hand conducting making use of different time signatures and at different tempos. For example: M.M. 60, 90, 112 (see Figure 8-11).

   Note: Use double-hand conducting only enough to set the tempo change. In this exercise, assume that it would take a downbeat plus one additional beat.

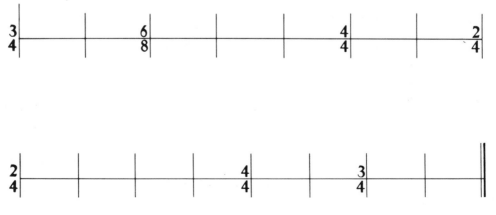

FIGURE 8-11

3. Practice the following exercise using double-hand conducting for a complete measure following the tempo change. Practice this at M.M. 60, 84, 120 (see Figure 8-12).

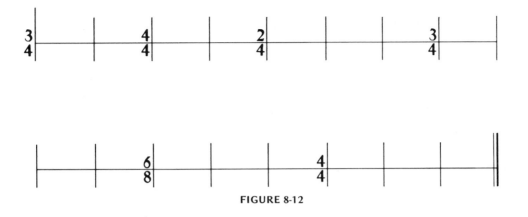

FIGURE 8-12

4. Practice double-hand conducting where necessary in the following exercises. The left hand should be used to indicate dynamic changes as well as an aid to understanding the time signature changes. When the two seem to conflict, choose the signature change on the assumption that this need be called to the attention of the performer more than the dynamic. The left hand should move smoothly from one assignment to the other (see Figures 8-13 and 8-14).

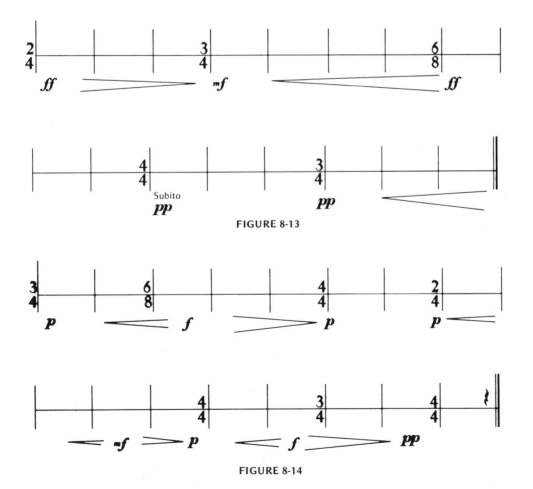

FIGURE 8-13

FIGURE 8-14

9

The Score:
Primary Considerations

It is now appropriate that we consider the score. A thorough knowledge and understanding of the score is a major component of conducting.

SIMPLE SCORES

Actually, the score of a piano composition is that from which the piano plays. The score for a solo song is that from which the singer sings. This type usually consists of three staves: one staff for the singer and two for the piano accompaniment. The score for an instrument sonata is also in three lines: one for the soloist and two for the pianist. Usually both the solo and the accompaniment part (the entire score) can be found on the pianist's copy to enable him to better follow the solo part.

Another type of score with which you are familiar is the vocal ensemble score. In some editions you will find a line for each part, but in the more simply written vocal music, two vocal lines are often combined, with the soprano and alto placed on one staff, and the tenor and bass on another. If there is an accom-

paniment to the vocal score, you will often see six staves in a brace. The dark line at the left of the music will indicate a brace, and enables the eye to see at a glance how many staves are within it (see pages 82ff.).

Despite the fact that performers regularly use and observe these simple scores, the beginning conductor is often at a loss with them. The instrumentalist is prone to work only the instrumental line in a sonata and disregard the piano accompaniment, particularly if he is not strong at the keyboard and does not easily read piano music. If a person plays the piano modestly well, often those particular staves get so much of the eye attention that one would not be justified in claiming that a score is being read. In other words, to really read a score one must be aware of all lines simultaneously and with the emphasis each is due. Of course this cannot be accomplished by merely wanting or expecting it, but through study that approaches the score from several perspectives.

To aid in this skill, carefully study the score of all music in which you are involved during the remainder of the course, even scores of piano music. Meticulously work with each to ascertain the particular musical meanings the composer has written into the work which a conductor must comprehend. If you are interested in the field of instrumental music, piano scores should be of interest to you, since many times band and orchestra scores are written in condensed form, giving an appearance similar to a complex piano score.

Observe either sonata scores or vocal three-line scores for solo singers, conducting those that you know well. If you were to help someone else to sing or play the score, take note of the points you would remember to mention to them. When you "know the score," you will hear in your mind without performance all the sounds of the composition, and this is what the phrase means: by looking at the printed page you re-create what the score can be when performed. The solo score will not be conducted publicly, but it serves as excellent practice material.

The simplest complete score that is used by a conductor is that for a vocal ensemble with two parts (SA), three (SSA) (SAB), or four (SATB) (TTBB). Although the score is simple, in order to conduct this type of vocal ensemble well, one also needs to study it carefully.

STUDY OF THE SCORE

Looking at the score, one should begin to think of it as a conductor might — as a visual contact with a work of art; as the only concrete representation of sounds chosen by this composer for expression of a musical idea. Do not consider it only a performance problem with technical challenges. More importantly, consider its form, the manner in which the phrases and sections have been arranged to create the whole, the rhythm that carries this form expressively, and the progression of melodic and chordal elements that speak to this movement.

Your first activity is to learn the score through study. Study of a score is of several types. All are valuable, and no single type will alone suffice. Taken together, they add to the total concept of the work. First is the study that comes through performance. As a performer in an ensemble, you have become familiar with a single line of the work or probably approached it more from a technical standpoint. Performance from the podium is different than from a section of the group, and rehearsal must become a part of your study, but in a special way. Your attention now must be toward the work as an artistic whole, and this new kind of approach is not easily acquired.

Second is the understanding and synthesis in the mind as one perceives the score and focuses on its theoretical and artistic aspects, storing information in order to bring it to bear upon the entire work as it is performed. Theory and music literature courses should have assisted you to begin this kind of study.

Third, even after you know the score, you must feel it within your conducting technique. You may have memorized the score, being able to advise each player of his notes or understand its style, but unless you feel the work in your body as a conductor, you might — as a visual contact with a work of art; as the only concrete representation of sounds formance from the podium is different from that of a coordination of these three areas, but particularly with developing your skill in the third.

By studying the score these three ways, the conductor ascertains how he can aid the individual performer in understanding his particular responsibilities and plans how he will work to aid the group in recognizing musical meanings, thereby producing a more completely satisfying musical experience.

Problems of Performance

Because you are a performer and will be confronting the amateur primarily as he performs, you should study your score during rehearsal (performance), considering the unique problems of your ensemble.

A few sample questions will be helpful.

1. What ranges are involved in the work? Are these within easy grasp of your group or do they challenge the limits of their ability? Do you hear a style deficiency because of range problems?

2. Is special equipment or are special effects involved? If these are not possible, is the aesthetic effect weakened?

3. To be musically satisfying, does the work demand balances that are not possible with the instrumentation or voices of your group?

4. Are the technical demands realistic? Are your performers so involved with technique that the musicalness evades them?

5. Does the work over- or underchallenge your performers and consequently defeat your musical planned growth pattern?

6. Do intonation problems rob the composition of its artistic qualities?

Some directors never go beyond the technical aspects of the performance to hear and analyze these items in terms of the pervading musical qualities.

Problems of Musicalness

Some elementary questions and comments will assist you in beginning to learn the score in a musical way.

1. Considering the title, type of material, composer or period of writing, and style, what are the appropriate performance practices for this composition?

2. What are the tempo and/or mood markings, and what relationship do these have to the style and form?

3. What is the time signature, and what relationship does it have toward an understanding of the rhythmic patterns involved in the composition?

4. The key signature should remind you to consider the keys or centers of tonality within the composition and their relationship to the form. Analyze the progression of tonality throughout the composition, noting the significance to melodic line and harmonic structure. A conductor must constantly be alert to the tonal relationships being performed by his group: the intervalic relationships as well as the broad perspective.

5. Study the compositional treatment and interplay of the voices.

   a. Do all the parts begin together? If not, when do they enter? If they enter together, what is the importance of each to the other?

   b. Is the melodic line or thematic material consistently in an upper voice (where it often is located) or in another voice?

   c. Do the accompanying parts follow the melodic line rhythmically, or are the parts more independent?

   d. Will the tempi assist the compositional balance or offer particular problems toward understanding the function of each voice?

Problems of Kinethesis

After studying the score in musical ways, the conductor then reexamines it to unite body technique with musical goals. He asks himself what movements should be involved to help the group best understand his in-

terpretation and the musical meanings that he wishes to convey as a result of his synthesis. Knowing the score brings security in the knowledge of where certain rehearsal problems might occur, and planning your conducting technique aids in overcoming such problems.

Ask yourself such questions as these:

1. Where will you use the left hand to better capture the style of the composition or indicate nuances that enhance its artistic qualities?

2. Do preparatories and releases indicate the tempo and character of each section of the work?

3. Through stance and movement does the body suggest an understanding of the composition?

4. Are there alterations of tempo that add to the meaning of the music? If so, what specific conducting techniques will best portray these meanings?

5. What techniques might assist the right hand in being more effective with the interpretive indications of patterns, phrasing, and rhythms?

Answer these questions by conducting the score for yourself alone. Too many conductors imagine that they must be in front of a performing group in order to practice. Problems that are worked out by the conductor with only a score will save much difficulty and many moments at the rehearsal.

To reiterate the main point, studying of the score is most important. Too many amateurs make too little attempt to know the score before a rehearsal. Can you imagine a director of a TV show coming to his first rehearsal without having read the script? Surprisingly, many conductors in our schools come to rehearsals without having studied the score beforehand. They falsely insist they must know how the score sounds before they know what to do. To this point, some band conductors travel with tape recorders to several band literature reading sessions before they will choose or conduct their concert and festival numbers. A good conductor will study the score so that he will know the music and be able to direct his performers in a more meaningful rehearsal.

SCORE PRACTICE PROCEDURES

Charles Munch, for a number of years conductor of the Boston Symphony Orchestra, suggests that a conductor need not feel intimidated about taking a score to a piano and playing it for himself.[1] This can be a great aid. A piano will only give you a representation of the sound, however, and will not help you completely to plan your work as a conductor. The sounds of the group for which the number is written must be reproduced in the mind's ear.

Another aid often used is the record player. This is an excellent aid in hearing interpretation, understanding the tempo, or aiding in memorization. I would caution, however, against using it as an aid to conducting technique. One develops conducting technique through study and practice, not by relying upon a record whose speed will not permit you to analyze your problems or to think carefully about the score as you work.

Consequently, I would suggest that you:

1. Study your score in private, planning your conducting technique.

2. Rehearse your score with a group as rehearsal time permits, noting conducting problems and performance problems.

3. Study your score again and replan your conducting technique for a new rehearsal, remembering problem areas. How can you help to solve the problems by your conducting?

4. Rehearse again.

[1]Charles Munch, *I Am a Conductor*, Oxford University Press, New York, 1955, p. 50.

5. At this point, if possible, listen to a recorded version, but do not conduct along with the record. Listen several times if you believe it will be helpful.

6. Return to your study of the score without the record, practicing your baton technique at the tempo needed by you to clarify your technique. As in practice procedures used by an instrumentalist, do not hesitate to practice at a somewhat slower speed if your technique is still not as you wish it.

7. Always conduct privately without performers or record two or three hours before a performance. Conduct each number completely. Omit no facet of your technique that will be needed in concert. Include even the simplest sections, because the overall rhythm of a phrase is just as important to feel in the conducting arm as the more intricate requirements.

This type of planning will assist in establishing a readiness for conducting details during a performance.

SCORE READING

In the exercises (not the musical examples) that you have conducted in the last few chapters you have begun to use a kind of musical shorthand which represents musical notation. Lines indicating measures are long lines crossing the horizontal line (see Figure 9-1).

FIGURE 9-1

The measures may be subdivided by short and longer lines. These short and longer lines should help you with conducting, for when a measure reaches the length that it can be partitioned, it then can be divided in conducting also with some beats to the left of the pattern and some to the right. For example, in a measure of quadruple meter this is indicated by a measure line, a short perpendicular line representing beat two, a longer perpendicular line representing beat three, and a short line for beat four (see Figure 9-2).

FIGURE 9-2

Most likely the eye will quickly see how the measures are divided in this diagram, but when a staff and notes are involved, sometimes it becomes more difficult. Good sight readers almost always quickly divide the measure at sight into parts or beats, enabling them to understand and comprehend the music immediately and keep abreast of the rhythmic movement of the music. Ensemble performers, particularly instrumental performers, usually are more adept at this than vocal and/or solo performers.

The conductor should have this ability even more than the performers. He should learn to read the score by making a habit of dividing the measures so that the notes on each beat may be quickly located. Measures of considerable length could have the beats subdivided. The length of the measure and the number of notes in the measure will act as a criterion. In each case the understanding of beat placement and note location will be considerably aided by this type of immediate visual division. This is a skill that can be developed, and the shorthand of each exercise is meant to underline this type of division for you so that you may more readily perform this function when confronted by a score and develop your skill in score reading. The purpose of this shorthand will become clearer as we progress through the next few chapters.

A conductor uses a score in two ways. First, during study, prior to rehearsal or at rehearsal when a problem arises and a detail must be observed, the score is read note by note or symbol by symbol. This type of score reading contributes greatly to the whole. Most of us have prepared for this type of reading by playing an instrument, singing from a vocal line, studying theory and orchestration, in fact, through almost every facet of our music study.

A second type of reading enables the conductor to overview the entire page of score and to be prompted in his responsibilities toward dynamics, phrasing, balance, entrances, ensemble, texture, and many of the necessary elements of the composition that will give it musicality. This type of reading is seldom developed by other classes and should be one function of a class for the beginning conductor. To encourage this development, a type of musical shorthand has been developed to lead you from simple to more complex score reading.

PRACTICE EXERCISES

1. The following examples (figures) should be considered as reductions of a score. Although consisting of two lines, they represent two parts of the performing organization. In one example they could represent the strings as opposed to the woodwinds and brasses; the brass as opposed to the woodwinds; or the male as opposed to the female voices. Other representations might be considered that would include the clarinets and flutes versus the low reeds, or the low brass versus the high brass. You may define these exercises as you wish and conduct them as you define them, using the location of the instruments as you find them in your college organizations.

    Figure 9-3: All eight measures should be conducted; the measures with no markings are void in specific items that should be called to the attention of the conductor. The third measure contains accents in the entire playing group. Measure four consists of a half note in some parts while the remainder of the organization continues with quarter notes. The composition ends with the entire organization playing a half note on beats three and four. The release should be on the point of one.

    Figure 9-4: This exercise features various types of cuing, since the somewhat antiphonal effect is continual throughout the 16 measures. Observe the dynamics and the ritard.

    Figure 9-5: The lines are similar in this exercise. Changes of tempo, meter, accents, cues, and releases are featured.

    Conduct the following score reductions:

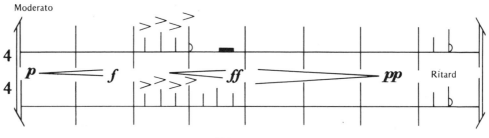

FIGURE 9-3

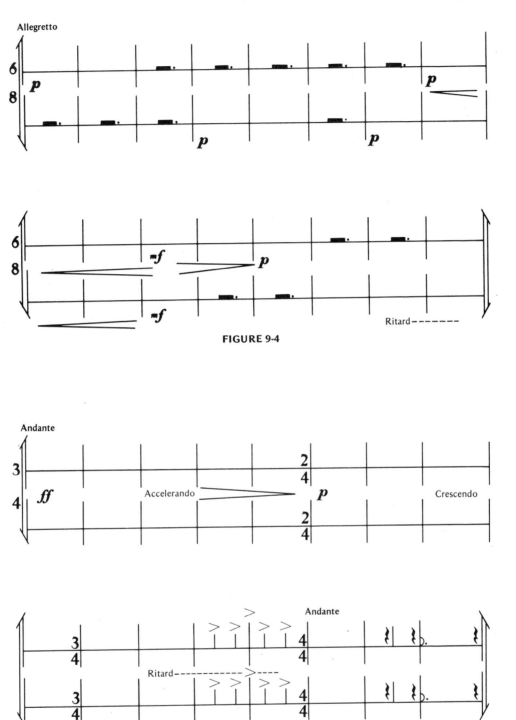

FIGURE 9-4

FIGURE 9-5

2. Conduct the following music examples after you have discussed the scores with your classmates and have created your own score reductions.

   Note: Many multilined scores may be reduced to one, two, or three lines.

4. LARGO

from *Celebres Sonatas*

G. Tartini, Op. 1, No. 5

COLOSSUS OF COLUMBIA
MARCH

by Russell Alexander
arranged for Concert Band by
Glenn Cliffe Bainum

Conductor

To the Townspeople
of Amherst, Massachusetts
1759 – 1959

Choose Something Like a Star*

Four-part Chorus for Mixed Voices
with Piano Accompaniment

Robert Frost   Randall Thompson

Danse des Bouffons

Dance of the Clowns

From the opera "Snegourotchka"

Piano - *Conductor*

N. Rimsky - Korsakow
Arranged by Adolf Schmid

Piano- *Conductor*

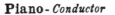

Piano - *Conductor*

10

Six Simple Cuing Devices

There are two attitudes toward the importance of the cue in conducting. Some professional and some amateur conductors give very few if any cues to the performer. Some high school directors rehearse so often on a given composition that cuing is not necessary. This is particularly true of choral conductors. However, I believe if one is to learn a good conducting technique, he should cue often during these formative stages. One can always perform fewer cues, but later it is difficult to build in these motions.

THE BODY CUE

The body is one way of alerting a section or individual to an entrance. The body as a whole is rarely used directly for a cue, but it can act as the alerting agent. When a conductor turns to a violin section, it should alert them to the approaching entrance. In turning toward a section, the conductor not only alerts the performers but also gives them a front view of the conducting pattern. A conductor who does not move a little on the podium will appear too timid and

too amateurish in approach. Most often the movement that removes this amateurism is executed at the time of cuing those sections which are located immediately to the far left or far right of the conductor. When the performer or section is more or less directly in front of the conductor, the conductor will usually take a small step forward in the direction of the person or section. This acts as a cue along with the regular conducting pattern.

CUES WITH THE EYES

The eyes are most useful in the giving of cues. In fact, good professional conductors who give few hand or body cues usually cue constantly with the eyes. The conductor should always look toward the person or section that he wishes to cue. Often this is sufficient for some obvious entrances or with skillful performers. In order to look at a section it is wise to turn the body somewhat in that direction. Merely turning the head quickly in one direction or the other will not act as a cue. It is an error for the conductor merely to lift

93

the eyes for a moment at the time of entrance. Even if this quick glance is executed a beat or two before the time of entry, it will be ineffective as a cue.

The method that will assure precision and understanding between conductor and performer consists of two steps. First, the conductor should look toward the performer for three or four beats prior to the entrance. This will enable the performer to make contact with the conductor some time during those few seconds. It is this contact that is essential. For faster tempi the contact should be made earlier, but in any event it should not be made regularly at the exact same place in the score. The irregularity of this contact actually establishes greater confidence.

Second, at the cue point the conductor should either nod the head slightly in the direction of the performer and/or give a slightly emphasized beat with the right hand while continuing to look at the performer. If a hand cue is needed, one of the cues discussed later could be used. In all cues the eyes should be used prior to the cue. In some entrances where persons or sections have recently been playing, only the eyes will be used.

When the cuing is for a section, the conductor will want to make the same contact with the section several beats before the entrance. In such a case it is advisable to move the eyes from person to person, making the contacts that you desire, so that as many of the section will be alerted as possible. It is this communion of performer and conductor that leads to sureness and precision.

Many times when the eyes are used in this manner for a cue of a section or performer, the head is also called into action. Eye contact is made as described, but in order to be assured of the entrance at just the correct beat, the conductor should move his head slightly in the direction of the performer. If this movement is obvious to any one in the audience, it is too large. In other words, it must be so small that it becomes an intimate thing between the conductor and the performer, imperceptible to any observer.

I have watched many well-known professional conductors execute this eye contact, and if one concentrates completely and knows the score well enough to be alerted to the cue possibilities, a viewer will be able to "see" this contact between performer and conductor. Perhaps the word should be changed from "see" to "feel," for many times it is just a feeling or an exchange of thought waves that makes the cue successful.

Another assist for the eyes is the act of breathing along with the entering performers, establishing another bond of reassurance. This is often used along with hand cues.

RIGHT-HAND CUES

Many cues can be executed by the right, or conducting hand. In this case the eye contact must be made beforehand as previously described. For these cues the right hand usually emphasizes that particular beat in some way.

In the case of the downbeat, if the conductor wishes to cue with the right hand, he could:

1. Use a larger downbeat than on previous patterns.

2. Slow the preparation as it approaches the beat point. In the case of a soft entrance cued by the right hand, the hand will delay arriving at the beat point by slowing itself just before that point. In this case there will be no perceptible delay of the rebound, and it probably will be normal in size.

3. Use a slower rebound from the beat point, hurrying to the next beat soon thereafter so as to arrive in time for the second beat.

In the case of a very loud or accented entrance to be cued by the right hand, the conducting hand will hurry toward the point of the beat and then will delay at the point and during the early parts of the rebound. The rebound is apt to be larger than if the entrance were without cue.

4. Misplace the beat point in the conducting space so as to more or less point to the section or person needing the cue.

This right-hand cue merely assists in giving security to the performer and does not of itself imply any dynamic. If given with an extra-small motion, it could imply a soft entrance; if with an extra-large motion, the entrance would be louder.

These techniques may be used for any beat.

PRACTICE EXERCISES

1. Practice the cuing exercises shown in Figures 10-1, 10-2, and 10-3 by turning the body or stepping forward at the appropriate cuing times. Use the same section arrangement for choir and instrumental ensembles that is used in your college groups. Let your classmates determine if they believe that your cuing has been effective.

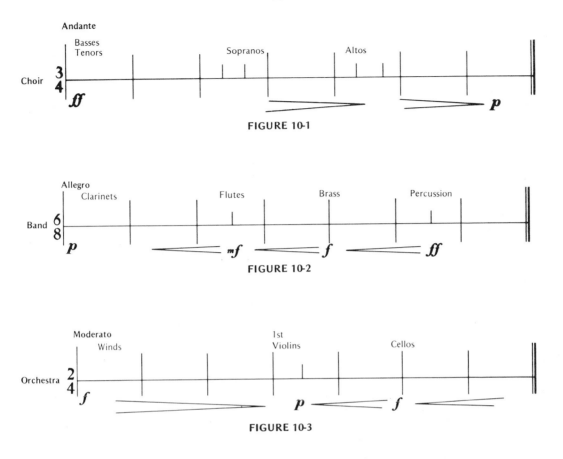

FIGURE 10-1

FIGURE 10-2

FIGURE 10-3

2. Practice the cuing exercises shown in Figures 10-4, 10-5, 10-6, and 10-7 by turning the body, using the eyes, and using the right hand as you believe would be appropriate for the demands of the music. Do not use the left hand for cuing in these exercises. Use the same section arrangement for choir and instrumental ensembles that is used in your college groups. Let your classmates determine how effective your cuing has been in each example.

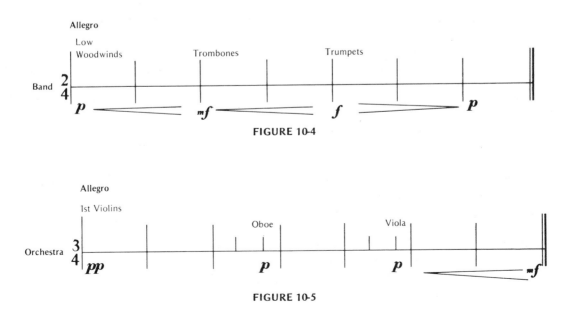

FIGURE 10-4

FIGURE 10-5

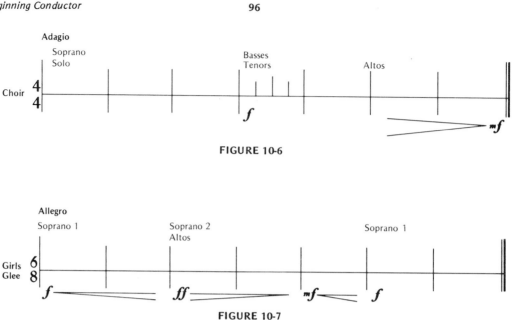

FIGURE 10-6

FIGURE 10-7

LEFT-HAND CUES

I suggest that cuing should be practiced as often as feasible by the student conductor. Cuing is especially important for the beginning conductor, particularly when we realize that this beginner will be working almost entirely with amateur performing groups. If the conductor wishes to place less emphasis upon hand cuing after some time, this can easily be accomplished. If we were to assume that very few instances in music really call for a hand cue and we placed little emphasis upon the motion, however, it would be a disadvantage to the beginning conductor and perhaps a detriment to his later technique in working with amateur groups. Cuing is missing from the technical vocabulary of too many amateur conductors.

Often during an amateur group's performance of a composition, a person or section will be confident that the time for his entrance has arrived but because of lack of experience will hesitate. This hesitation will lead to a lack of precision of the attack or no attack at all. How much easier it would be for the conductor to assure the performers by a simple hand cue.

On one occasion, I was listening to and watching a concert given by a summer band camp organization. The conductor was a college band conductor who apparently had done a commendable job with the group. Nevertheless, in the introduction of one number the entire cornet section missed an entrance, leaving eight or more measures with only a background of rhythm. It must have been obvious to even the

most amateurish listener that no composer had written a number in this fashion and that something had gone awry. It probably would never had happened had the conductor thought to give a hand cue to the section. Undoubtedly he had been in the habit of working with college-age students who had more confidence of entry and had less need of a cue. In other words, it often is better to give a few more cues than necessary than not enough.

The purpose of the cue is threefold: to act as a reminder for an entrance; to enable performers to enter with precision; and to help to indicate the volume, nature, and quality of the attack and entrance. All these ideas can be conveyed by a left-hand cue. Although some cues can be successful with the right hand (the baton) or the eyes, other cues are left-hand operations.

The Pointed Index Finger

One simple left-hand cue is the pointed finger. Here the index finger is used to indicate the entrance by pointing to a person or section involved.

These rules will guide in the execution.

1. The palm of the left hand is perpendicular to the body.

2. The index finger is pointed a bit more than other fingers of the hand but is not completely straight. A perfectly straight finger gives the appearance that you are trying to imitate a child playing cowboys and Indians.

3. Other fingers of the hand are cupped in a relaxed fashion.

4. The thumb is held on the same level as the index finger and does not point upward in any way.

5. The hand is brought into the conducting space from the waist one to two beats before the attack.

6. Leading into the attack beat, the left hand moves outward from the body toward the performer needing the cue. At the same time it moves downward about 3 or 4 inches. The bottom of this movement should be reached at the beat of the cue and the beat of the entrance.

7. The left-hand motion should have a rebound which moves upward about half the distance of the downward motion, and the hand should continue to move toward the performer and away from the body.

8. This is a forearm motion and not a wrist motion.

   This type of cue is used when no volume change is imminent and no difficulty is expected. It is a good cue and is used by many conductors. It should not be used too often or to the exclusion of all other left-hand cues, since it becomes quite monotonous if not used interchangeably. This type of cue is better for an individual than for a section.

PRACTICE EXERCISES

In the exercises below (see Figures 10-8 and 10-9), use the pointed finger cue as indicated by the X. Use other types of cuing for other entrances.

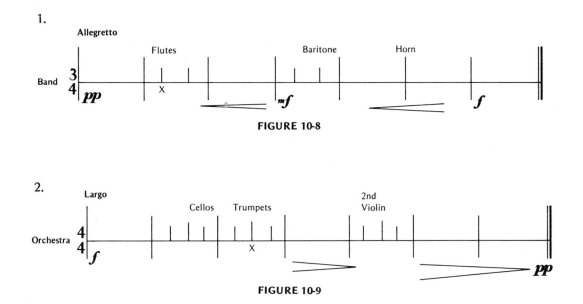

FIGURE 10-8

FIGURE 10-9

The Relaxed Hand

A second type of left-hand cue is often used when a conductor wishes a person or section to make a secure entrance that is not necessarily loud. Here the left hand is turned with the palm toward the body and remains so during the entire motion.

These rules will guide in the practice and development of the motion.

1. The palm of the left hand is toward the body.

2. The fingers of the left hand are relaxed but not cupped.

3. The thumb is just above the index finger with the first knuckle parallel to the fingers.

4. The hand is brought into the conducting space from the waist one to two beats before the attack.

5. Leading into the attack beat, the left hand moves slightly inward toward the body and downward about 3 or 4 inches. The bottom of this movement should be reached at the beat of the cue or the beat of the entrance.

6. The left-hand motion should have a rebound which moves upward about half the distance of the down-ward motion, and the left hand should continue to move in a direction opposite to the right.

This cue is equally good for a single performer or an entire section. If the section to be cued is near the rear of the performing group, the cue should be given at eye level or above. It will be given lower to a section nearby.

PRACTICE EXERCISES

In the exercises below (see Figures 10-10, 10-11, and 10-12), use the relaxed-hand cue as indicated by the letter *Y*. Your classmates will assist you in determining if you have made a distinction between the pointed finger cue and the hand cue just discussed.

1.

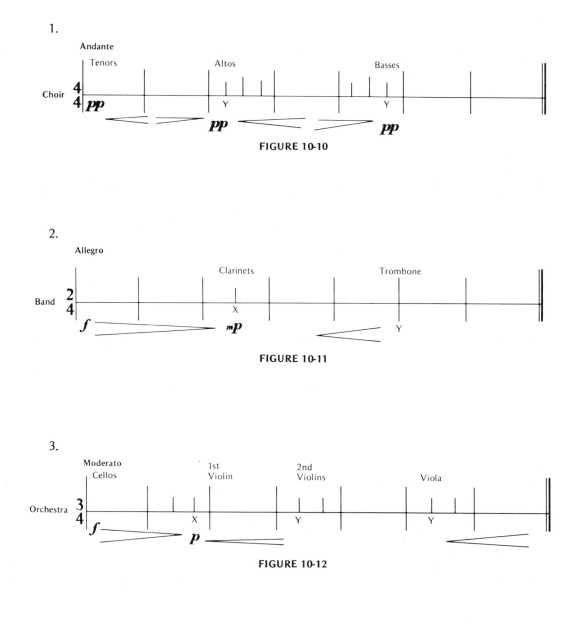

FIGURE 10-10

2.

FIGURE 10-11

3.

FIGURE 10-12

The Fist

If the music calls for great volume at the time of entrance, a left-hand cuing technique may be the closed left hand first.

These rules will guide and assist in developing the motion.

1. Use the same type of movement as described in the preceding left-hand cue: outward toward the performers, the bottom reached at the point of entrance, with rebound.

2. Although this may be used at a low conducting level for sections close by, it is most effective when used for percussion or brass sections which almost always sit at the rear of a performing group.

3. This motion may be used for choral groups and is most effective also at a higher level (eye level or above) and for an entrance involving the entire group or a large section.

PRACTICE EXERCISES

Practice the fist left-hand cue with the following exercises where marked Z.

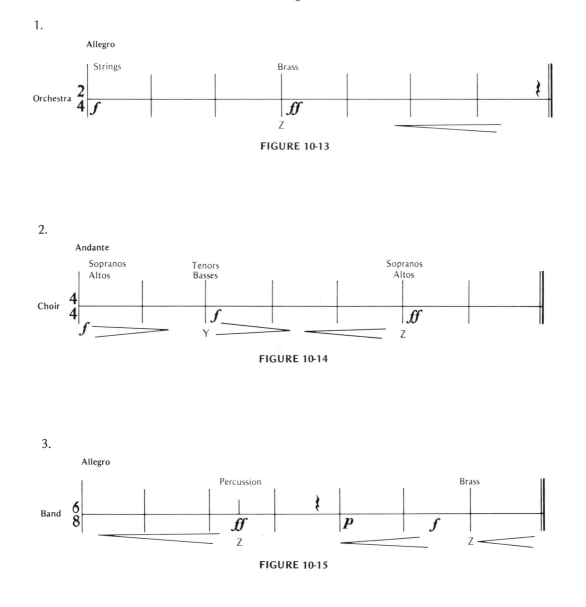

1.

FIGURE 10-13

2.

FIGURE 10-14

3.

FIGURE 10-15

Sometimes more than one method of indicating a cue is advisable for the same entrance. This depends, of course, on what has gone on before, what the size and experience of the group is, what the music is trying to portray, and what number of people are involved in the entrance. It is conceivable, therefore, that a conductor might turn toward a section, make eye contact with the group, and use the left and right hands to make the cue. During a later rehearsal he may feel that it is sufficient to make only an eye contact or to make eye contact and use only the right hand. Each instance must be worked out individually by the conductor so that his technique will be clear and obvious. When the group immediately comprehends what the conductor wishes and communion is established, then the conductor will have good, clean entrances, and the volume of each entrance will be satisfactory.

PRACTICE EXERCISES

Note: Before working with these exercises be sure that you understand just where each section of your group will be located. Be sure to make eye contact with this location each time you cue. Execute body and hand motions in that same direction.

Look over these examples of music that you will find in the literature of amateur groups. Decide how you will cue these entrances and then perform them for your class.

FAEROE ISLAND DANCE
for Concert Band
PERCY ALDRIDGE GRAINGER

Inter Vestibulum

Kneeling Between the Hall and the Altar

Motet for Mixed Voices, A Cappella

(S. A. T. B.)

JOEL 2:17
Paraphrased by P. S. B.

GIACOMO ANTONIO PERTI
(1661-1756)

The following example is the first 22 measures of the fugue section from "Psalm and Fugue for String Orchestra" of Hovhannes.

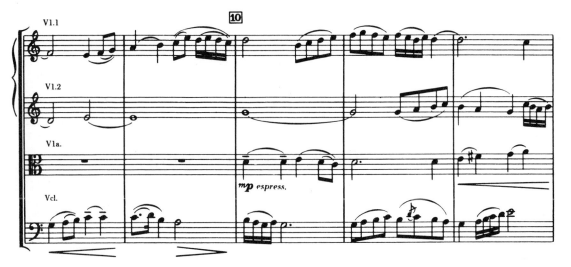

11

Rests: Six Common Problems

RESTS IN MOST PARTS

The rest offers little problem to the conductor when it is printed in one or more parts for short periods of time while other parts, at least one, are still performing. The conductor, watching the score in such a case, sees that at least one part is still required to perform and knows that he too must continue to conduct for this person or section.

SHORT RESTS IN ALL PARTS

If a problem occurs, it usually develops when all parts rest simultaneously. Then the amateur conductor believes that he too must do something different, since the music ceases and conducting is meant to lead the music. But this is an error. For small value rests that are to be found throughout music, the conductor should understand that he should do nothing but continue conducting. Many times, for example, phrases of music are separated by an eighth rest. This merely is an indication to the performers that a bit more obvious phrasing is intended; hence, the conductor

should only phrase his beat. Any hesitation at this point will merely confuse the performers into believing that the conductor wishes a longer value rest than one sees.

AT CHANGE OF TEMPO

When most of a measure contains rest in all staves, the conductor should decide in his own mind if the tempo is to be continued or if it is to be changed. It is not uncommon for these longer rest indications to come at the end of a section or phrase accompanied by an obvious change of tempo. When this occurs, the conductor would release with the last note in the one phrase and begin anew with the newer tempo at the beginning of the following section or phrase. To try to beat through these rests will only be more confusing than not. In most cases it will not be necessary even to describe your technique to your performers, for it will be obvious what you are doing unless you are conducting an elementary school group that is learning to count measures and rests for the first time; then an explanation might be necessary.

The following example, a band arrangement of a Bach "Toccata and Fugue," indicates rests at rehearsal 5. Follow the suggestions above.

Toccata and Fugue in d minor
J. S. Bach, arr. Leidzen

A portion of the "Hansel and Gretel Overture," arranged by Isaac, beginning andante 4/4, offers two additional examples.

Overture to *Hansel and Gretel*
Engelbert Humperdinck, arr. Isaac

Andante (♩ = 60)

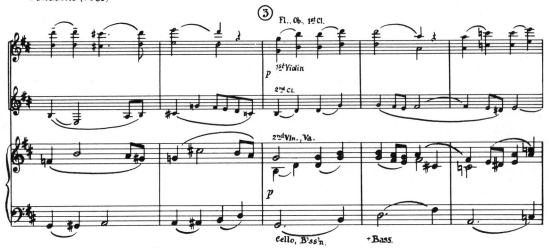

Piano - Conductor

CONDUCTING THROUGH RESTS

When most of the measure contains rests in all parts but the music is not involved in a change of section, the conductor will usually continue conducting. In this way he will help the performers to count the rests correctly and to begin again without mishap. Usually it is advisable to make the pattern smaller when no one is performing, indicating your awareness of the situation. A smaller beat pattern also reassures the audience that nothing is awry, for often when music stops for any length of time, particularly with an amateur group, an audience is apt to suppose that something is amiss. A conductor whose patterns are as prominent when no music is being played as at other times will appear to be overdoing the situation as much as a conductor with a large pattern for pianissimo music.

Although conducting with a smaller pattern during these rather short rests, the conductor should maintain the same style. The legato style should not become sloppy, and the agitato or marcato style should not become legato. In addition, the conductor ought to prepare the group for reentry after the short rest by enlarging the rebound just before the group begins again.

There are instances when, prior to a rest in all parts, one will find that the parts are so written that it is extremely easy for the performers to hang across into the rest. Even though you rehearse this spot carefully and often, at the performance, one person may be trying with such diligence to achieve high quality that the rest may be overrun. The wise conductor will give some aid to the performers in this type of situation, usually by increasing the size of the beat leading into the rest so as to attract more attention to himself and less to the spot approaching or by giving a release or cutoff. Both means are used to good effect.

STOPPING AT RESTS

From time to time a conductor may find rests that are longer than one complete measure. These may be indicated by rests, by a fermata over a rest, or by a break (caesura) in the music. In any of these situa-

tions a conductor may wish to indicate this type of rest without continuing the beat. When doing this, he should hold his conducting hand motionless during the value of the rest because any motion may give the performers some idea of reentry. Usually it is advisable for the conductor to count the rest accurately if the rests are measured. In indicating the unmeasured rests, the conductor may be less strict, and the performing group should expect a difference of value in each rehearsal and performance. Indeed, what is dangerous — and some conductors do this regularly — is to be strict during all rehearsals and irregular at a concert.

Usually the conductor will meticulously follow the indications of the composer if the rests are in measures. Although a conductor has the prerogative of making the rests shorter or longer than indicated on the printed page, it is advisable aesthetically for him to observe the rests as indicated in the music. Performers will expect a rest of an indicated length, and the conductor who does not conduct during a rest should remain motionless, counting strictly in his mind, not with his lips, and should indicate a new attack at the proper time.

COUNTING THE RESTS

The amateur conductor may need to help the young performer understand the counting of rests, for many unskilled performers sit in ensembles and guess at the rest's duration. For this reason many students do not like to see rests in the music, and many prefer to play an instrument which will not confront them with rests continually.

The usual manner for counting rests is to number the first beat of each measure according to the number of measures that have passed since the rest began. Young players need to be helped with this kind of counting until it becomes familiar. When performers have been resting for some time, it is advisable to give some cue to them so that they may be assured that the entrance is correct. When amateurs are playing or entering on parts of measures, counting often is misleading for the young player, and a look of assurance may be of considerable assistance.

PRACTICE EXERCISES

Conduct the following scores making use of the suggestions given in this chapter.

The first example, a portion of Bruckner's "Locus Iste" from *Liber Usualis* in 4/4 andante (page 109), contains numerous rests used in various ways.

Locus Iste
Anton Bruckner

Themes from
SYMPHONY No. 6
(Pathetique)

P. I. TSCHAIKOWSKY
Arranged by Clair W. Johnson

Conductor

12

The Fermata

The fermata is commonly called the "hold" or "bird's eye." Conductors of school groups as well as of adults should use the correct term for this symbol rather than a nickname or colloquial term.

This symbol generally is used to indicate that the note over which it is placed should be given additional time value or some special consideration. There are exceptions.

FERMATAS IN THE BACH CHORALES

The fermata is a common symbol in the Bach chorale, with one occurring almost at every phrase. Some sources claim that these should not lengthen the note over which they are placed since the fermatas at that time merely indicated to those who could not read music and words well that a phrase of music had ended. Singers could then associate a phrase of music with a phrase of the printed words at the bottom of the page. Contemporary meanings for this symbol probably should not be used. Others state that in actual usage the choir and organ did hold these notes longer so that the less-trained congregation could catch up.

Today it is common to consider all fermatas in relation to the music. The conductor must approach each fermata with general principles in mind, and then his musicianship must come into play.

An appropriate role for the Bach chorales, as well as other selections, could be that a conductor should consider the fluidity of the phrases involved in interpreting each fermata.

There are instances in the Bach chorales when a fermata should not be elongated. This is usually ascertained by the words and their phrasing. There are other occasions, of course, in conducting fermatas when it is best to elongate the note to double or triple value. The determination is often a matter of taste and text. Band directors using chorales as practice or program material are advised to study the text and context of the chorales to ascertain correct procedures for fermatas.

USE IN SCORES

Fermatas may be found in all types of music placed over notes and at times over rests. The music rarely gives direction as to the correct interpretation of this symbol, so the conductor must make it clear exactly how he intends to interpret it. Usually, careful use of the baton will suffice. Occasionally the conductor may have to explain how he expects to conduct this symbol.

Fermatas that are placed over notes are either (1) followed by notes; (2) followed by rests (this includes final notes of a section or composition); (3) placed over a long-valued note in some parts while other parts are still moving. In the case of the last type, some parts may never carry the fermata. One can immediately understand the confusion that may arise if the conductor does not prepare himself carefully for conducting in these situations.

OVER NOTES FOLLOWED BY NOTES

Fermatas as Elongation

The conductor must decide just how much longer than normal the note with a fermata must be performed and still retain the musical meaning that the composer intended. In some cases the fermata will probably mean an elongation of double or sometimes even triple value. As a rule of thumb, however, it might be easiest to remember that fermatas over notes followed by notes will tend to elongate less than other types of fermatas. In some instances, I have found music where fermatas actually sound best if they are treated as if they were not printed in the music at all. In other words, the music should proceed without a break or even a ritard. In general, the amateur has a tendency to overconduct a fermata of this type, trying to make sure he is giving every symbol in the music its just due. This is particularly true in festivals or contests where amateur conductors often believe (and perhaps rightfully so) that judges are prone to criticize a performance if the conductor does not respect every symbol completely.

Fermatas As a Ritard

There are times when a fermata should be treated as a ritard. In these situations, it would be possible to indi-cate the slowing of the tempo without using the left hand. However, the use of both hands for the ritard will assist amateurs in realizing the exact beginning of the ritard and the amount of ritard the conductor wishes for this particular performance.

Usually both hands are involved during the time of a fermata if it is considered as a ritard. As the beat of the fermata approaches, the conducting pattern is followed by the left hand. Both hands slow the tempo of the pattern as they approach the beat of the fermata and the process of rebound. The right hand continues the pattern slowly so that the next beat or note may be arrived at without a break. The left hand may follow the conducting pattern for the left hand, or it may be occupied with dynamic levels or other left-hand problems during the fermata.

Fermatas and the Release

The conductor may decide that, even though the fermata is followed by another note, the music should not proceed without a break. In such a case, the right hand executes the pattern at proper speed until the fermata is reached. The right hand indicates the beat point of the fermata in tempo but continues with the rebound at a slower speed, the exact speed being determined by the length of the fermata. If the fermata is to be long, the rebound will be slow; if short, it will be quicker. After a proper fermata length a release is given, a preparatory for the following beat is used, and the pattern and music continue.

At no time during the fermata should the right hand stop and wait until the conductor decides that the fermata has lasted long enough. Usually a stop of the baton means a stop in the music. At best, some performers will decrescendo, some may stop, and others will continue. Many times the fermata over the note calls for no decrease in loudness and could require a slight increase. Indecision on the part of the performers will not aid this effect. Consequently, if the baton is in motion until the release is requested, the conductor will communicate correctly to his performers.

PRACTICE EXERCISES

1. Practice the fermata exercise shown in Figure 12-1 using the right hand only and executing the fermata as a ritard.

    Commentary: In this exercise the first measure should be conducted as usual. In the second measure the rebound for the first beat should be slower than usual and should become progressively slower as the second beat is approached, reaching the slowest point just at the second beat point. The re-bound to the second beat should regain some of the tempo, and by the beat point of three the

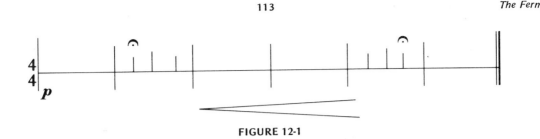

FIGURE 12-1

original tempo should be completely regained. The process for the second fermata should be similar. The last measure should end with a release after beat four.

General rule: Begin the ritard for the fermata before the actual beat where it is placed so that it does not seem awkward or abrupt. Regain the tempo gradually.

2. Practice the exercise shown in Figure 12-2 using both hands, treating the fermata as a ritard. When involving the left hand, follow the conducting pattern for the left hand.

FIGURE 12-2

Commentary: In this exercise the left hand should be at correct waist position during the first complete measures. The left hand will come into the conducting space during the rebound of the first beat of the second measure, moving off to the left and upward in almost exact imitation of the right hand. It should move to the left so that it will have room to move inward in the conducting space as beat two is approached and as the right hand moves toward the left of the pattern, while the right hand moves inwardly toward the right or center. Both hands together should slow the tempo, indicate the exact beat point for the second beat, and rebound with slightly increasing speed. When the right hand moves to the right for the approach to the third beat, the left hand should move to the left at a similar speed. The third beat point should be given by the right hand only, and as the rebound is indicated, the left hand should be returned to the waist.

Remember: The two hands are closest at the beat point of two. The hands and baton should not cross, and it is for this reason that the left hand moved to the left on the rebound of the first beat. The left hand should remain at the waist position during the third measure.

For the second fermata on the fourth beat, the left hand should leave the waist immediately after the third beat point has been reached by the right hand. It should move to the left so that it balances the right hand position on the other side of the body. As the right hand rebounds for beat three, slowing in the process, the left hand should also move upward on the left side of the body in exact tempo, calling attention to the ritard. Both hands should move toward the center for the fourth beat point and execute the fourth beat rebound upward simultaneously with hands close together at the center of the conducting space. Before the right hand reaches the top of the rebound, the left hand should be returned to the waist position, leaving the right hand to execute the next downbeat without assistance.

Remember: If you are dealing with insecure performers, the left hand may be needed for a somewhat longer time before and after the ritard in order to regain the original tempo. The foregoing description may be altered to fit style or tempo. The same basic procedures should be used, and the drill will act as a basis for your development.

3. Practice the exercise shown in Figure 12-3 using the right hand only but indicating a break or stop after the fermata before indicating a preparatory for the next note.

FIGURE 12-3

Commentary: The first measure should be conducted with a simple standard pattern.

In the second measure the rebound for the third beat should be slow but in proportion to the original tempo and to the length of the fermata as decided by the conductor. The release and preparatory of the next beat are diagramed in Figures 12-4 and 12-5.

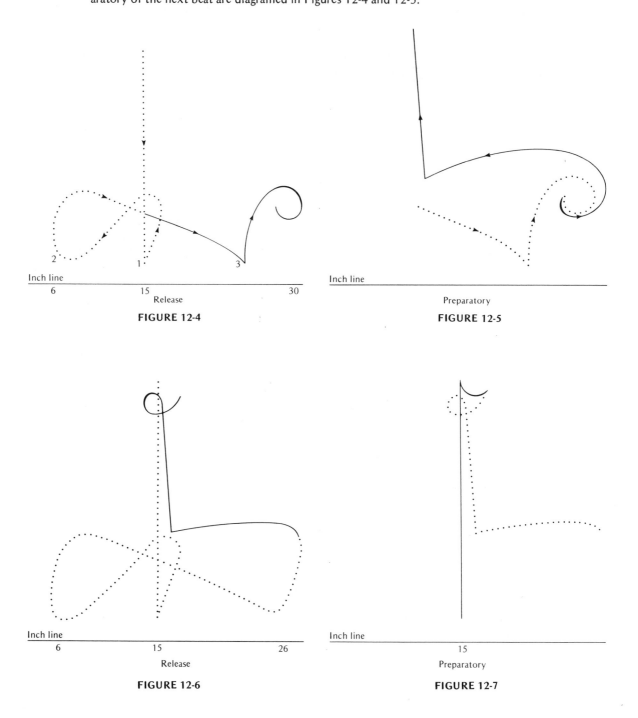

FIGURE 12-4

FIGURE 12-5

FIGURE 12-6

FIGURE 12-7

In the fifth measure the rebound for the fourth beat should be slower than the preceding tempo, and the baton should not stop until the release has been given. The release for beat four and the preparatory for beat one are diagramed in Figures 12-6 and 12-7.

4. Practice the exercise shown in Figure 12-8 using the right hand to execute the fermatas as a ritard and the left hand to indicate the dynamic markings shown. If the left hand is not needed for dynamics, decide whether it should be used to aid the fermatas or remain momentarily idle.

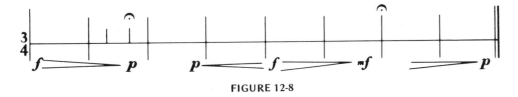

FIGURE 12-8

5. Practice the exercise shown in Figure 12-9 using the right hand to execute the fermatas as one calling for a definite break afterward. Use the left hand for the dynamic markings.

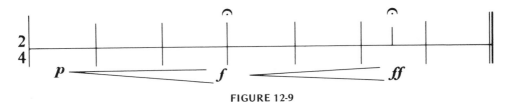

FIGURE 12-9

FERMATAS AND NOTES FOLLOWED BY RESTS

The fermata placed over notes followed by rests gives the conductor fewer problems. The fermata is generally elongated, and there will be a release where the conductor indicates before moving into the next note.

Fermatas at the End of Compositions

When the score contains a fermata over the last note of a composition followed by a rest, it is obvious that the composer could have written the note longer and not used the rest and the fermata. Then what is the meaning of the fermata? The best rule is to elongate the note as you desire, which is probably what you would have done in any event, considering that it was the last note of the composition or a section. It seems

an unwritten law with conductors that the last note of a composition or section may generally be treated with some liberty.

Fermatas in Some Parts

When the rest follows the fermata, observe whether all performers have the same type rest at the same location. This rarely will be a problem for the singer, since choirs and choral groups almost always use common scores. The instrumentalist, however, has only his own part, and there is often a discrepancy between parts. For example, suppose that the strings are playing for the first eight measures of a composition in 4/4 meter. During these eight measures a fermata is involved on an eighth note on the second beat followed by an eighth rest. The strings will continue on beat three (see Figure 12-10).

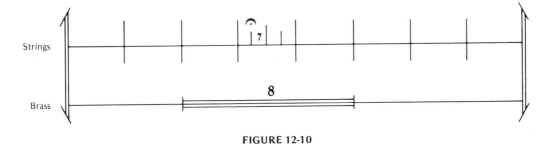

FIGURE 12-10

The brass players may not have this fermata indicated in their part; they may only carry the indication that eight measures are not being played. In this case, the conductor should clarify for the brass players what must be in the string parts: the fermata is on the second beat, a cutoff or release occurs, and the music begins again on the third beat.

FERMATAS AND LONG-VALUE NOTES

The third type — fermatas placed over a long-value note in some parts while other parts keep moving — is not as difficult as it seems. In such cases the conductor must proceed with the pattern until all members of the group arrive at a fermata in each part. At that point, and only at that point, may an elongation be made.

The beginning conductor errs by not watching all parts of the score and thus executing the fermata too early. This only leads to some confusion, which often takes precious rehearsal minutes to alleviate. Generally, he should use the left hand to indicate to the section that arrives at the fermata first that he is aware of the fermata in their part, and yet is still conducting. Performers are centered upon their own part enough to believe that when they have a fermata, all persons playing must have the same symbol. The left hand can reassure the section that arrives at the fermata first, and at the same time the right hand may conduct the remainder of the group toward their own fermata. The left hand in this case will be extended toward the section involved, palm usually upward, and will remain almost motionless.

PRACTICE EXERCISES

1. Conduct the following vocal score that is part of a version of the Twenty-third Psalm.

   Commentary: In the fourth measure after rehearsal C the alto and tenor have a fermata over a half note while the soprano and bass have three quarter notes in that measure with a fermata over the second one. The comma over each staff and the comma after the word "me" seem to indicate that a break after the fermata would be in order. No ritard is indicated as we approach the fermata. Here is a good example of type three discussed above.

   For a good execution, the left hand should indicate to the altos and tenors that the fermata is being realized continuously from the downbeat to the release after two. The right hand should execute the second beat before the fermata is given with that hand, and following correct procedure, the right hand should rebound slowly until the conductor believes that a release is proper.

2. Study the score for other conducting problems.

   Commentary: Note the syncopated rhythm for the sopranos and altos and, in a lesser way, for the basses in the fifth measure of the example. In order to assist the syncopated parts so that a good ensemble will result, overemphasize the rebound in one of two ways: *(a)* Pull the forearm quickly to the top of the rebound of beat two and hesitate momentarily before moving to the third beat point. *(b)* Pull the hand backward at the wrist after the second beat point so as to arrive at the peak of the rebound exactly on the half beat. Hesitate only momentarily before moving to the third beat point. This device is sometimes known as the *cue of provocation*.

   In the first suggestion the wrist and arm are kept in the usual hand and arm position. The second beat point is emphasized by a small downward arm movement, and the stop at the top of the second beat rebound should come precisely on the half beat so as to emphasize the syncopation. The same idea may be used for the third beat.

   In the second suggestion only the wrist and hand move on the second beat rebound. The first and second beats are executed as usual. On the second beat rebound, however, hold the arm in the same place as for the second beat and move the wrist so that the top of the hand is closer to the elbow. This movement will turn the hand so that the baton and the palm of the hand will be perpendicular to the floor. This should be executed quickly and exactly on the half beat and will accentuate the syncopation.

The choice of *(a)* or *(b)* will be determined by the approach you use to the music and the type of conducting used in preceding measures.

a. All parts are somewhat even in the second measure. The right hand will continue in an even, regular pattern. The left hand could indicate the crescendo.

b. The bass part in measure seven sings alone on the last half beat. This could be indicated by the conducting hand again emphasizing the rebound of the third beat. Follow the suggestions under 2*(a)*, but with less obvious right-hand motion.

c. The eighth measure contains the fermata. The left hand should be used and should be brought into the conducting space during the downbeat for the measure. The left hand will be used with palm up, toward the center but in the general direction of the alto section, and a little higher than the waist. When it is about 15 inches from the waist, it will be motionless until the right hand has passed the second beat point. Notice the crescendo during the fermata. This may be executed by the left hand when the right hand is in the rebound for the second beat. It is executed by lifting the hand upward as any crescendo would be indicated. The rebound to the second beat for the right hand will also require that it be lifted slowly upward, indicating an elongated beat but at the same time assisting with the crescendo.

The release for the fermata should be in proportion to the crescendo and to the outside of the body. Use both hands. The regular motion for attack on beat three should be used, bringing the right hand in toward the center of the body in a small circle, and then up for the rebound. After a small hesitation, the downbeat should be given. Since the crescendo is continuing, the downbeat should be more vigorous.

Yea Though I Wander   *Georg Schumann, arr. Christiansen*

★ Top notes may be omitted.

Yea Though I Wander - 5

FERMATAS OVER RESTS

Fermatas placed over rests offer less of a problem than those involving notes. When a rest is involved, the conductor must decide how much silence the fermata indicates. A fermata over an eighth note in one selection or over a half rest in another selection may not indicate anything other than the composer desiring to treat his measure, melody, and rest in a metrical manner.

The conductor must understand the music, trying to make the melody and harmony carry as much meaning as possible for the listener, and must incorporate the fermata into this meaningfulness. Every fermata over a rest will involve the stopping of the music at least for a second of time. There may be times when a conductor would consider it proper to emphasize the silence by making it considerably longer. In some cases a release or cutoff will be required, and in others the rest will be so short that the conductor should indicate nothing with the baton to avoid complicating matters. There may be instances when a fermata is placed over a rest in most parts but where it would be placed over a note in other voices of the same measure. Again the left hand should be used to reassure those holding the note while the right hand would release the other performers from their last note. Normal preparatory, probably using both hands, would then follow, and the pattern would be continued.

PRACTICE EXERCISES

1. Conduct the portion of the score for the Guentzel "Intermezzo."
   Commentary: This score offers some interesting work with the fermata. In measure eight we see an example of the third type of fermata that we discussed earlier in the chapter, where at least one voice is moving and others have a fermata.

   The left hand could best be used to indicate to the upper voices that you are aware of their fermata until such time as the bassoon reaches the fermata in his part.

   Because of the nature of the music and the method of using the fermata in this measure, a fermata of ritard rather than one of holding followed by a release is a possible interpretation. In such a case the rebound for beat three of measure eight would be quite slow, allowing for the extent of the fermata but with the baton in continual motion so that the bassoon would not break or breathe. If a break after the same fermatas is desired, this execution would produce another interpretation. Practice both procedures.

2. Study this score and plan your conducting technique for observation by your classmates.
   Commentary:
   a. The first two measures should be conducted in a legato style. Since only one person is playing and since this is a soft dynamic level, the pattern should be of modest size. The left hand might give a small indication of volume increase in the second measure.

   b. At the entrance of the other instruments in measure three, decide if you wish to cue these instruments, and if so, whether the cue will be given with the baton only, with the eyes only, or with the left hand.

   c. Note the difference of style in measure five where most of the parts are staccato. The score indicates that a little more speed is desired. We have reached a forte marking. All these items can be handled by the baton, and the difference in style should be evident to the performers.

   d. In measure six the fermata is placed over a rest on the last half of beat three. No release should be necessary, and unless you are working with a very young group, no left hand should be needed. The conductor should determine the length of the fermata, but a wait equivalent to three beats at M.M. 96 would not be overdone, provided the poco anima measures were also taken at the same tempo.

   e. The left hand would probably be needed in measure seven to indicate a piano staccato entrance, since in the preceding measure the performers had been performing at forte.

   f. As indicated above, the eighth measure may be treated as a ritard without a break. The left hand could indicate the diminuendo after beat three has been played and while the fermata is being held. As it approaches the waist position, the left hand can also be used to indicate the downbeat for measure nine, which could double as a release for the upper four parts.

g. With these ideas in mind rehearse the score for yourself and then for your classmates. If players are available, it might be advisable to conduct this work, but the greatest value to you can be obtained by your own practice with yourself and one or more observers.

INTERMEZZO

Flute, Oboe, Clarinet, Horn and Bassoon

Conductor

GUS GUENTZEL, Op. 68

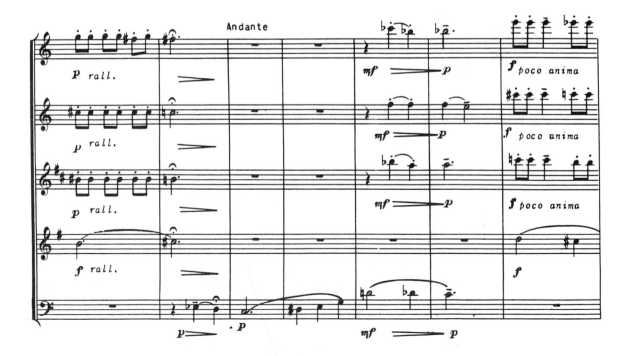

3. Conduct the first three Bach chorales (pages 121–123). Work out your interpretation before conducting. Keep in mind the points made early in the chapter. Remember that not all chorales need be taken slowly and ponderously; some by their very nature and the sentiment of the text require a bright tempo. After working through the chorales, read the following comments. If you disagree, what would be the basis for differing?

Commentary:

a. Chorale 1: Conduct this at M.M. 92 for the half note with no indication of tempo change or hold for any of the fermatas. This is a good example of fermatas in music that need no tempo change. If you do not agree with this interpretation, work out your own using the various styles indicated.

b. Chorale 2: Conduct this at M.M. 84 for the half note. The fourth and fifth fermatas may be considered as ritards. Possibly the performers would not breathe after the fourth fermata, but this would make little difference to the conducting. Work out other fermatas in this chorale and conduct as your class sings. They should comment on whether you have captured the tempo, the style, and a good fermata interpretation.

c. Chorale 3: Conduct this at M.M. 108 for the quarter note. Conduct the first two fermatas as definite holds with a release after each one. To be precise, hold the fermatas three beats, rest for one beat, and indicate the beginning of the next phrase on the next beat. No ritard is used in approaching the fermatas because this would weaken the style of the chorale.

4. Work through other chorales in the following group and be clear in your mind which of the three types of fermatas you would use at any one location. Practice these before your classmates and discuss the different interpretations that come from different student conductors.

All Glory Be To God On High
(Gloria in Excelsis)
(Allein Gott in der Höh' sei Ehr)

N.D., 1529
Translated by CATHERINE WINKWORTH

Melody by
NICOLAUS DECIUS, 1526
Arr. by JOHANN SEBASTIAN BACH

friend - ed! To us no harm shall now come nigh, The
ev - er, O Fa - ther, that Thy rule is just, And
Fa - ther, Who didst for all our sins a - tone And
fail - ing, O'er Sa - tan's snares our souls up - lift, And

strife at last is end - ed; God show-eth His good will to men, And
wise, and chang-es nev - er: Thy bound-less pow'r o'er all things reigns, Done
the lost sheep dost gath - er, Thou Lamb of God, to Thee on high, From
let Thy power a - vail - ing A - vert our woes and calm our dread; For

peace shall reign on earth a - gain; O thank Him for His good - ness.
is what-e'er Thy will or - dains; Well for us that Thou rul - est!
out our depths, we sin - ners cry, Have mer-cy on us, Je - sus!
us the Sav - ior's blood was shed, We trust in Thee to save us!

How Bright Appears the Morning Star
(Wie schön leuchtet der Morgenstern)

P. N.

Translated by JOHANN C. JACOBI

Melody by PHILIPP NICOLAI, 1599
Arr. by JOHANN SEBASTIAN BACH

Andante

f 1. How bright ap - pears the Morn - ing Star, With mer - cy beam - ing
O right - eous Branch, O Jes - se's Rod, Thou Son of Man and

p 2. Though cir - cled by the hosts on high, He deign'd to cast a
The whole cre - a - tion's Head and Lord, By high - est ser - a -

from a - far; The host of heav'n re - joi - ces;
Son of God, We, too, will lift our voi - ces.
pit - ying eye *p* Up - on his help - less crea - ture;
phim a - dored, As - sum'd our ver - y na - ture.

Je - su, Je - su, Ho - ly, ho - ly,
Je - su, grant us, Thro' Thy mer - it

yet most low - ly, Draw Thou near us, Great Im - man - uel, come and hear us!
to in - her - it Thy sal - va - tion: Hear, O hear, our sup - pli - ca - tion!

Praise To The Lord, The Almighty
(Lobe den Herren, den mächtigen König der Ehren)

J. NEANDER, 1679
Translated by CATHERINE WINKWORTH with modifications

Melody from
STRALSUND H.B., 1665
Arranged by JOHANN SEBASTIAN BACH

1. Praise to the Lord, the Al - might - y, the King of cre - a - tion! O my soul,
2. Praise to the Lord, who o'er all things so won - drous - ly reign - eth, Who, as on
3. Praise to the Lord! O let all that is in me a - dore Him! All that hath

praise Him, for He is Thy Health and Sal - va - tion! Join the full throng;
wings of an ea - gle, up - lift - eth, sus - tain - eth; Hast thou not seen
life and breath, come now with prais - es be - fore Him! He is thy Light;

Wake, harp and psal - ter and song; Sound forth in glad a - do - ra - tion.
How thy de - sires all have been Grant - ed in what He or - dain - eth?
Soul, keep it al - ways in sight, Glad - ly for - ev - er a - dore Him!

O Sacred Head, Now Wounded
(Salve Caput Cruentatum)
(O Haupt voll Blut und Wunden)

BERNARD of CLAIRVAUX,
1091-1158

Translated to German by PAUL GERHARDT, 1656
Translated to English by JAMES W. ALEXANDER, 1830

Melody by HANS LEO HASSLER, 1601
Arr. by JOHANN SEBASTIAN BACH

Wake, Awake, For Night Is Flying!
(Wachet auf, ruft uns die Stimme)

P. N.
Translated by CATHERINE WINKWORTH

Melody by PHILIPP NICOLAI, 1599
Arr. by JOHANN SEBASTIAN BACH

mar - riage-feast pre - pare, For ye must go to meet Him there."
call we ans - wer all, And fol - low to the nup - tial hall.

Draw Us To Thee
(Zeuch uns nach Dir)

F. FABRICIUS, 1668
Translated by AUGUST CRULL

Melody by C. PETER, 1655
Arr. by JOHANN SEBASTIAN BACH

Moderato

mf

1. Draw us to Thee, For then shall we Walk in Thy steps for - ev - er, And
2. Draw us to Thee, Lord, lov - ing - ly; Let us de - part with glad - ness, That
3. Draw us to Thee, That al - so we Thy heav'n-ly bliss in - her - it, And
4. Draw us to Thee Un - ceas-ing - ly, In - to Thy king - dom take us; Let

has - ten on Where Thou art gone, To be with Thee, dear Sav - ior.
we may be For - ev - er free From sor - row, grief, and sad - ness.
ev - er dwell Where sin and hell No more can vex our spir - it.
us for - e'er Thy glo - ry share, Thy saints and joint - heirs make us.

Praise God, The Lord, Ye Sons Of Men
(Lobt Gott, ihr Christen alle gleich)

N. H. 1560
Translated by AUGUST CRULL

Melody by
NICOLAUS HERMANN, 1560
Arr. by JOHANN SEBASTIAN BACH

Festively

ff 1. Praise God, the Lord, ye sons of men, Be - fore His high-est throne, To -
mp 2. He leaves His Heav'n-ly Fa - ther's throne, Is born an in - fant small, And
p 3. He lays a - side His pow'r di - vine, A ser - vant's form doth take, In
ff 4. He o - pens us a - gain the door Of Par - a - dise to - day; The

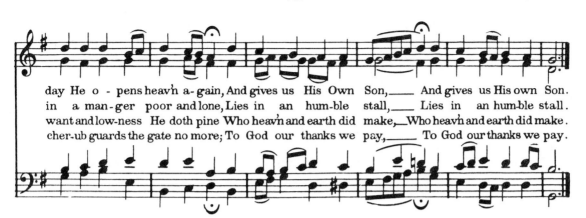

day He o - pens heav'n a - gain, And gives us His Own Son,___ And gives us His own Son.
in a man - ger poor and lone, Lies in an hum - ble stall,___ Lies in an hum - ble stall.
want and low - ness He doth pine Who heav'n and earth did make,___ Who heav'n and earth did make.
cher - ub guards the gate no more; To God our thanks we pay,___ To God our thanks we pay.

Abide, O Dearest Jesus
(Ach, bleib mit Deiner Gnade)

DR. J. STEGMANN, 1632
Translated by AUGUST CRULL

Melody by MELCHIOR VULPIUS, 1609
Arranged by JOHANN SEBASTIAN BACH

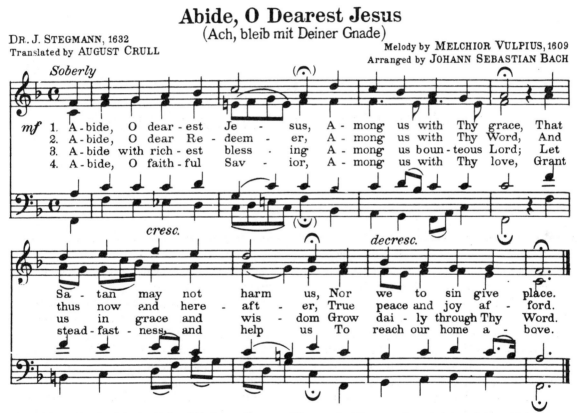

1. A - bide, O dear - est Je - sus, A - mong us with Thy grace, That
2. A - bide, O dear Re - deem - er, A - mong us with Thy Word, And
3. A - bide with rich - est bless - ing A - mong us boun - teous Lord; Let
4. A - bide, O faith - ful Sav - ior, A - mong us with Thy love, Grant

Sa - tan may not harm us, Nor we to sin give place.
thus now and here - aft - er, True peace and joy af - ford.
us in grace and wis - dom Grow dai - ly through Thy Word.
stead - fast - ness, and help us To reach our home a - bove.

13

Conducting Patterns: Compound Meters

By working through the preceding chapters, you have been preparing for increasingly difficult assignments and challenges. One of these is the compound meter signature, or the signatures of 6/8, 9/6, and 12/8, where the eighth note is the unit and beat determinate. Students who begin practice on these meters before they have mastered the patterns for the simple meters usually weaken their technique. These patterns require a precise understanding of fundamentals but are then easily included in one's technique. The student having most difficulty with compound meters will be weak in the earlier concepts.

GENERAL CONSIDERATIONS

If more beats are conducted in a pattern, logic could argue that more space would be required. Since this is not true, the conductor must control his patterns so that some beats take a disproportionate amount of space. The lack of practice and feel for this disproportionment is the sole reason for unsteady beat patterns and uncomfortable-looking amateur conduc-

tors with patterns of five, six, seven, or more units to the measure.

Many beginning students of conducting fail to understand that the conducting hand often travels at different speeds as it progresses through the pattern. For example, in conducting the simple patterns the distance covered by the hand in the conducting space is approximately the same for the downbeat as it is for beats two and three in a triple-meter pattern. Contrast this with the distance covered by the hand in a multibeat pattern such as a twelve-beat measure. In the latter, the downbeat is of normal size as if the pattern were to be a simple one, but then the pattern distance is reduced, since three beats must now be placed in the conducting space that would normally be covered by a downbeat and its rebound.

When the pattern is first practiced, the student might make some beats too large or fail to indicate a consistent tempo. These problems can easily be corrected if a metronome is used during practice and if the student is placed close to another person or a wall so that his conducting patterns must fit into a prescribed space. These limitations should exist only for a short period of time, since no beginning conductor should feel restricted.

In the diagrams that follow, the complex patterns are considerably more intricate and florid. If these patterns are to be meaningful to the performer, they must be articulate and precise enough to be followed easily. This is particularly true when one considers that most of us will be conducting amateur groups that need a simple directing pattern. All patterns should follow meticulously the intended style and have the beat points carefully placed. The patterns can be clear and easily understood if these items are practiced.

When beginners are faced with more complex patterns, they often omit beats. In order to overcome this, they will resort to counting the beats aloud or inaudibly but with moving lips. Never practice these bad habits, since you will find it almost impossible to eliminate them later. If audible counting is necessary, a nonconducting person should do the counting rather than permit the conductor to count them for himself. The goal here is for the conductor to feel the pattern as an entity, as a rhythmic unit, and not be distracted by the business of counting. The mind must be somewhat free and ready to accept the overall impression created by the complete pattern as well as those of the inner units. The neuroresponses must be so practiced that when a conductor sees a time signature, he will feel an overall rhythmic compulsion to conduct automatically the correct pattern. This comes from much practice and a constant awareness of the pattern as a unit.

The more complex the pattern, the more tempted one becomes to swing the right hand and arm toward the body on those beats that are on the left of the pattern. This is true since we are adding more beat points in the same conducting space. Try to remember that the pattern must be kept on a plane in front of the conductor parallel with the downbeat.

A review will be of assistance before considering the patterns:

1. A conducting pattern need not be broader or larger in scope because it contains more beats to a measure.

2. The speed of the hand must vary according to the amount of space covered in the pattern.

3. Try to make each pattern distinct by careful attention to style and beat point placement. With the addition of more beat points and more loops, patterns quickly become unclear.

4. Do not count beats for yourself either audibly or silently with lip movement.

5. Do not permit the hand and arm to swing toward the body as the beats are pointed on the left side of the pattern.

THE SIX-BEAT MEASURE

The patterns shown in Figures 13-1 and 13-2 may be used for the slower 6/8 measures.

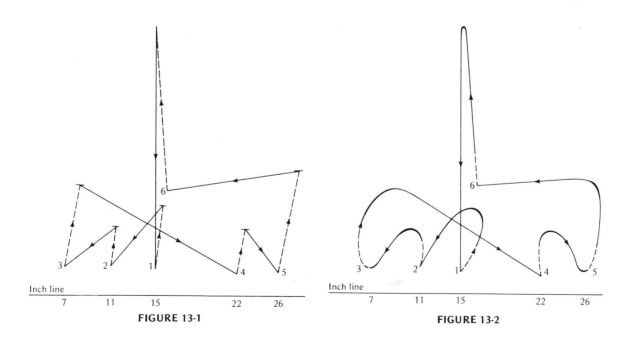

FIGURE 13-1   FIGURE 13-2

Some rules for these patterns are:

1. Start the pattern with the baton about eye level and lower the hand to the waist for the downbeat.

2. Keep the good posture and good arm movement that you have been practicing for the simple patterns.

3. Beats two and three are usually smaller than one and four and cover considerably less distance but the same time in space.

4. Beat four should always receive an obvious movement. It should be obvious in height as compared to beats two and three and obvious in length of line from beat three to the beat point of four. This is because it subdivides the measure for the performer's eye and indicates a secondary accent in the same way as the secondary accent is indicated in a 4/4 measure by a similar crossover.

5. Most 6/8 meters use the two-beat pattern. When the tempo becomes slower than 84 M.M. for the eighth note, a six-beat pattern should be considered. When the tempo is faster than 84 M.M. for the eighth note, a two-beat pattern will usually be more comfortable. A six-beat pattern may be used, however, up to M.M. 112 for an eighth note. A determinate for your choice might be that the use of a divided beat tends to make performers emphasize each beat.

6. The right side of the pattern should not swing toward the body. Imagine that the tip of the baton needs to write constantly on a board in front of the conductor.

7. This pattern may also be used for less common 6/4, 6/2, or 6/16 meter signatures.

PRACTICE EXERCISES

1. Practice the exercises shown in Figures 13-3, 13-4, and 13-5 making use of the six-beat pattern.

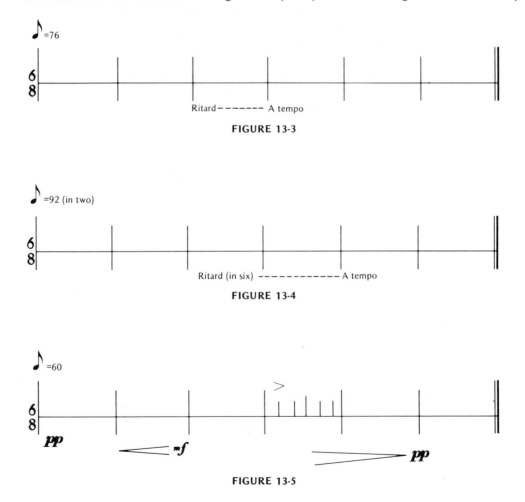

FIGURE 13-3

FIGURE 13-4

FIGURE 13-5

2. Conduct "Drink To Me Only With Thine Eyes" thinking of phrasing, tempo, and dynamics. Later conduct as your classmates sing. Have you conducted in the style of the composition?

DRINK TO ME ONLY WITH THINE EYES

Ben Jonson   *Old English Air*

1. Drink to me on-ly with thine eyes, And I will pledge with mine;
2. I sent thee late a ro-sy wreath, Not so much hon'ring thee

Or leave a kiss with-in the cup, And I'll not ask for wine; The
As giv-ing it a hope that there It could not wither'd be; But

thirst that from the soul doth rise, Doth ask a drink di-vine;
thou there-on didst on-ly breathe, And send'st it back to me,

3. Conduct "Silent Night" in two tempos: once in a two-meter pattern as slowly as you believe you can conduct in two and still maintain your pattern and evenness of beat, and once again in six. When in six, do not permit the beat to become so slow that it is difficult to sing, especially the latter measures, or permit your beat to cause the performers to emphasize each pulsation.

SILENT NIGHT

Franz Gruber

Si - lent night, Ho - ly night, All is calm, All is bright,

Round yon Vir - gin Moth - er and Child, Ho - ly In - fant so ten - der and mild,

Sleep in heav - en - ly peace, _____ Sleep in heav - en - ly peace. ___

THE NINE-BEAT MEASURE

The patterns shown in Figures 13-6 and 13-7 are used for the 9/8 measure.

Some 9/8 meters may be conducted in three beats to the measure and some will follow the nine-beat patterns above. Notice that the nine-point patterns are really a subdivision of the three patterns. They should always appear so.

1. Beats two and three are always slightly to the left of the downbeat line.

2. Beats five and six are always to the right of the fourth beat.

3. Beat nine should always lead naturally into the downbeat.
   Note: The crisscross patterns suggested for beats seven, eight, and nine in some texts place too much emphasis upon these beats.

4. To be most successful, beat nine should be an upswing slightly to the right of the downbeat line so that the baton may come naturally into place for the downbeat.

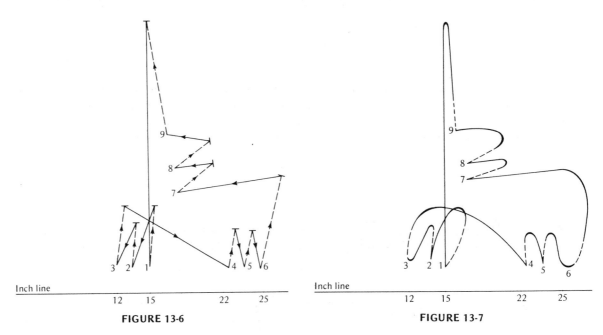

FIGURE 13-6   **FIGURE 13-7**

5. Beats four, seven, and one should appear as obviously larger to the performer to assist in the proper eye-division of the measure.

6. The three-beat pattern probably will be used for most 9/8 measures. When the tempos become slower than 84 M.M. for the eighth note, a nine-point pattern should be used. When a tempo is faster than 84 M.M. for the eighth note, usually a three-beat pattern is more comfortable. You may find that your control will demand a somewhat different break point.

7. This pattern may also be used for slower 9/4, 9/2, or 9/16 measures.

PRACTICE EXERCISES

1. Practice the exercises shown in Figures 13-8 and 13-9 using the nine-point pattern.

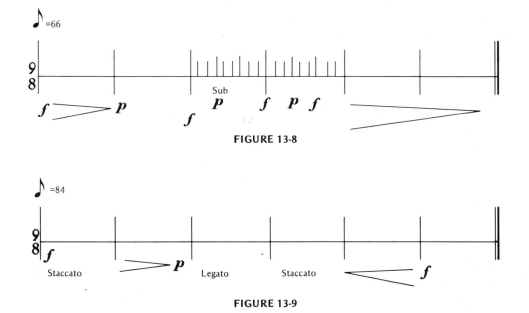

FIGURE 13-8

FIGURE 13-9

2. With a metronome locate the exact point where you feel comfortable using a three-beat pattern for a 9/8 measure. Be sure to place three metronomic beats between each beat point of the pattern. Is your pattern smooth and controlled?

3. Conduct "Down in the Valley" using the nine-point pattern. Practice your upbeat or preparatory until you are satisfied that you can obtain the results that you wish.

DOWN IN THE VALLEY

Kentucky Mountain Ballad

1. Down in the val - ley, the val - ley so low, ____ Hang your head o - ver,
2. Ros - es love sun - shine, ____ ros - es love dew, ____ An - gels in heav - en
3. Build me a cas - tle, ____ for - ty feet high, ____ So I can see you

hear the wind blow; _____ Hear the wind blow, dear, hear the wind blow, _____
know I love you; _____ Know I love you, dear, know I love you, _____
as you go by, _____ As you go by, dear, as you go by, _____

Hang your head o - ver, hear the wind blow. _____
An - gels in heav - en know I love you. _____
So I can see you as you go by. _____

4. Conduct "Beautiful Dreamer" in both a three-point and a nine-point pattern. Which do you prefer for the usual performance?

Beautiful Dreamer

Serenade

STEPHEN C. FOSTER
(His last song)

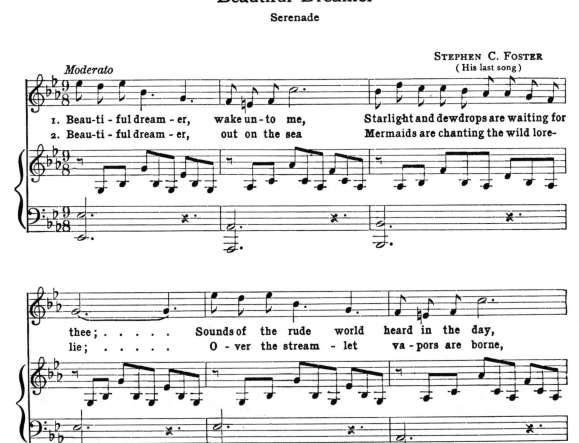

1. Beau-ti - ful dream - er, wake un-to me, Starlight and dewdrops are waiting for
2. Beau-ti - ful dream - er, out on the sea Mermaids are chanting the wild lore-

thee; . . . . . Sounds of the rude world heard in the day,
lie; . . . . . O - ver the stream - let va - pors are borne,

Lull'd by the moonlight, have all pass'd a - way! . . . .   Beau-ti - ful dream - er,
Wait-ing to fade at the bright coming morn. . . . . .   Beau-ti - ful dream - er,

queen of my song,   List while I woo thee with soft mel - o - dy;
beam on my heart,   E'en as the morn on the streamlet and sea;

Copyright © 1950 by Joe Mitchell Chapple, Inc., Boston. By permission of the publisher, The World Publishing Company, 2231 West 110th Street, Cleveland, Ohio.

THE TWELVE-BEAT MEASURE

The patterns shown in Figures 13-10 and 13-11 are used for the 12/8 measure.

The following rules for these patterns will be of assistance:

1. Beats two and three are to the left of the downbeat point even though we have a number of beat points to the left of the downbeat. In some cases beat points two and three may be slightly to the right of the downbeat to allow for a greater sweep into four. This would be of particular benefit if beat point four carried an accent or entrance.

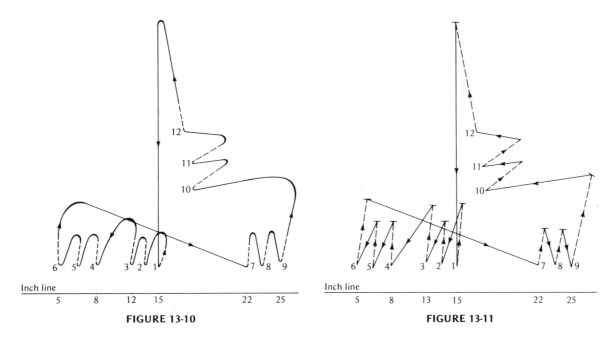

FIGURE 13-10   **FIGURE 13-11**

2. Beat four should be obviously larger than two, three, five, or six. When this occurs, the performer is assured that he is accurately interpreting the subdivision.

3. Move to the left only a little farther for beats five and six so that the proportion of the pattern is not lost. The left side of the pattern should have some proportion with the right side.

4. To be most successful, beat twelve should be an upswing slightly to the right of the downbeat line

so that the baton may come naturally into place for the downbeat.

5. The four-beat pattern will probably be used for most 12/8 music. When tempi become slower than 84 M.M. for the eighth note, a twelve-point pattern should be used. When a tempo .is faster than 84 M.M. for the eighth note, a four-point pattern is advisable.

6. This pattern may also be used for less common 12/16, 12/4, or 12/2 signatures.

PRACTICE EXERCISES

1. Practice the exercises shown in Figures 13-12 and 13-13 using the twelve-point pattern.

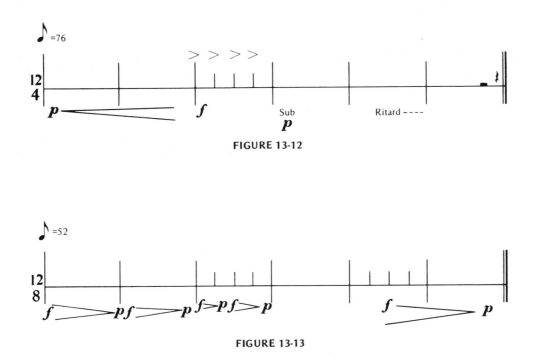

FIGURE 13-12

FIGURE 13-13

2. Conduct the "Pastorale Symphony" from the *Messiah* by Handel. This composition is usually conducted in twelve, but there have been times when amateur players were not able to sustain the line so that some conductors have been forced into a four-beat pattern.

Pastorale from "The Messiah"   *G. F. Handel*

13 Pifa

3. Also from the *Messiah* is the aria "He Shall Feed His Flock." Usually this composition is begun in twelve to secure the eighth note, and then the conductor moves into a four-point beat. Practice this procedure, since it means that this composition is usually performed at a borderline speed where it could be conducted either way.

Note: The 9/8 and 12/8 patterns described above should be understood as variations of the three- and four-beat measures. In the case of the nine-point pattern, one could easily consider it as being a three-point pattern with variations. In the case of the twelve-point pattern, one could assume this to be a varied four-point pattern. If the beginning conductor will make these associations, he will find that he will be more apt to feel at ease with them. This is not true, however, with the six-point pattern.

14

The Score: Additional Problems

It now is time to turn from simple nontransposing scores to more complicated ones. Before doing so, emphasis should again be placed upon proper score study. What follows is devoted to some of the technical concerns, all of which are vitally important and become one aspect on conducting knowledge and score preparation. Attention to these details should in no way supplant our previous suggestions but only add to them. The study of instrumental scores for quartets, quintets, octets, etc., as well as brass and woodwind choirs and string ensembles, will aid the beginning conductor in becoming familiar with scores before turning his attention to the more complex orchestral or band score. Consequently, we will review some of the problems found in the various families of instruments and study appropriate scores.

THE STRING FAMILY

The string ensemble or string orchestra score is the simplest of the three types of family scores for study. In this score instruments are all of concert pitch even though they are not all reading the same clef. No time here will be spent on the acoustic qualities of the various instruments in this family, which would be a part of an instrumentation or orchestration class. Let us, however, review the transposition of the instruments and the clefs used from the viewpoint of the beginning conductor since he is continually confronted by these problems. The vocalist should be familiar with these problems also, since this information is part of the general background of a musician and since choral conductors are often involved with the study, discussion, or conducting of instrumental groups.

The Alto Clef

In the string section we should be aware that there are two violin parts, a viola part, a cello part, and a string bass part. Both first and second violins play the same clef (g clef) and play at the same pitch (concert pitch).

The viola plays in the alto clef and sounds a fifth below the violins. For the beginning conductor one immediate solution to pitch names in this clef is to think the g clef and read each note one step higher.

This at least will give you the pitch name of the note. *Remember*: The viola will sound just one octave lower than the note you are reading as being in the g clef. In other words, if the note is written on the second line of the alto clef, you should call it by the name of the next step in the g clef, or concert a. Instead of sounding a¹, the viola will play this note sounding small a. (See Appendix 7 for note names.)

A second method of approaching the alto clef makes use of the great staff, which is the g and f clefs connected by the inclusion of the c¹ line between the two. In Figure 14-1, the g and f clefs on the left are drawn as usually seen in the piano score and the c¹ line has been dotted in place to show its connecting possibilities. On the right the c¹ line becomes the center line for the alto clef which uses the bottom two lines of the g clef and the top two lines of the f clef. Reading in this manner places the pitch exactly.

By reading several lines from this clef you will soon be able to quickly understand the pitch relationships.

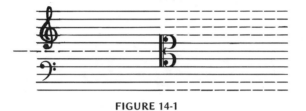

FIGURE 14-1

PRACTICE EXERCISE

1. Read aloud by name of note the viola part for the following example taken from the Beethoven String Quartet, Opus 132, first movement. The viola plays the third line from the top of each brace.

String Quartet, **Op. 132** *Ludwig van Beethoven*

180

190

The Tenor Clef

The remaining two instruments of the string family are the cello and the bass viol. Both of these instruments usually read the f clef, and many times the cello and bass are written on the staff with the conductor reading the notes in unison. When scores are printed in this fashion, remember that the bass viol will be sounding exactly one octave lower than what the conductor is reading.

When the cello plays in the upper part of its range for a number of measures, usually the part will be written in the tenor clef. So that this clef need not delay a young conductor in thinking of pitch, a quick way to name the pitches is to think of these notes as if they were written in the g clef and then read them one note lower. In other words, when a note is written on the top line of the tenor clef, think momentarily of this as being in the g clef (which would name the pitch f) and then mentally adjust it down one step to the pitch name of e. Keep in mind that it will sound one octave below your present reading pitch of the g

clef. For example, what appears to be e^2 will sound e^1 when played in the tenor clef.

A second approach to tenor clef uses the great staff as before. The figure is similar except that the tenor clef uses only one line from the g clef. When reading from the great staff the pitches are exact (see Figure 14-2).

Note: The best manner for the reading of clefs is to learn the clef completely, so that it can be thought and named without manipulation. Many vocal students do not find daily use for these clefs, however, and a quick formula is often useful.

FIGURE 14-2

PRACTICE EXERCISE

Read aloud by name of note the cello part in the following example.

String Quartet, **Op. 132**   *Ludwig van Beethoven*

The String Choir

Now let us turn our attention to a string orchestral score. Many items about string playing are idiomatic with these instruments. Some of these are covered in Appendix 5, "Bowings." If you are not a string player, you may not know a great deal about strings and string problems. Do not hesitate to conduct strings. Many professional conductors have been pianists and have not known strings from the standpoint of a player. These conductors did have help from the concert master, however, and the amateur conductor can gain some assistance from his concert master. From the podium or prior to a rehearsal talk to your string players advising them of the type of sound you as a conductor may desire. You may wish the effect to be somewhat different from what you heard; perhaps singing for them or demonstrating in some way would be possible. Before too long you will learn the technical terminology for the effects that you wish.

Some basic items to remember are these:

1. Most measures begin down-bow on the downbeat.

2. Phrases that begin on the upbeat begin on the up-bow.

3. Any note to receive some emphasis should be played down-bow. This may mean some adjustment in bowing for a few previous measures. This is the conductor's prerogative.

4. With amateur players do not expect phrases to run too long without changing bows.

5. As a conductor, try to assist your performers in differentiating between bowing and phrase markings. This is not always clear even in string parts, and a conductor should be prepared to assist his string players with this. Many times for the amateur these are not the same since the phrase marking will be much too long for his bowing technique.

6. If bowing and pizzicato follow each other quickly, be sure the last bowed note is taken up-bow so as to be ready immediately for the pizzicato. The next played note after pizzicato should probably be down-bow.

7. To obtain as full a sound as possible, insist that your strings use long, full bows. Amateurs often forget this unless reminded regularly.

8. When conducting strings as an accompaniment to vocal or stage works, rehearse the strings at least once by themselves before adding winds or voices. If this is a major production, several string rehearsals might be necessary. In these rehearsals you will be able to work out many problems that would be lost in the full rehearsal. These details will make a tremendous difference in the performance. This is much more the case with strings than with winds. The problems in the winds are obvious to almost every conductor immediately. Some inner string parts may present difficulties that are not quickly heard when winds or voices or both are performing.

9. Do not hesitate to make a decision for a particular bowing based upon sound. Remember that many professional violinists disagree on exactly which bowing to use under some circumstances.

10. Listen carefully to the strings as they play. If no phrase or bowing markings exist, string players will usually play each note with a separate bow. This could make the music too jerky or rough. If this is not what you wish at a particular moment, be sure to add bowings to the music. It may have been obvious to the professional that it should be played in such a manner, but the amateur may never realize it unless told to do so.

11. Some obvious items that string players know but sometimes fail to do:
    a. Make sure that the bow is parallel to the bridge.
    b. Play a bit nearer the fingerboard than the bridge.
    c. Use the flat of the hair. Some professionals will not play in this manner, but for the amateur the best tone is obtained in this manner.

12. If you wish the strings to play more loudly, ask them to do one or more of the following:
    a. Use more bow (longer strokes per note).
    b. Bow a bit closer to the bridge.
    c. Use the lower half of the bow, if possible.
    d. Push the bow a bit into the strings.
    e. Be sure that the bow is flat on the string.

13. If you wish the strings to play more softly, ask them to do one or more of the following:
    a. Use less bow, by moving it a bit slower.
    b. Bow a bit farther from the bridge.
    c. Use the upper half of the bow, if possible.
    d. Lighten the bow weight on the strings.
    e. Tilt the bow a bit on the string.

14. Listen to ascertain if your players crescendo on each up-bow and descresendo on each down-bow. They should not, and this points to uneven bow weight.

15. Do not use the term "legato" to a string player as you would a wind player. Strings use this word to mean slurred; winds use it to mean softer tongue.

16. Unless the note is accented, the bow should begin on the string.

17. Normally, use the middle of the bow for a tremolo effect.

St PAUL'S SUITE.
For String Orchestra.

Jig
1

GUSTAV HOLST

THE WOODWIND FAMILY

The woodwind family of instruments actually takes on different concepts depending on whether the woodwinds are playing in an orchestra, a band, a woodwind ensemble, or woodwind quintet. The conductor should know just what is expected from the woodwind instrumentation in each of these organizations. Then he will be aware of deviations and his responsibility to each.

Woodwinds for the Orchestra

The woodwind group of instruments in the orchestra usually consists of two oboes, two flutes, two clarinets, and two bassoons. In some of the more recent orchestrations the woodwind family has been enlarged to include three flutes (most often the third flute doubles on piccolo and rarely on alto flute), two oboes and one English horn, two Bb clarinets and one bass clarinet (occasionally a score will call for a soprano Eb), and two bassoons and a contrabassoon. Most scores played by amateur groups will request only the standard eight instruments.

A word of warning: Follow the instrumentation for woodwinds as suggested by the composer, using one instrument per part. Do not pad the orchestra with additional members of the woodwind family. To do so will not give the desired effect and will overbalance the strings. One may add string players to an orchestra almost indefinitely without harming the color of the group, but this will not be true in the case of woodwinds or brasses.

With the eight woodwinds that one normally finds in an orchestral score, the oboes, flutes, and bassoons all play concert pitch. This means that when you read a woodwind note from the printed score, it sounds exactly as if you were to read this note from a piano score. The flutes and oboes use the g clef and the bassoons mostly use the f clef. Occasionally, the bassoon uses the tenor clef if the music is consistently written in the upper range of the instrument.

The Clarinet in the Orchestra

Of the usual orchestral woodwind family the clarinet is the only instrument not in concert. Usually in the score the part will read "Clarinet in Bb" or "Clarinet in Si flat." Rarely the part will be labeled "Clarinet in B." The indication is the same except that it is written for the European musician.

The clarinet in Bb indicates that the instrument is built one step below that of the piano or concert pitch. Since this instrument has a lower pitch center than other instruments of the woodwind orchestral family, the printed music must be altered to take care of this discrepancy. The music, therefore, is printed one step higher than it would be for a concert instrument. The key signature is also changed. Therefore, when you look at a Bb clarinet part in a score, the key signature differs from the key signature of the concert instruments. The key signature will always add two sharps for the Bb clarinets as compared to the flute, oboe, or bassoon.

For example, if the oboe and flute were to play in the key of one flat, the Bb clarinet will add two sharps to this signature and will be playing in the key of one sharp. The reason for this is that the oboes and flutes are playing in the key of F major, and the Bb clarinet must play in the key one step higher than F, or the key of G. The conductor must think the pitch lower by one step to establish a unison if he is reading the woodwinds on a transposed score.

Sometimes in orchestral literature the score and parts have been written for clarinets in A. The pitch center of these clarinets is a minor third below that of concert instruments. If we are to have the instruments play in unison, we must alter the printed music for the instrument which is not playing at concert pitch. The part and usually the score will be transposed. Since the clarinet in A is a minor third below concert, then we must pitch the part a minor third above concert to reach a unison. For example: If the oboe and the flutes are playing in the key of G major, the clarinet in A must play in a key a minor third above this, or Bb. When the conductor looks at a score containing a part for an A clarinet, he should imagine the pitch down a third to place it in correct relation to other concert instruments. Other problems might exist if one were to discuss the instruments from the standpoint of composition or orchestration. Our main concern is that of score reading and understanding why the parts would be written as we will discover them in the scores.

Additional Orchestral Woodwinds

In some scores a conductor may find woodwind instruments in addition to those eight in the normal orchestral score. One of these instruments could be the piccolo. In most orchestral scores the C piccolo is called for, and this instrument plays at concert with the exception that it will sound one octave above where it is written.

Another woodwind instrument might be the English horn. It uses the g clef, but it plays in the pitch center of F. This means that it plays a fifth below the pitch of concert woodwinds. Being pitched a fifth below concert, the parts and score must be written a fifth above and must carry a key signature equivalent to a fifth above concert signature. For example, if the concert instruments were playing in the key of D major, the English horn part would be written in the key of A major, or a fifth higher. A conductor looking at a score containing an English horn part must realize that the part is written a fifth above concert pitch and think it a fifth lower to achieve a unison.

The contrabassoon uses the F clef and is in concert pitch except that it will sound one octave below the pitch that is read.

PRACTICE EXERCISES

1. Suppose that you wish all woodwinds to play at unison if possible, or at the octave.
   What would the Bb clarinet play if the bassoon played d^1, f#, G?
   What would the oboe play if the English horn played f^1, a^2, d^2?
   What would the bassoon play if the A clarinet played g^2, $f\#^1$, eb^2?

2. Originate your own questions of this type for other members of your class.

3. Conduct the woodwinds in the following score taken from the orchestral literature. Be sure to read the clarinet part first by concert pitch names. All other sections have been screened to stress the woodwinds.

Copyright © 1962 by Neil A. Kjos Com., Publisher, Park Ridge, Illinois. By permission of the publisher.

The Woodwind Quintet

The woodwind quintet consists of one flute, one oboe, one clarinet, one bassoon, and one French horn. The inclusion of the French horn with the other woodwinds is a concession to tonal color rather than the material from which it is made. Except for the French horn, score reading involved with each of these instruments has been discussed.

The French horn is an instrument with a tonal center of F. As with the English horn, the part and the score have been written a fifth above where it would sound for a concert instrument, and thinking a fifth lower will achieve concert. The French horn plays in several different tonal centers, so that the performer is truly a transposing artist. This is discussed more in detail in the section on brass instruments.

PRACTICE EXERCISE

1. Conduct the following excerpt of woodwind music taken from the second movement of Tomasi's "Quintette." Note the fermatas and cue possibilities. (The woodwind quintet usually does not require a conductor for public performance. A teacher-conductor will conduct many groups in rehearsal that would not require a conductor at the professional level. This type of practice is invaluable for the beginning conductor.) See page 162.

Woodwinds in the Band

In the band the woodwind family comprises a large group of instruments with no apparent numerical limit on instrumentation. Many of the newer scores and organizational standards for the wind ensemble set arbitrary standards on instrumentation in some instances.

Scherzo fantastique

Publie avec l'autorisation des Editions Henry Lemoine, Paris. Copyright 1952 by Editions Henry Lemoine.

The Bb clarinet is the primary woodwind instrument of the concert band. This instrument has been to the band what the violin is to the orchestra. In recent scores its function is more nearly tailored to its particular character.

Usually there will be from six to twenty-six Bb clarinets in a band, depending on the size of the organization. Music for this instrument, as you know, is written a step higher than concert. This does not offer a major problem to the band conductor since so many instruments are playing in a tonal center of Bb. When one studies a band score, the predominance of those instruments in the Bb tonal center almost gives one the impression that they are concert. It is advisable, however, to keep concert clearly in mind and to determine all instruments from that tonal center. This procedure will aid the beginning conductor in future work.

Another member of the clarinet family regularly used in the band is the soprano Eb clarinet. The pitch center of the instrument is a minor third above concert, so that the instrument must play notes that are written a minor third below concert. For example, if the concert pitch is Ab major, the Eb clarinet will be playing in a key that is a minor third below Ab. This key would be F major. The key signature on the part would be altered to accommodate this tonal difference. (For all Eb instruments add three sharps to con-

cert.) The instrument reads the g clef but sounds a minor third higher than noted.

The saxophone family usually consists of three prominent instruments in the band score. These instruments are usually the Eb alto, the Bb tenor, and the Eb baritone. All these instruments use the g clef, and all sound an octave or two octaves below concert pitch with the proper transposition taken into consideration. These transpositions have been discussed earlier in the chapter.

At first, the amateur conductor might find it difficult to read the various transpositions of a band score. Realize, however, that they follow a pattern of Bb or Eb, and constant use will aid your ability to read these scores at sight.

In the band, oboes, flutes, and bassoons are used in different quantities from the orchestra's. The only tonal center difference might be in the case of the piccolo. In earlier band music a conductor will find a scoring for Db piccolo. Although Db piccolos are still used in some circumstances, the C piccolo has replaced it almost completely. The Db piccolo is given a tonal center that is one-half step above concert pitch. This means that the music must be written a half step below concert pitch. For example, if the band is playing in the key of Eb, the Db piccolo will be playing in the key of D. As with all piccolos the sound will be one octave higher than the written notes.

PRACTICE EXERCISES

1. Imagine that you wish all woodwinds to play at unison if possible or at the octave.
   What would the alto saxophone play if the oboe played b^2, c^1, f^2? What would the Bb bass clarinet play if the Bb soprano clarinet played c^3, e^1, f^2? What would the Baritone saxophone play if the flute played $c\#^1$, eb^2, g^3? What would the bassoon play if the Db piccolo played g^3, ab^2, bb^1?

2. Originate your own questions of this type for other members of your class.

3. Conduct the woodwinds in the following score taken from the band literature. Read each part, and give the names of the notes for the concert pitch. All but woodwind sections are screened.

Scherzo

HERBERT ELWELL
Arranged by Robert E. Nelson

3
C Piccolo
C Flutes
Oboes
Eng. Horn
1st Bb Clarinet
2nd Bb Clarinet
3rd Bb Clarinet
Eb Alto Clarinet
Bb Bass Clarinet
1st Eb Alto Saxophone
2nd Eb Alto Saxophone
Bb Tenor Saxophone
Eb Baritone Saxophone
Bassoons
3
Solo
1st Bb Cornet
2nd Bb Cornet
3rd Bb Cornet
1st & 2nd Horns in F
3rd & 4th Horns in F
1st Trombone
2nd Trombone
3rd Trombone
Baritone
Basses
Timpani
Percussion

The Woodwind Ensemble

Woodwind ensembles are of various types including homogeneous trios, mixed trios, and homogeneous and heterogeneous quartets. For years the clarinet quartet has been popular in two types: one with four Bb soprano clarinets or three Bb soprano clarinets and one Bb bass clarinet and one with two Bb soprano clarinets, one alto, and one bass clarinet. Note that the latter group is more nearly like the string quartet in color. The clarinet duet and trio is popular in school contests. Recently, the clarinet choir has become prominent. This organization makes use of all the types of clarinets in various numbers, including the Eb or Bb contra. There is no problem for the conductor in any of these organizations from the standpoint of score reading that has not been covered previously. The newest woodwind ensemble is the flute quartet using 2 C soprano flutes, 1 alto flute in G, and 1 bass flute in C. The alto is a fourth below concert, and the bass is an octave below.

PRACTICE EXERCISE

1. Conduct the following clarinet choir score.

Divertimento I
Transcribed for Clarinet Choir

JOSEPH HAYDN
trans. by ROBERT W. HINDSLEY

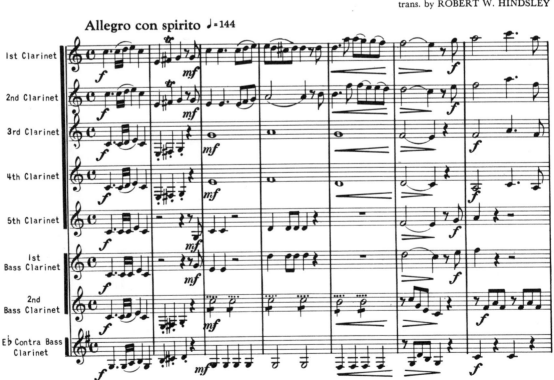

THE BRASS FAMILY

The Brass Choir

This grouping of brass instruments was popular in the sixteenth century, only to fall into disuse until a comparatively few years ago. Brass choir instrumentation is set by the composition that is being performed. In most cases trumpets, horns, and trombones are used, with baritones and tubas added if called for in the score. The brass choir usually has a conductor.

The easiest brass instrument to read and comprehend could be the tuba. Tubas are built in almost every tonal center, but the player transposes. Most common in orchestras is the tuba in C, although the Eb, F, or G tuba may be called for occasionally. The Eb tuba may be used in bands or brass choirs, but normally school organizations use Bbb tubas reading f clef concert and sounding the pitch as written.

The trombone uses three clefs: most often it uses the f clef, many times it uses the tenor clef if the phrase is written toward the upper range, and under some circumstances in orchestras it will use the alto clef. These clefs have been discussed in the string material. The instrument reads the note at pitch, so that if you read the key signature and the correct

clef, you will be reading the notes as they sound.

In the present brass choir, the baritone may use either the f or g clef. This depends somewhat upon the performer, his instruction on the instrument, and occasionally upon the composition. If the instrument is playing in the g clef, it will be treated as if it were in a Bb tonal center, and one would then read the score a ninth lower. If the instrument reads the f clef, no transposition is necessary because it is playing at concert pitch.

The French horn in the brass choir is usually treated as an instrument with a tonal center of F, resembling the English horn in this respect. Therefore, the conductor will need to read the part a fifth lower if he is to bring it to concert pitch. Occasionally, the French horn part may be written in Eb, in which case the Eb transposition rule would apply, sounding a major sixth below the g clef written pitch.

The trumpet or cornet in the brass choir will usually play in the Bb tonal center. At times one will find a part written in C so that the trumpet player must transpose if he is playing on a Bb instrument. Trumpets in the C tonal center play at concert pitch, while parts in Bb need to be transposed downward one step. The C trumpet is usually considered an orchestral instrument.

PRACTICE EXERCISE

Read the following brass choir score. If possible conduct this with a group of performers.

MUSIC FOR BRASS No. 72

SPECTRUMS

[Second Prize - 1952 Thor Johnson Brass Composition Award]

Paul Shahan

The

177   *The Score: Additional Problems*

Copyright © 1955 by Paul Shahan. By permission of the publisher, Robert King Music Co., North Easton, Massachusetts.

2. Make a score condensation (see pages 80–81 as an example) of the above which would include the concerns of a conductor during rehearsal.

Brass in the Band

In considering the brass section of the band, we find no additional problems from those listed for the brass choir. Trumpets are found in Bb, the horns usually are round in the tonal center of F, baritones are playing either the f or g clef, and the trombones rarely if ever will be placed in the tenor clef. In other words, a conductor will meet fewer problems in a brass section of a band score than in other scores.

PRACTICE EXERCISE

Conduct the brass parts from the first 25 measures of the band score beginning on page 189. Notice how the instruments are used and how one moves the eye through the score to pick up important information for the conductor.

Brass in the Orchestra

The brass section of the orchestra contains transposition problems not found in other scores. In most cases these are in the horn or trumpet parts.

The trumpet in the orchestra is seldom found in the Bb tonal center unless the score is of a more recent period or unless you are conducting a selection which has been arranged for school groups. Many times orchestra scores call for the trumpet in C. This is not a difficult transposition for the Bb trumpet. In some cases orchestral scores request trumpet in D. If attempting to aid a performer playing the part on a Bb instrument, recognize the difference between the Bb instrument and the D part, raising the pitch a major third from that printed.

Occasionally one finds trumpet parts in Eb or A. Both of these transpositions have been discussed earlier in this chapter.

French Horn Transpositions

Usually selections played by school orchestras place the French horn in F. Standard repertoire orchestra scores, however, use almost any pitch center. Reminiscent of the days when the natural horn necessitated a number of crooks or slides to accommodate concert keys, older French horn parts carry no key signature as other instruments, but only a designation for a pitch center. In some compositions it is common for them to change pitch centers during the work or between movements of a longer work. Rarely the first two horns are written at one pitch while the third and fourth are at another. Present-day double horns with valves make chromatacism easy, but the horn player must learn his transpositions to play compositions written in various pitch centers. A difficult transposition is the horn part written in E.

Usually the lack of key signature for the horn part is more confusing than if one were given. The accidentals written into the part in lieu of the signature often require thinking by interval. Practice of a given interval will bring familiarity.

One further note concerning the horn. Pedal tones often are written in the f clef a fourth below concert rather than a fifth above making the part appear very low in pitch on the printed score. To achieve concert, the conductor must read this part a fourth higher than printed.

Assignment of Parts

In scores written after the mid-nineteenth century the third horn plays the second highest part. This unusual assignment of parts could disturb the beginning conductor, for he might feel that he is misreading the score. It has the advantage of being easy to read, since the notes of the horn parts are almost always well spaced.

In the case of the brass choir, trumpets are assigned two or three parts, two to four parts for the horns, two or three parts for trombones, and one part each for the tuba and baritone.

In the band, conductors will usually find three parts for the cornets. Some conductors believe the cornet is truly the band's instrument. Most publishers respond by giving the first soprano brass part the title "Cornet 1." If the score makes an obvious difference between cornets and trumpets, the parts will be assigned by taking the tonal qualities of the instruments into consideration.

Usually in the band there will be four horn parts, three parts for the trombones, and one part each for the baritones and tubas. It is common practice in the band to double or triple performers per part. If one has nine cornet players, it is not too unlikely for a conductor to place three on a part. Other brass instruments duplicate parts similarly. This would be less likely in the brass choir or orchestra.

There is no question but that the trumpets are the instrument for the orchestra. In simpler or older orchestrations only a pair of trumpets will be scored, but three parts were used regularly after 1850. In some classical compositions horns are requested in pairs, but in later orchestrations four horns will be required.

Although the trombone is one of the oldest of brass instruments, it was not used in orchestras as early as as the French horn. However, if the composer has written for the trombone, he usually calls for three, the third being a bass trombone. Only in more recent scores does the tuba come into much use. More than one tuba is rarely used in the orchestra.

PRACTICE EXERCISES

1. Read through the brass parts in the following orchestration and name the concert pitch for the horn parts. As you read the horn parts, be sure that you understand the pitch location of these parts on the great staff.

2. Conduct the brass portions of the following score for orchestra.

Menuetto from "Music for the Royal Fireworks"
G.F. Handel

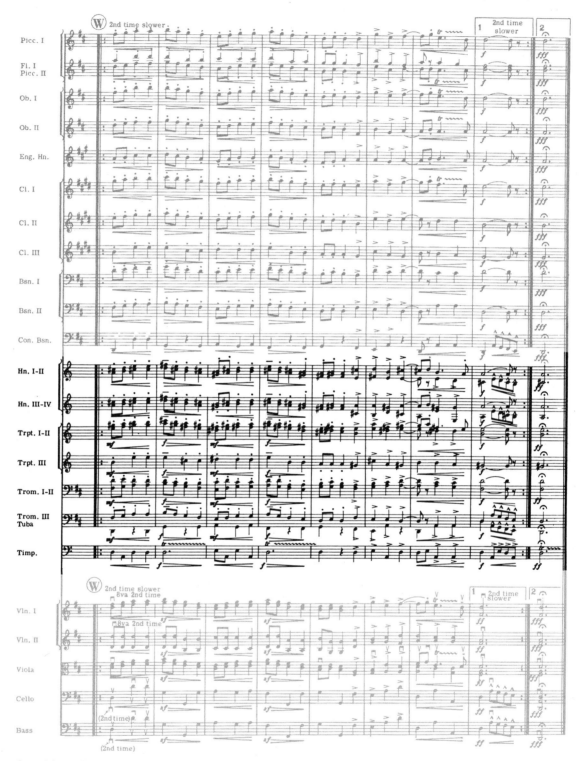

THE PERCUSSION FAMILY

Although the percussion instruments used in the modern score are many and varied, the conductor's reading problems are usually quite simple. No transpositions are called for, and many of the instruments do not use a five-line pitching staff.

The xylophone and celeste sound an octave higher than written, whereas the orchestra bells sound two octaves higher. All are concert pitch. The conductor needs to be alert to two items in particular.

1. The terms used for the various percussion instruments are often varied and sometimes written in foreign languages. For this reason you will find a complete list of these in Appendix 2: "Percussion Terms." Memorize the most commonly used ones even in two or three languages, and do not hesitate to refer to this text or a music dictionary when confronted by the less common terms.

2. The rhythm written for some percussion instruments can be complex looking with many notes and appoggiaturas. It is best to work out these rhythms carefully when practicing your score alone. Sing the rhythms to yourself, noting the accents and how the rhythms accompany the melodic line or assist the rhythmic line of other instruments. Do not permit your percussion players to fake a percussion part because you have not taken the time or trouble to learn the percussion lines. Have a particular reason for any ad libitum.

Once you have become familiar with the percussion parts you will be more alert to them in rehearsal and will be able to decide upon their balance within the section and their balance in comparison to the remainder of the group. It is difficult for the amateur percussion performer to understand style enough to be able to balance this loudness against the group. The conductor should be of constant assistance as to loudness. Related to this is the type of stroke used, the type of mallet, and the location of the stroke on the instrument. Studying a good percussion manual will be of great assistance in these areas. A percussion course taught by a professional percussionist will be of greater value.

The scores of the classical period often requested only tympani. Do not add percussion parts to these scores. If conducting a band arrangement of an orchestral score, it is often wise to refer to the original version of the score to ascertain exactly what and how much percussion should be used. Some arrangers add many percussion parts to a score just to keep the large band percussion section busy, leaving the amateur conductor of this type of arrangement wondering why the composition sounds ponderous and out of proper style. A study of the original percussion parts would supply at least part of the answer.

The percussion ensemble has become quite popular during the last twenty years. Most high schools as well as universities provide this type of musical experience for members of the percussion section. In some schools where the number of percussionists might be smaller than the required number of players for a composition, it is possible to enlist ensemble members from other sections to play mallet instruments or parts that require less intricate technique but an exacting sense of rhythm. Serious compositions for this group have increased almost one hundred times over the past twenty years, and many well-known composers have written for the group. Percussion ensembles appeal on a broad base to children and adults and to the trained and untrained. The amateur conductor should take every opportunity to conduct or perform with such a group to gain valuable experience for his conducting career.

PRACTICE EXERCISES

1. On a neutral syllable sing the percussion parts listed below as you conduct. Follow this by conducting them without singing being sure to consider style, cuing, and dynamics.

2. Conduct the percussion ensemble score given below. After practice alone, work with a percussion group if possible. If that is not convenient, members of your class could sing and talk through the score as you conduct. (For the present, conduct in a fast three.)

TAKE - OFF

Full Score

Full Score

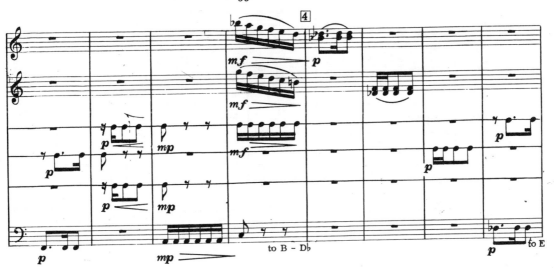

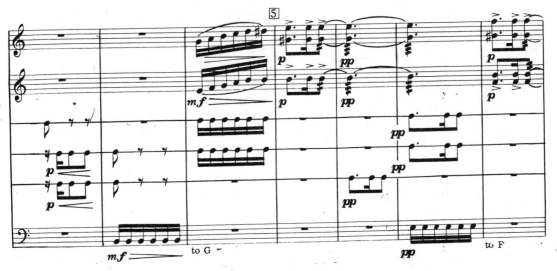

Full Score

THE FULL SCORE

You are now prepared to study and conduct from the full orchestra score. Notice that the woodwinds are at the top of the page, the brass and percussion near the center, and the string section at the bottom. Because of the simplicity of the classical orchestral score, it would be best to study this type of score now.

If a soloist or chorus is used with an orchestra, you will find the solo part or parts located between the percussion and the string section. The score that we study first will have no vocal parts.

One score for study is the first 100 measures of the Haydn Symphony No. 101. Since this type of instrumentation is feasible for an amateur ensemble, this score offers a good opportunity to use the information that we have discussed in previous chapters. It also uses a basic classical orchestra with which you should be familiar. The recorded version of this music is readily available.

At this point it would be advisable to review Chapter 9 and follow the suggestions given there for score study. Remember when studying a score, it is impossible even for a professional conductor to comprehend all its musical meanings and possibilities in one or two study sessions. Consequently, the amateur need not hesitate to work with a page of a score for a considerable time. Many small items may be seen at a glance, but true musical study that leads to comprehension involves vigorous attention to numerous details.

Remember: First, study your score without the aid of recorded reproduction or keyboard instrument. If you desire to make use of these instruments later, all well and good, and you should expect to do so. At first, however, make every effort to capture as much of the score as possible without aids.

Remember: Considerable assistance may be obtained from an analysis of the lines of the score. This is not a theoretical analysis but rather a study of what each part is doing and how this part fits into the whole. Many times in musical compositions scores can be separated into three or four simple lines if the conductor will only take a few moments to study them with this in mind. For this reason we have worked with a representational score diagram in earlier chapters.

PRACTICE EXERCISES

1. Complete a diagram score of the introduction of Haydn's Symphony No. 101. Conduct from the diagram, then conduct from the musical score.

Symphony No. 101
(The Clock)

Joseph Haydn
1732-1809

*) Die Klarinettenstimmen sind mitgedruckt; vergl. jedoch den Vorbericht.

2. Complete a diagram score of the allegro section of the preceding Haydn symphony. Practice conducting from the diagram, then conduct from the musical score.

3. Compare your diagram score with that of others in your class. Where do you differ? Are the differences significant?

4. Complete a diagram score of the *Transylvania Fanfare,* measures 103 to 148 (pp. 197-201).

5. Compare your diagram score to those of others in your class. Where do you differ? Are the differences significant?

6. Examine the score for the *Hallelujah Chorus* (pp. 205-220). Do you find sections where a diagram score could be of assistance? Prepare a diagram score of these portions for your personal practice.

7. Ask a classmate to check over the diagram score for the *Hallelujah Chorus* which you have completed to ascertain if he understands it and agrees with your indications of the conductor's problems.

8. Without further assistance, prepare the score of an entire composition. After preliminary check sessions with your teacher, obtain fellow students for a rehearsal and/or performance.

Transylvania   Fanfare

Performance time:
Approx. 3 minutes.

Warren   Benson

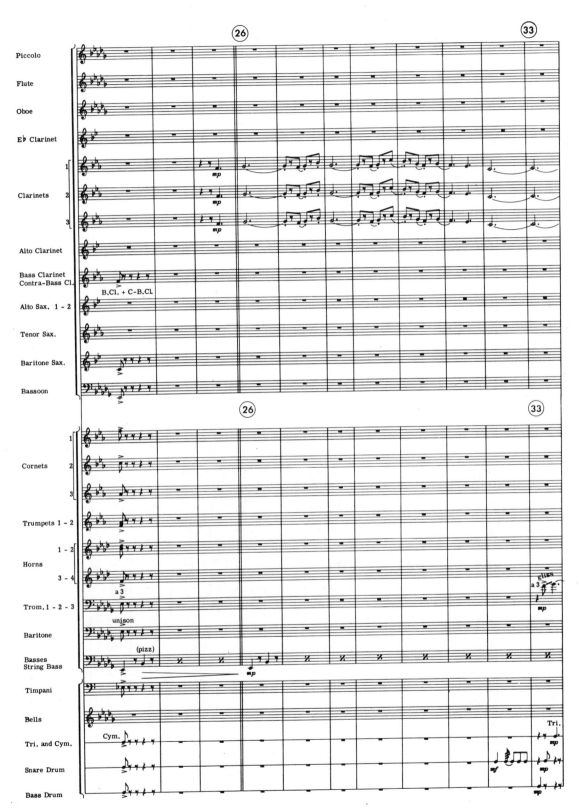

108
115
Piccolo
Flute
Oboe
E♭ Clarinet
Clarinets 1 2 3
Alto Clarinet
Bass Clarinet
Contra-Bass Cl.
C-B. Cl.
B.Cl.
Alto Sax. 1 - 2
Tenor Sax.
Baritone Sax.
Bassoon
Cornets 1 2 3
(Horn cue)
Trumpets 1 - 2
unison
Horns 1 - 2 3 - 4
a 2 soli
Trom. 1 - 2 - 3
Baritone
Basses
String Bass
Timpani
Tri. and Cym.
Cym.
Snare Drum
Bass Drum

138
(Enharmonic spelling in parts)
144
Piccolo
Flute
Oboe
E♭ Clarinet
Clarinets 1 2 3
Alto Clarinet
Bass Clarinet
Contra-Bass Cl.
Alto Sax. 1 - 2
Tenor Sax.
Baritone Sax.
Bassoon
138
144
Cornets 1 2 3
Trumpets 1 - 2
Horns 1 - 2 3 - 4
Trom. 1 - 2 - 3
Baritone
Basses
String Bass
Timpani
Bells
Tri. and Cym.
Snare Drum
Bass Drum
(To Tri.)
soli
Cym.
ff
mp
E♭♭ to E♭
F♭ to F♮

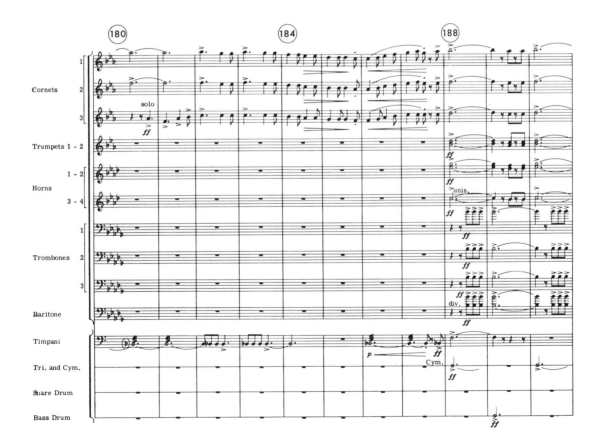

42. Coro.

***Hallelujah Chorus,* from "The Messiah"**
G. F. Handel

✱ *Händel's Trumpet parts; rewritten by Mozart.*

✱✱ *Original Timpani parts.*

a 2.
a 2.
a 2.
Gott, und er re - giert von nun an auf e - - wig, Herr der Herrn, der Göt - ter
Lords, and he shall reign for e - ver and e - - ver, King of Kings and Lord of
Gott, und er re - giert von nun an auf e - - wig, von nun an auf ewig, von nun an auf
Lords, and he shall reign for e - ver and e - - ver, for e - ver and ever, for e - ver and
Gott, und er re - giert von nun an auf e - - wig, von nun an auf ewig, von nun an auf
Lords, and he shall reign for e - ver and e - - ver, for e - ver and ever, for e - ver and
Gott, und er re - giert von nun an, von nun an auf e - - wig, von nun an auf ewig, von nun an auf
Lords, and he shall reign for e - ver, for e - ver and e - - ver, for e - ver and ever, for e - ver and

Fine della seconda parte.

15

The General Pause and the Caesura

Two symbols indicating pauses or breaks in the music deserve our attention. They usually do not present the conductor with difficult problems, but decisions must be made concerning the approach and reentry.

THE GENERAL PAUSE

Occasionally one may find the two letters "G.P." written in a particular measure. Certain styles of writing favor this symbol more than others, so that it is possible for a conductor not to meet one for months or years and then find several in a short period of time.

The letters are an abbreviation for the words "general pause." In some areas they are termed "grand pause." In the latter case the word "grand" means extensive or all-inclusive. Some conductors mistakenly have been taught that "grand pause" means an unusually long pause.

This symbol is another method of assigning a complete rest or silence to the entire group of performers. It will often appear in unlikely places, not necessarily at the phrase end, so that the music may come to a rather abrupt and inconclusive stop. At other times it is placed in the music by some composers apparently to alert the ensemble to the fact that a silent measure has been reached and that the conductor will probably react to this measure by waiting.

Since the symbol may appear in mid-phrase, the conductor must be certain that his indication for release or cutoff is adequate to enlist the attention of the entire group. No problem need be anticipated here, since it is merely an execution of a release of those notes immediately before.

Usually the letters "G.P." are placed in a measure by themselves rather than in a part of a measure. It would appear, then, that the composer intends that a full measure of silence be used. The conductor must rely completely upon his sense of musicianship, and if the situation could use a longer or shorter break, he then should conduct it in such a manner. At times the deviation from a strict rhythmic rest would be reason enough to use this symbol rather than an ordinary rest of one measure, since the latter is interpreted generally as a complete measure, no more or less.

221

PRACTICE EXERCISES

1. Plan your conducting of the two scores considering tempi and interpretation. Discuss these items with your classmates. After this, listen to a standard recording of one of these numbers to ascertain how your study and the recording has differed and how it was similar.

   First, the final page of the Holst "St. Paul Suite" which uses one type of G.P. The tempo is vivace and the meter is 6/8.

St. Paul Suite
Gustav von Holst

2. The introduction of the Schuller Quintet includes a G.P.

Score

SUITE
I PRELUDE

Gunther Schuller

THE CAESURA

Occasionally one will find two vertical lines placed close by each other and near the top of the staff slanted into the left. This is the caesura and indicates a break in the music. By students and conductors alike these have been known as slash marks, railroad tracks, or other colloquialisms. As in the case of the fermata, the correct term for this symbol should be used with students.

Caesuras are sometimes found in unlikely places. At times they appear to be placed in error or in poor taste and deserve to be disregarded altogether. Other times they seem to call for a ritard in the music as approached. Different interpretations might be considered.

SCORE STUDY

Usually the caesura is a type of unexpected hesitation or break in the music that obtains its advantage from the surprise element, but this is not always the case. In the Giovannini example that follows, the caesura is used to indicate a break, but little surprise is involved.

In conducting this example, one should indicate the length of the eighth note in measure seven by the speed of the baton's rebound and the length of rebound for that beat. If the rebound is fast, the note will be played quite short; if the rebound is longer and slower, the eighth will also be longer. Decide in your practice if the release for the caesura should be on beat four or beat one.

In the second example, which is an excerpt from Clifton Williams' "Festival," the meter signature and the tempo have been changed just a few measures before the caesura. As we approach the caesura, the loudness increases, and the music is broken and then begins again more quietly.

In conducting the caesura in this example the conductor beats a simple pattern, increasing slightly in size to suggest the crescendo. The baton should conduct the third beat of the measure and execute the rebound. At the height of the rebound the baton should almost jerk to a stop. After a momentary break, the downbeat is given and the music resumes. Another procedure would execute the third beat at the conducting center, almost at the beat point for the first beats, and with the rebound moving almost horizontally to the right. This permits the hand to end low rather than high so that a false reentry is not as likely.

Unlike the first example, do not use a release or cutoff for this measure unless you find the performers holding over. Where the last measure before a release contains short notes, the release is partly built into the rhythm of these notes. In other words, the players tend to release partly through the rhythmic drive of these notes played toward the end of the measure. Correct conducting procedure would necessitate only an energized rebound for the third beat of the measure and an abrupt stop at the top of the rebound. The top of the rebound should be reached simultaneously with the last note of the horn triplet. The flute and oboe should play their last eighth during the rise of the baton on the rebound, stopping the note as the baton comes to a stop at the top of the rebound.

PRACTICE EXERCISES

1. Study the following scores, considering the comments given above.

2. Work out the conducting procedures for the scores, including the tempi, style, and dynamics. Use the left hand with discretion.

3. Study the caesura in the Williams' selection. Conduct it as suggested above and also with a release at the top of the rebound. Which way do you prefer? Have members of your class sing the rhythms of the various parts so that you may practice both releases and the following attack. Do you notice a difference in the performer's ability to release?

Sonatina for Band
Caesar Giovannini

II

Festival
Clifton Williams

4. Have you seen a G.P. or caesura recently in the music being performed by your school organizations? If so, how have they been executed? Could you have conducted them in the same manner?

16

The Preparatory: Less-used Patterns

For a number of years my conducting classes had been simultaneously introduced to all the preparatory patterns somewhat early in the course. Two of these patterns were assimilated into the technique rather quickly, but the two other patterns remained practically unlearned. The students, not ready to conquer all preparatory problems at that point of their learning, were not absorbing them into their technique. Therefore, it is advisable to postpone until this point the introduction of the less-common preparatory patterns. Since fewer compositions make use of them, they become more difficult in the mind of the conductor, affecting his ability to assimilate them.

Many conductors state that there is no need for them to learn to give a preparatory on beats to the right and left of the downbeat, since their students could not perform this attack even if conducted correctly. After working with amateur groups in all kinds of ensembles, this reasoning appears to me to be false and only an excuse for the director. Most student groups can be taught to follow these preparatory patterns in a few minutes, even without the use of verbal directions, if the conductor will permit them to ob-

serve his technique and then practice four or five entrances with the group. The conductor should insist the performers attack as cleanly as for the downbeat.

Nothing is more amateurish than watching a conductor move through a pattern silently so that his group may enter upon the proper beat. Worse yet is the conductor who counts almost audibly through a preparatory measure while conducting with a small pattern during those introductory beats.

PREPARATORY FOR BEATS TO THE LEFT OF THE DOWNBEAT

Some helpful rules follow:

1. Most preparatory beats to the left are begun with the right hand and with the baton held a bit toward the center of the body, a little lower than a regular preparatory. About three inches below the normal preparatory line is a correct position in most instances.

2. The elbow should be bent slightly and placed about five or six inches from the rib cage.

3. The baton should point inward toward the center line of the body.

4. The forearm is almost parallel with the floor.

5. The baton should be held motionless for a moment or two before the motion is begun.

6. The motion of the preparatory should be upward into the preparatory loop and then fall into the motion toward the left.

7. The upward motion should not be draggy but deliberate and in tempo with the music that is to follow.

8. The upward portion of the preparatory should be timed so that the right hand reaches the top of the motion on the downbeat or the preceding beat to the attack.

9. The sweeping motion to the left should be direct but in tempo.

10. The lowest point to the left should be followed with a good rebound that will indicate precisely where the beginning attack should be made.

11. The rebound should be in proportion to the type of attack you are requesting.

12. The wrist should move in proportion to the loudness and style of attack requested.

PRACTICE EXERCISES

1. Practice the preparatory to the left with and without a baton according to the diagrams below. When working without a baton, be sure that the hand is equally expressive as with a baton. Practice by counting for yourself or by working with a metronome, being sure that the beats occur as indicated in Figures 16-1 and 16-2.

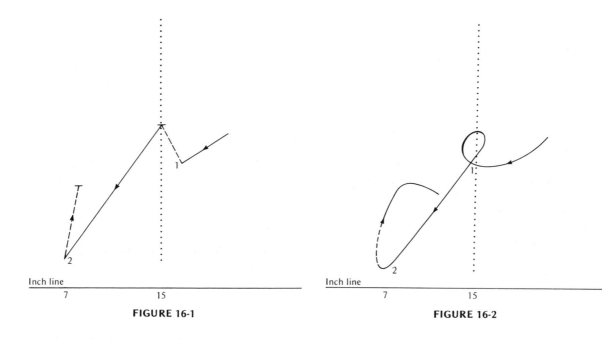

Inch line
7   15
FIGURE 16-1

Inch line
7   15
FIGURE 16-2

2. Practice this preparatory for both conducting styles that we have been learning: smooth, or legato, and disconnected, or marcato.

3. Practice this preparatory using the music examples below. Try purposely not to use the same tempo for each practice example. A variety will offer a range of practice opportunities.

Symphony No. 3
Vittorio Giannini

49

O Jesu So Sweet

O Jesulein süss

Sacred Chorus for Mixed Voices, A Cappella
(S.A.T.B.)

UNKNOWN
English version by P. S. B.

SAMUEL SCHEIDT
(1587-1684)

Praise God, from Whom All Blessings Flow

Chorale for Mixed Voices, A Cappella
(S. A. T. B.)

THOMAS KEN

Maestoso

Genevan Psalter
Harmonization by
JOHANN SEBASTIAN BACH
Edited by WALTER E. BUSZIN

Praise God from whom all bless-ings flow; Praise Him all crea-tures here be - low;

Praise Him a - bove ye heav'n-ly host; Praise Fa - ther, Son, and Ho - ly Ghost.

4. See also the "Hansel and Gretel" overture, page 106, and the last phrase of "Locus Iste," page 109, M44.

5. Practice these preparatory beats with a group of players or singers. This is important, since amateurs often believe that they have mastered their problems, only to find that a performer does not believe that the preparatory is clear.

PREPARATORY FOR BEATS TO THE RIGHT OF THE DOWNBEAT

This preparatory is used more often than is the one to the left of the downbeat, but it is fairly easy after you have learned the former pattern.

    Follow these suggestions carefully.

1. Most preparatory beats are begun with the right hand and baton held toward the left center of the body and somewhat lower than a regular preparatory. To be exact, for preparatories to the right the beginning point may be lower than for any other pattern. About nine to twelve inches below the chin would be correct in most instances.

2. The elbow should be bent slightly but closer to the rib cage than before, for this pattern about four inches between elbow and ribs.

3. The baton will point to the left of center, since the right hand is to the left of center of the body.

4. The right forearm is almost parallel to the floor.

5. The baton should be held motionless for a moment or two before the motion is begun.

6. The motion of the preparatory should be upward into the preparatory loop and then fall into the motion toward the right.

7. The upward motion should not be draggy but deliberate and in tempo with the music that is to follow.

8. The upward motion of the preparatory should be timed so that the right hand begins the upward motion immediately after the preceding pulsation.

9. The motion to the right should be smooth, direct, and in tempo.

10. The lowest point to the right should be followed with an appropriate rebound.

11. The rebound should be in proportion to the type of attack you are requesting.

12. The wrist of the rebound should move in proportion to the loudness and the style of attack requested.

PRACTICE EXERCISES

1. Practice the preparatory with and without a baton according to the diagrams below.

2. Notice that again two styles of pattern are given. Practice both styles, being sure to make an obvious difference between them.

3. Two types of preparatory are given in Figures 16-3 through 16-10 in each style. Which of these do you prefer?

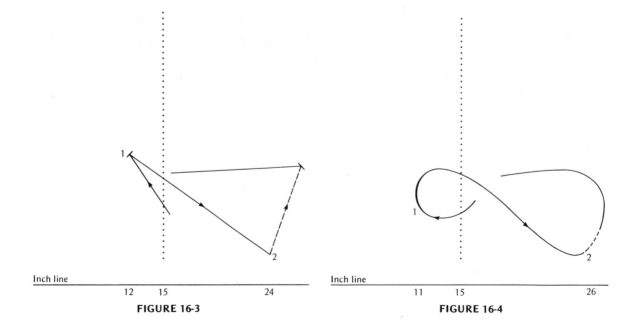

Inch line
　　　　12　　15　　　　　　24
FIGURE 16-3

Inch line
　　　　11　　15　　　　　　26
FIGURE 16-4

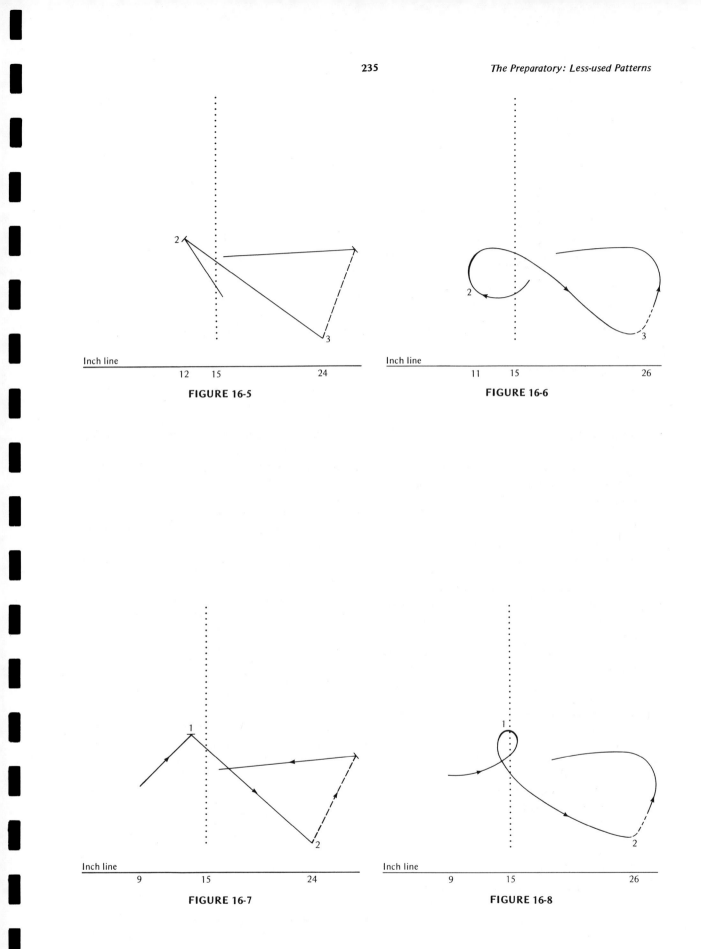

Inch line

        12   15   24

FIGURE 16-5

Inch line

        11   15   26

FIGURE 16-6

Inch line

     9   15   24

FIGURE 16-7

Inch line

     9   15   26

FIGURE 16-8

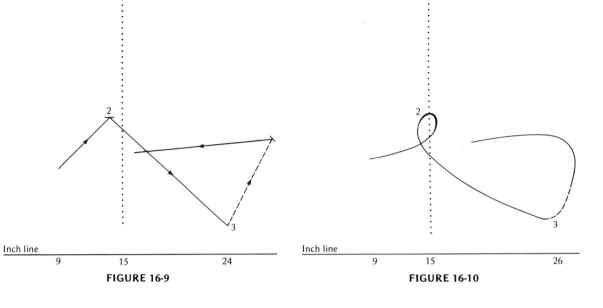

Inch line
9   15   24

FIGURE 16-9

Inch line
9   15   26

FIGURE 16-10

GENERAL RULES

1. The preparatory for any attack begins its movement immediately after a pulsation. Note the diagrams above.

2. Move the arm at the tempo of the composition to be performed until you reach the loop of the attack beat and begin the rebound.

3. The rebound will be executed faster than the preparatory motion. If the tempo is slow or modest, the amount of increased speed in the rebound will be very little, in fact just enough to let the performer understand that you have arrived at the beat point and have moved away from it. If the tempo is quick or very fast, the rebound speed will be obviously faster than the preparatory movement. For the performer, this creates at that exact moment a definite pull into the performance.

4. For the conductor, the only hesitation will come at the top of the rebound. Any hesitation before that point will result in indecision in attack and possible confusion. The tempo of moving from the beat point to the top of the rebound in any given attack will be faster than the preparatory motion but in proportion to the speed of the composition to be performed. It is this proportion that must be practiced by the amateur so that the performers feel comfortable with the attack. What is sometimes forgotten by the amateur is that professionals must rehearse an attack more than they might any other portion of a composition. This is particularly true if the composition were not of standard repertoire.

5. When the tempo is on the slow side, performers will begin to play or sing almost immediately after the bottom of the beat point has been indicated. During the faster compositions, performers will not begin until the top of the rebound has been reached. In very fast tempi the conductor may be forced to wait a fraction of a second at the top of the rebound before the music begins. If the conductor diminishes the intensity of his right hand during this hesitation, the attack will lack uniformity. The conductor must realize that this will happen and have confidence that the attack will begin. This sureness in your own technique is often the difference between the experienced and inexperienced conductor on this point.

PRACTICE EXERCISES

1. Practice the following literature to assist you with these patterns.

   Note: In the Thompson selection the preparatory for beat two is as defined earlier. The fermata affects only the rebound, which moves slowly upward and to the right until you are ready for beat 3, which is treated similarly. Conducting in a quick three, move the baton upward for the rebound of the second beat of measure two stopping abruptly to indicate the fermata on the last half of the beat. When you are ready to proceed again, give a preparatory for a pickup and continue in tempo.

At the Beach

Concert Waltz

VIRGIL THOMSON

CONDENSED CONDUCTOR

J587

Trumpet Solo with Band Accompaniment

2. Another example of a preparatory to the right is found in Mozart's *Eine Kleine Nachtmusik* at the beginning of the second movement. Conduct in four.

ROMANZE.
Andante.

By permission of the publisher, Breitkopf and Hartel, Weisbaden.

3. See also "Yea Though I Wander," page 117, rehearsal D and two measures before D, and phrases of "Wake, Awake," page 125.

These preparatories may be used for all signatures. A pattern beginning on beat three in a six-beat measure would use an attack to the left of the downbeat. Also it could be used for a second- or third-beat attack for a five-beat measure. The attack on beat four or five of a six-beat measure will use the patterns to the right of the downbeat. Examples for other meters will be obvious.

PREPARATORY FOR PART OF A BEAT
There may be times when one may wish to conduct a preparatory for half a beat or part of a beat. This is usually not necessary if the tempo is fast. As the tempi become slower, an entrance on the half beat becomes more difficult to execute together. It is at times such as these that such an attack becomes important.

Even when the tempo is rapid, a subdivision of the preparatory might be important depending upon the location of the partial beat to the entire composition. For example, if the partial beat begins a concert or begins a composition when the conductor is not sure that the exact tempo is remembered, then a divided preparatory would be appropriate.

PRACTICE EXERCISES

1. Practice the diagrams shown in Figures 15-11 through 15-15 for subdivided preparatory patterns if the tempi are slow. These will be particularly important for the choral conductor.

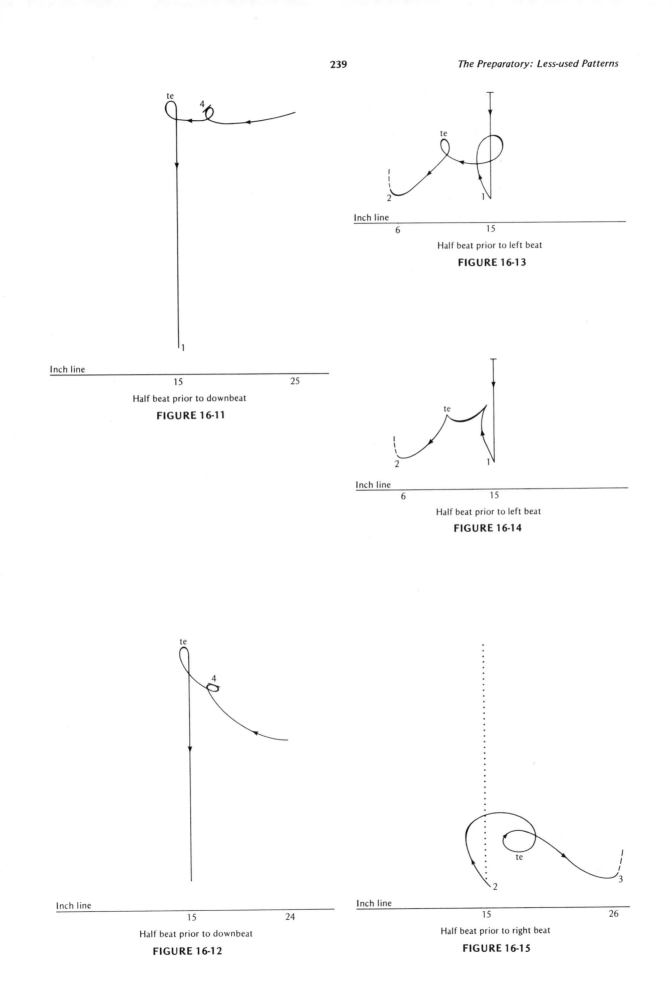

te

4

1

Inch line

15   25

Half beat prior to downbeat

FIGURE 16-11

te

4

Inch line

15   24

Half beat prior to downbeat

FIGURE 16-12

te

2   1

Inch line

6   15

Half beat prior to left beat

FIGURE 16-13

te

2   1

Inch line

6   15

Half beat prior to left beat

FIGURE 16-14

te

2   3

Inch line

15   26

Half beat prior to right beat

FIGURE 16-15

Note: The beginning point for patterns in Figures 16-13, 16-14, and 16-15 should be adhered to strictly. These are lower than the starting point for any previous pattern.

Note: These patterns may be used for numerous signatures.

Note: Try 16-15 with "Hansel and Gretel," page 106. Would you prefer 16-18?

2. Practice the diagrams in Figures 16-16 through 16-19 for subdivided patterns if the tempi are quick, These will be particularly important to the instrumental conductor.

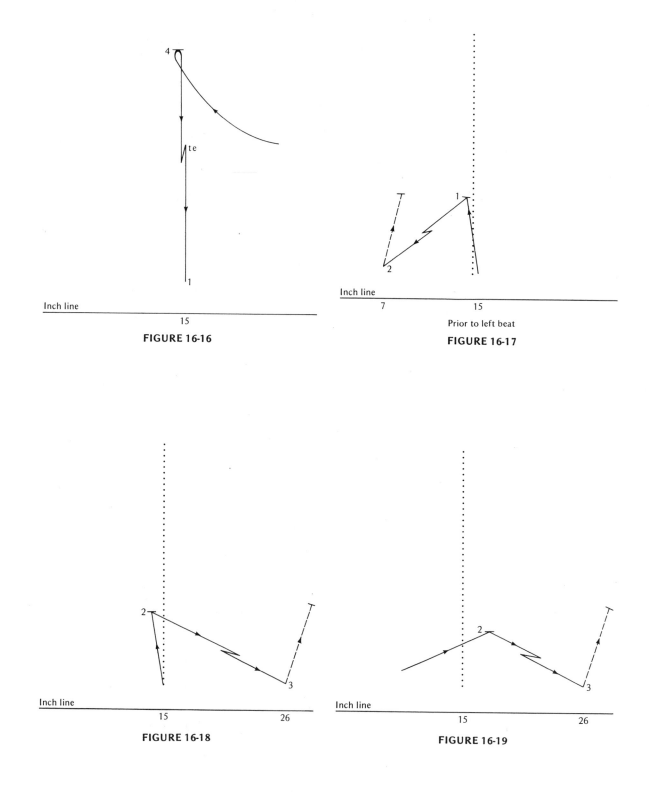

FIGURE 16-16

FIGURE 16-17

Prior to left beat

FIGURE 16-18

FIGURE 16-19

3. Practice the examples written in musical notation in Figure 16-20. Which of these need a subdivision and which do not? Which type of subdivision would you prefer for these examples?

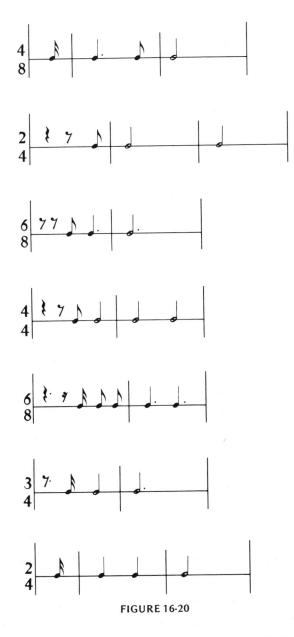

FIGURE 16-20

Some rules might be helpful.

1. Do not subdivide the preparatory for every attack on the divided beat. Some will not need it, since the attack will appear obvious to many performers almost immediately, particularly where the rhythm of the selection will be easily remembered. Only more difficulty will be introduced by subdividing where not necessary.

2. Be sure the right hand is held almost at eye level for every new attack. Even though the preparatory beat is to be made in a lower beat point position, raise the hand if the attack is a part of a new beginning. Unusual preparatories diagramed under Exercise 2 above should still begin almost at eye level but will use a short downbeat or a short upstroke carried higher.

3. With subdivided preparatories the inclination is to push the tempo of the hand so that it appears to the performer that the attack will be made at a faster tempo. Be sure that any preparatory is in tempo with the music that is to follow. Practice the subdivided preparatory by using it in the first two measures of the examples below.

SONATINA FOR BAND

CAESAR GIOVANNINI
Scored for Band by
WAYNE ROBINSON

I

Duration: I = 3:10
II = 3:50
III = 2:45
Total: ca. 9:05

Has Sorrow Thy Young Day Shaded

Irish Melody

THOMAS MOORE

MORTEN J. LUVAAS

17

The Left Hand: Additional Uses

In Chapter 8 the left hand was discussed in some detail in connection with five particular functions: in a rest position, for the preparatory, during the release, with dynamics, and in connection with some patterns. In Chapter 10 the left hand was used in cuing. Four additional ideas will be discussed in this chapter: style, shading, pauses and breathing, and accents and sforzandos.

Some comments about style have already been made. Many amateur conductors do little with style in conducting. This can be remedied if consideration is given to it from the very beginning of the conducting class. In the chapter on patterns, two obvious styles were practiced. Throughout the text, reference has been made to these two styles. This does not mean that there are only two styles but rather that these styles are at the extreme ends of the possibilities and, once the conductor has worked with the extremes, the more subtle concepts will probably be possible.

These two styles deserve first consideration again in connection with the left hand.

LEFT HAND AND STYLES

Smooth, Legato Style

The left hand may be of assistance with a legato style if the conductor so desires. To portray this flowing concept to the players, the left hand may be moved in a rolling and smooth fashion from time to time during the music. This rolling motion may be in a horizontal plane and may take on the configurations of a portion of a figure eight.

Most often, if the right hand is moving to the right side of a pattern, the left hand may move toward the left (see Figure 17-1).

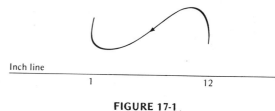

FIGURE 17-1

If the right hand is moving toward the left of a pattern or toward the top of the pattern, the left hand may move toward the right (see Figure 17-2).

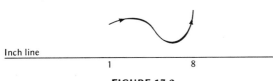

Inch line

1   8

FIGURE 17-2

For the upbeat of any pattern, the left hand may mirror the right in the upward sweep that one uses for the last beat of any pattern (see Figure 17-3).

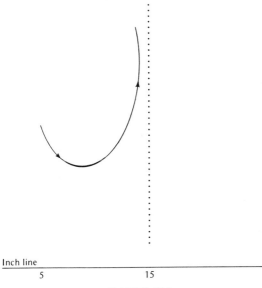

Inch line

5   15

FIGURE 17-3

If executed with finesse and smoothness, the legato will be aided considerably as compared with patterns that involve only the right hand.

Note: Do not overuse this kind of motion. The usual problem with these motions is that they can be overused once the hands feel at home with double execution. Exercise them if the ensemble needs a reminder of the style of the selection or if you are changing concepts in the progression of a selection.

An occasional treatment of these motions may be found when a legato melodic line is performed with a staccato accompaniment. The left hand can express the feelings of the melodic line while the right hand can convey the mood of the accompaniment.

Marcato Style

The left hand can also be of assistance in marcato styles. When the music is extremely heavy and/or staccato, the left hand may assist with the interpretation by executing small, quick, jerky movements in the direction of the performers. These are executed either with the fist in a closed position or with the hand open but with the index finger slightly pointed toward the performers. In the latter case, the palm of the hand should be toward the floor or toward the performers. These small, jerky motions should be made in the shape of the letter "V" and with considerable intensity.

Note: Do not use this motion for a light staccato, since it will only create a heavy effect.

Increase in Intensity

Often the conductor wishes the performers to increase the intensity of the music or to keep it at a high peak. The favorite motion for most conductors is almost the same as that used by string performers in executing a vibrato. The left hand should face the conductor with the palm open and with considerable looseness and flexibility at the wrist. The wrist is moved back and forth so that the left hand moves away and toward the body of the conductor. Speed of the movement should be only a bit slower than the speed of the vibrato, or about three or four per second.

PRACTICE EXERCISES

1. In legato style, conduct several measures in triple meter. Use the left hand to assist in the feeling of legato as indicated above. Practice extensively, since both hands must be independent of each other and yet appear as if both are indicating the same general feeling.

2. Conduct other meters and practice similarly with the left hand.

3. Practice all meters in a marcato style, and use the left hand occasionally to assist with the overall feeling.

4. Practice the left hand alone, giving the vibratolike motion for the increase of intensity. Do not move the hand too low or too high during this exercise. After considerable practice, when you seem confident that the left hand is quite skillful with this movement, practice both hands together (see Figures 17-4 through 17-7).

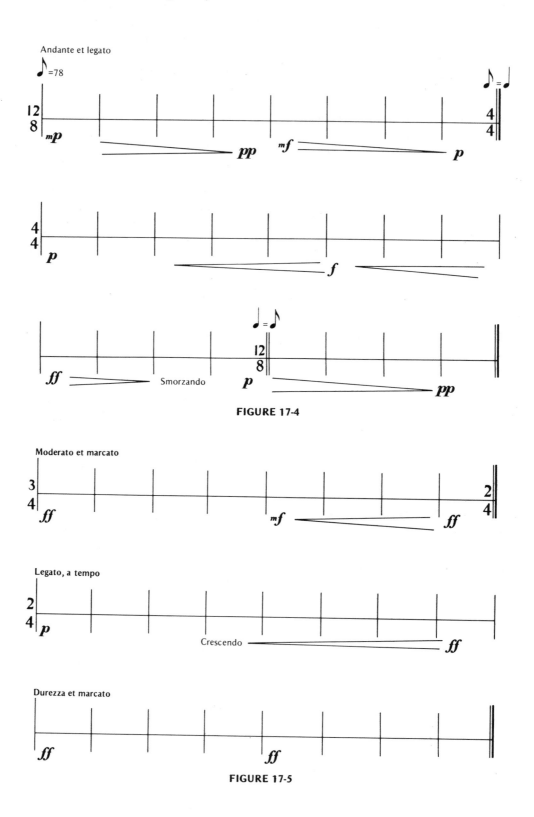

FIGURE 17-4

FIGURE 17-5

Allegro scherzando

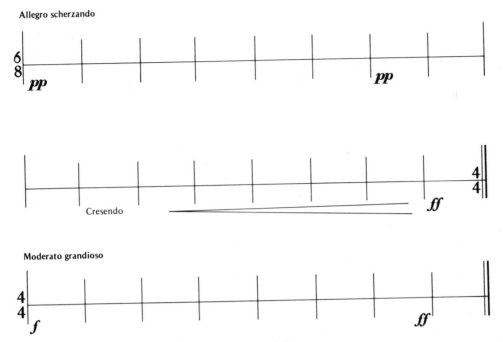

Moderato grandioso

FIGURE 17-6

Andantino expressivo

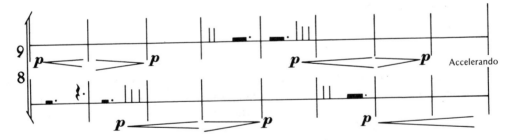

Allegretto

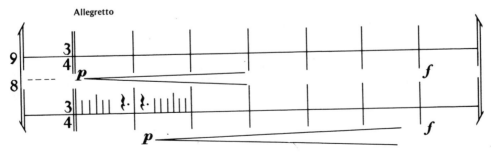

FIGURE 17-7

SHADING

Many lines in music require subtle shading to reach maximum effectiveness. The left hand can be of considerable assistance. The motions are similar to those used in a change of loudness; in fact, shading a line requires a change of volume along with other items. By using the left hand in smaller but similar motions, the shading of a line can be affected, particularly if one is conducting a person or section. Larger motions and less-subtle dynamics probably will be necessary for large groups.

As the line increases toward its aesthetic peak, the left hand should rise somewhat from a previous position. When this occurs, the palm will usually be open and upward. When the intensity of the line becomes less, the left hand will turn over, and the palm will be more toward the performer. The careful movement of the left hand in these motions will be able to guide the performers in interpreting the nuances of the musical line. No diagrams are necessary here, since the movements are too similar to those used for the control of dynamics. The hand must move easily, and with no abruptness or roughness. The distance moved by the hand will be small and, in some cases, almost insignificant. Practice these movements with the left hand while the right hand is conducting different patterns.

PHRASING AND BREATHING

From time to time, a good conductor will prefer to interpret the music so that it gives the listener the impression that a tiny pause has been placed in the music. These small breaks often are used to separate one phase of music from the next so that the entire composition takes on more meaning for the listener. At other times, even in instrumental groups, the melodic line should breathe, so that the music will be phrased and bring more meaning to the listeners.

The left hand can assist with both of these ideas. The motion used is similar to the shape of a reversed comma, which means it is usually performed from left to right. The left hand moves into the conducting space immediately after the preceding beat point has been indicated. It is brought almost shoulder-high unless the direction is meant particularly for persons directly under the conductor's podium. The motion is executed at the exact moment when the conductor wishes the phrase to end or wishes the breath to be taken. This may not be on a beat, and it may come very near the end of one beat. If the conductor wishes to allow for a short interval, he may slow the right hand between beat points, so that the next beat will not be arrived at quite in tempo. This in itself will bring a kind of phrasing to the music. At no time should the conductor stop the right hand.

PRACTICE EXERCISE

The exercises in Figures 17-8, 17-9, and 17-10 will give opportunity for you to practice the use of the left hand in indicating phrasing, breathing, and shading. Do not omit any of the indications. Are you performing easily, smoothly, and with independence of hands? Add your own dynamics to each exercise. Were these obvious to your classmates?

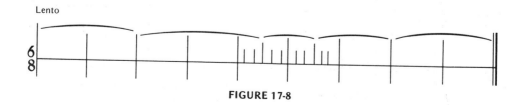

FIGURE 17-8

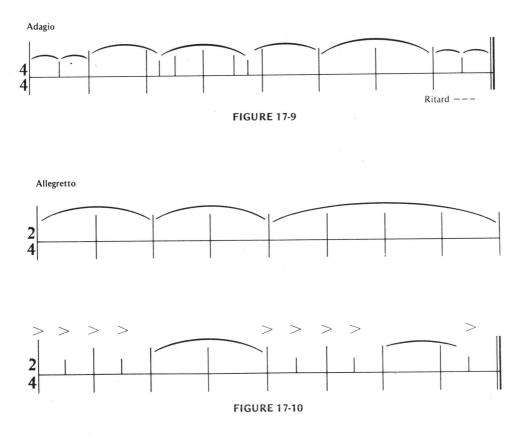

FIGURE 17-9

FIGURE 17-10

ACCENTS AND SFORZANDOS

Another good use for the left hand is to aid in the conducting of accents and sforzandos. A conductor must decide in his own mind when faced with an accent just how much of an emphasis he wishes the group to make. If the composition is slow and soft during a particular section, and if an accent is placed over a particular note or notes, usually a small accent will suffice. This push or leaning on a note can be overdone, making the music seem distorted in style. The conductor's taste must be the guide. Some conductors will desire little, and others may wish for more. During accents where a small leaning on the note is often sufficient, most conductors conduct these with the right hand alone. This is usually executed by increasing the intensity of the right arm and pushing downward with the right hand at the time of the accent. Some conductors will push the right hand downward and at the same time toward the performing group a little. Both methods are effective.

If this accent falls on the first beat, the beat point will usually be lower than usual and the rebound of the beat will be larger. This is true of the other beat points as well. When the rebound is executed quickly, much more quickly than the other parts of the pattern, the accent will be executed with more strength. When the rebound is slow, the accent will be less. In both cases the conducting hand will slow down or seem almost to stop as it reaches the top of the rebound.

If the accent is less subtle, accompany the right hand pattern with a motion by the left hand. It is easy for the left hand to accompany the right hand in a downward motion on the downbeat and to execute a small rebound. This will emphasize the accent. After the accent has been completed, the left hand will either return to the waist position or indicate that the group should return to a softer dynamic than that played during the accent (Figure 17-11).

For an accent on a beat to the left of the pattern, the left hand will move to the right, also executing the rebound indicated in the following pattern for the right hand (Figure 17-12). In most cases conductors feel more at ease in having the left hand move toward the center of the body. The left and right hands should not cross, and the left hand will execute the rebound in an almost perpendicular position.

For an accent on a beat to the right of the pattern, the left hand generally moves to the left of the pattern so that the hands are at opposite ends of the conducting space. Seldom does the left hand move to the right for such an accent. The rebound is indicated by both hands (Figure 17-13).

When the accent appears on the upbeat, the left hand often moves parallel with the right, as indicated in the pattern diagrams of Figure 17-14. The accent is given emphasis by having the left hand move from the left toward the center, as if it were conducting a preparatory. When the center is almost reached, the left hand then executes the rebound with the right hand.

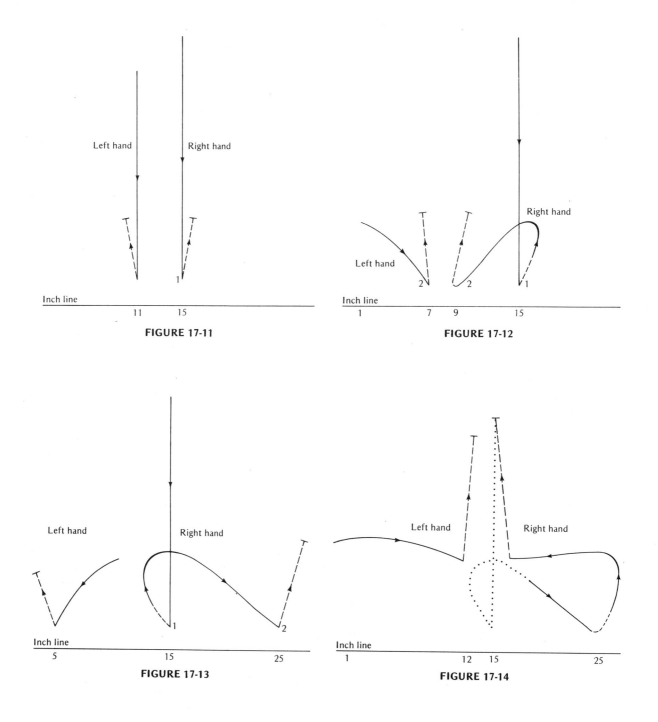

FIGURE 17-11

FIGURE 17-12

FIGURE 17-13

FIGURE 17-14

Some conductors prefer the left hand to move upward for large or emphatic accents. This means that as the right hand is moving downward or sideways for the beat point, the left hand is executing a motion similar to that normally used for the upbeat. This truly calls attention to the accent. This method is used if the accent is one where the members at the back of a group are particularly involved, such as a percussion section. This same motion can be used for an accent on any beat. The conductor must decide whether the accent calls for that much emphasis by the performers.

Accent on the Half Beat

When an accent or sforzando falls on the half beat, it can be indicated by the left hand alone. In this case the right hand continues conducting the pattern with no attention given to the accent. The accent is indicated by the left hand moving to the left of the body after it has made a preparatory for the accent by moving away from waist position almost directly in front of center of the body. The result is almost like the letter *V*. This motion can be used with any beat or pattern (see Figure 17-15).

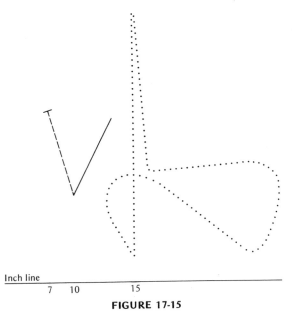

Inch line

7   10   15

FIGURE 17-15

This type of accent direction is most effective if the accent occurs in one section rather than throughout the group. The left hand then indicates the accent in the direction of the section having the accent while the right hand carries the regular pattern for the re-

mainder of the group. In this manner, both melodic and rhythmic ideas of the composition are satisfied.

Between-the-beat accents may be conducted with the right hand alone. In these cases it should be assumed that the accent is a minor one. To execute these, use the wrist rebound patterns described in Chapter 18, "Rebound-type Subdivision." The difference from normal patterns comes in the speed of the rebound. When the accent occurs on the beat, the rebound is faster than any other movement in the pattern. When the accent is between the beats, the rebound is stronger and slower, so that the conductor reaches the culminating point of the rebound at midpoint of the beat or just as the accent takes place. This execution gives a more angular look to the pattern for at least that one beat. This is sometimes called the *cue of provocation* and may be used for unaccented afterbeats as well.

Many times the left-hand position is determined by what is immediately before it. It is not necessary to return the left hand to waist position if, just before the accent, the left hand is involved in other activities. In addition, these other activities will control the type of accent movement that the left hand will use and where the left hand will move for the accent. Remember that the hands should move with meaning and should never appear to move awkwardly from one position to another. An amateur conductor often looks studied if he tries to follow slavishly the motions that are suggested and if he accepts them as the only solution to a conducting problem. Too often, however, this kind of advice is taken to mean that no careful thought should be given to conducting and that anything that comes to mind at the moment will be satisfactory. At times a person may get by with an improvised solution, but that is far from saying that it is a good solution. It is best for a young conductor to work out a conducting problem without a group so that he may carefully watch what is happening with both hands and may focus attention on the step-by-step process of conducting a specific problem.

There is a school of conducting which believes that a conductor is in error to indicate stress or accents which occur off the beat or between beats. A conductor might not desire to conduct a particular accent or stress since it occurs in such a manner that the performers never omit it. Under such conditions, I too would agree that no special effect by the conductor would be necessary. Then again, if the accent continues for a series of measures, the conductor should not feel compelled to conduct all the accents. In that case, perhaps the first one or two would be sufficient.

In working with amateur groups it is always wise to

give them some feeling for the music and not take for granted that they will perform the accent just because it has been performed repeatedly during rehearsals. Under the strain of performance a student group may forget the very items that have been rehearsed so carefully. It behooves the conductor, who is expected to bring more reserve and experience to the podium, to continue in such a manner that the student performers will feel as comfortable as possible during a public performance. In other words, if the conductor will conduct in his usual style, using the accents as part of his conducting if he deemed them necessary at rehearsal, he will probably be rewarded for his extra care.

PRACTICE EXERCISES

1. Practice the exercises in Figures 17-16 through 17-19, planning carefully beforehand the manner of executing each accent.

2. Conduct these exercises for your classmates so they may observe your pattern, if your accent is obvious, and if your accent is excessive for the size of your pattern.

3. Conduct these exercises using only the right hand to indicate the accents and then conduct them so that both hands indicate the accent.

4. Conduct these exercises and use the left hand at least once during each example to indicate a heavy accented stress for members at the rear of the performing group.

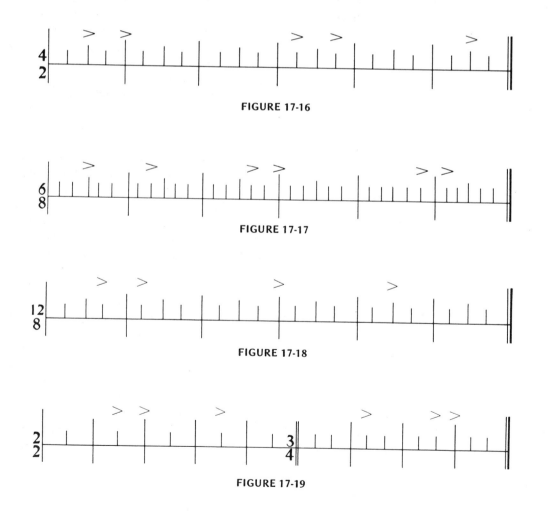

FIGURE 17-16

FIGURE 17-17

FIGURE 17-18

FIGURE 17-19

5. Conduct the exercises in Figures 17-20 through 17-23. Experiment with various left-hand movements to move better from accent to dynamic change to accent. Conduct these exercises at different tempi.

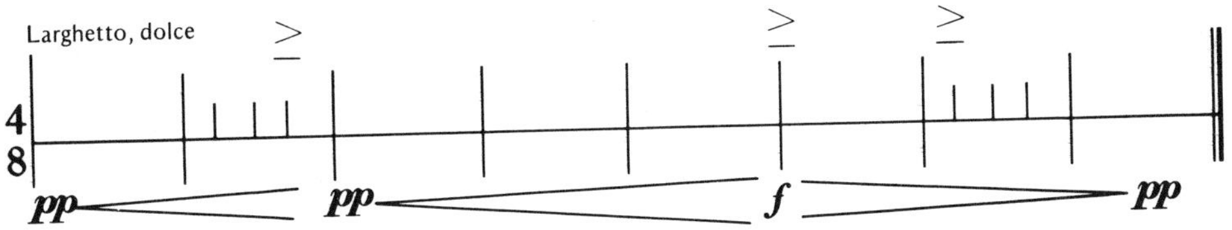

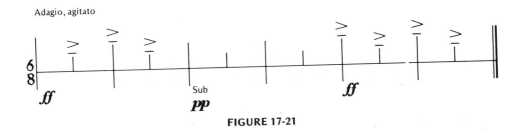

FIGURE 17-20

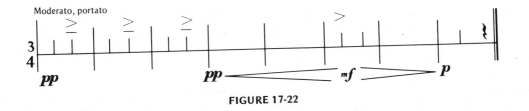

FIGURE 17-21

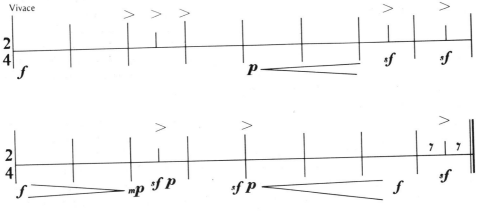

FIGURE 17-22

FIGURE 17-23

18

Augmentation and Diminution

In the broadest sense, augmentation and diminution deal with an alteration from the time values specified by the printed signature and notes. Augmentation indicates an extending or drawing out; diminution indicates a lessening or pushing together. For conducting purposes *augmentation* means a drawing out of the music despite the time signature. The conductor will handle this by what is commonly called a *subdivision*. *Diminution* means just the opposite: The music is played and conducted faster than it would appear from the notation or signature.

AUGMENTATION

First, let us consider augmentation, or the subdivision. Three reasons could be given for subdividing a measure or passage of music.

1. A measure may be subdivided to assist with a ritard. Many measures that call for a ritard will not use the subdivision; some will be aided by it. Two items would determine this. First, the measure contains notes that are faster than the unit expressed in the conductor's pattern. Secondly, the ritard is to be prolonged or of a greater slowness than the performers might expect. The first reason is the most used and most obvious.

For example, if the measure that calls for a ritard were to contain eighth notes and the conductor has been beating the quarter note as his unit, then in order to assure that the eighth notes will be played together and the ritard executed simultaneously, the conductor will probably subdivide the measure. What had been conducted in three would be subdivided three. This subdivision should not be spoken of as a six-beat measure since a six-beat measure will pulsate differently from a subdivided three. It will also be conducted differently.

2. A tempo might be better expressed by a subdivided beat than the regular pattern called for by the time signature. This usually occurs when the tempo must be slow and yet the intensity maintained. The subdivision will assist the conductor in regulating the true tempo, since it often is difficult to keep a steady, slow pattern moving at the same

254

pace from measure to measure. It will also assist the performers, since they will feel the intensity of the motions and will be better able to master the variances of dynamic that should go into the elongated notes of a slower-paced composition.

For example, imagine a slow choral number that is marked about M.M. 58. The signature might be 2/4, and at first glance the amateur conductor might assume that this composition would move along at a modest to fast pace. However, the metronomic marking would indicate just the reverse. If the conductor tried to conduct this composition in two beats to the measure, he might find that the conducting movements are so slow that he would feel uncomfortable. Even if he were able to conduct this with a smooth, slow beat, the performers might find that this pattern in no way assisted them with the interpretation of the work. A satisfactory answer to the problem would be a subdivision.

3. A measure or two may be divided in the interest of clarity of ensemble. This statement may appear to cover the two other cases listed above, and yet the two specific ideas above might not cover some measures that would fall under this general heading.

Occasionally there are measures whose rhythmic continuity must be broken; the tempo following them may not be obvious to all members of the group. If at such a time the conductor finds that the next entrance is on the half beat, it could be

to the advantage of the group to subdivide that measure or part of a measure.

For example, imagine arriving at a fermata involving all members of the group. Following the fermata is a three- or four-note cadenza or solo so that the tempo is obviously altered. The ensemble then enters on a pickup to a beat. That part of a measure might best be conducted with a subdivision so that the clarity of the ensemble will be always consistent and intact.

The following might be of assistance in thinking of subdivision:

When the signature is a	The subdivision may be executed by
two-beat pattern (2/4, 2/2, 2/8)	a divided two- or a four-beat pattern
three-beat pattern (3/4, 3/2, 3/8)	a divided three-beat pattern
four-beat pattern (4/4, 4/2, 4/8)	a divided four-beat pattern

Other signatures have a potential for subdivision, but the possibility of needing these is so slight that we need not discuss them here.

The subdivision for a two-beat measure usually is conducted as a subdivision. There are times, however, when the subdivision may be executed as a four-beat measure. The flow of the musical line will assist the conductor in making this decision.

The divided two, three, and four patterns are given in Figures 18-1 through 18-6.

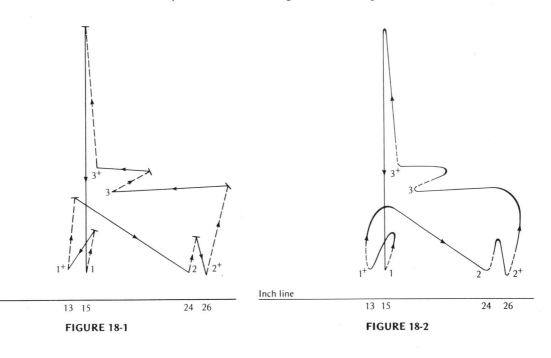

FIGURE 18-1   FIGURE 18-2

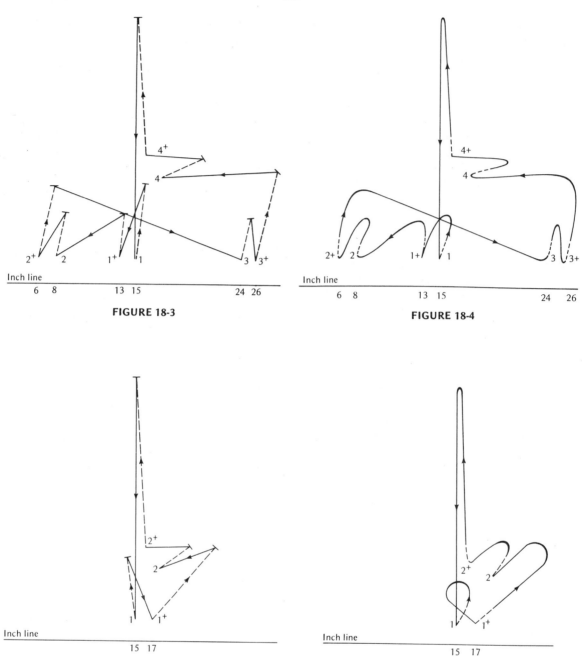

FIGURE 18-3

FIGURE 18-4

FIGURE 18-5

FIGURE 18-6

REBOUND-TYPE SUBDIVISION

There are times when the above patterns are too complicated and difficult to originate on short notice with a quick change that may be needed in some music or when subdivision may be inconvenient for just a measure or part of a measure. At these times it is appropriate to use the rebound-type pattern, shown on page 257, for the subdivision.

These patterns are executed by a quick throw of the wrist. To understand these motions in a different context, refer to Chapter 12, "The Fermata," in the section "Fermatas and Long-value Notes," practice exercise 2.

Remember: the dashes at the vertexes mean a stopped motion (see Figures 18-7, 18-8, and 18-9).

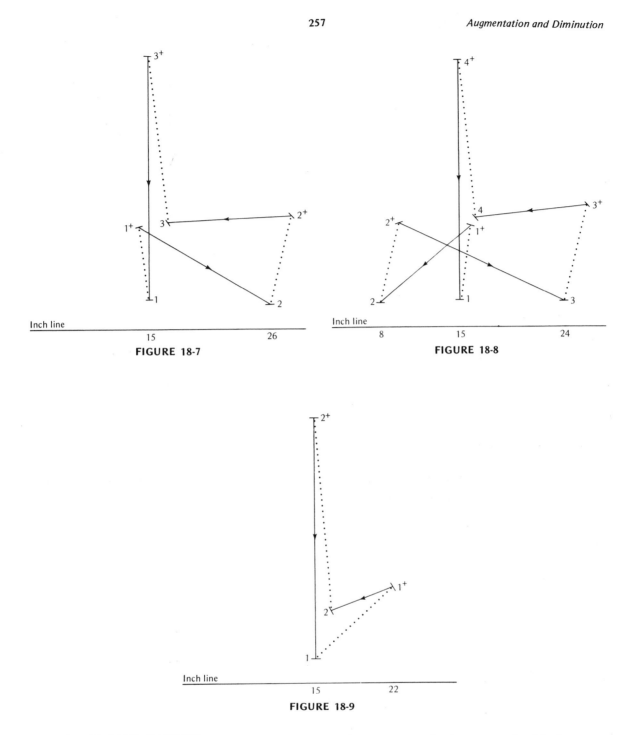

FIGURE 18-7

FIGURE 18-8

FIGURE 18-9

SUBDIVIDED PREPARATORY

The subdivision of the preparatory has been discussed in Chapter 16. Some conductors insist on this for a clean attack when the first note of a composition is a part of a beat preceding a downbeat. If this is desired (it is not really necessary, and some professional conductors never use it), the baton identifies this attack as indicated in Figures 18-10 and 18-11. (Also see Chapter 16.)

The preparatory is given as usual, with the exception of the small rebound about halfway down the vertical stroke. The tempo of the composition and consequently the conducting pattern will determine the speed of the rebound as well as the speed of the preparatory and down-stroke. If the pickup note is of small value, or if the tempo is rapid, no need for the subdivision will exist. It may be used on other beats than just the downbeat by subdividing those preparatory patterns also.

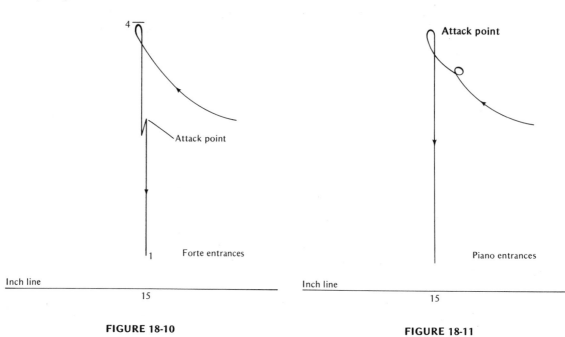

FIGURE 18-10

FIGURE 18-11

PRACTICE EXERCISES

1. In the following examples (Figures 18-12 and 18-13) practice the subdivision for the beat patterns for the three- and four-beat meters.

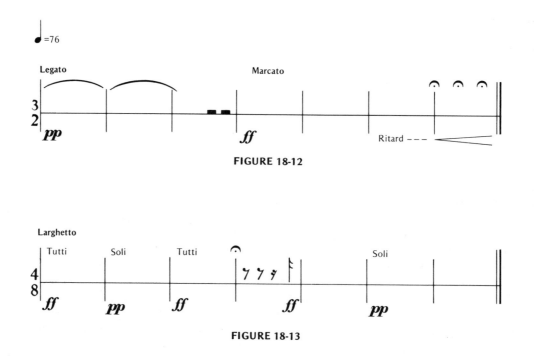

FIGURE 18-12

FIGURE 18-13

2. Practice the examples in Figures 18-14 and 18-15 using the subdivided beat as called for.

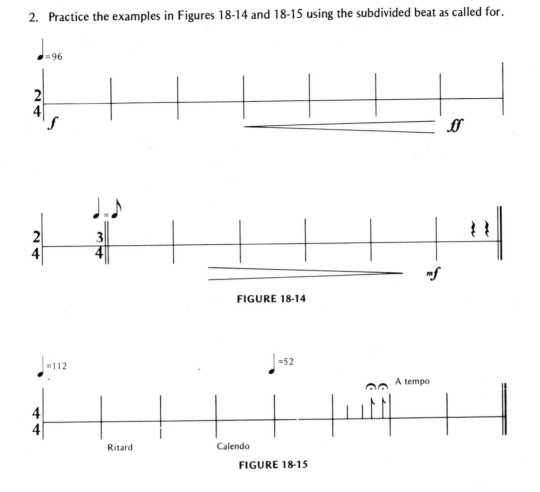

FIGURE 18-14

FIGURE 18-15

3. Also practice Mozart's *Eine Kleine Nachtmusik* on page 238.

4. Practice the following from Caylor Bowen's arrangement for string orchestra.

ADAGIO AND COURRENTE
from Sonata IV

F. Francoeur

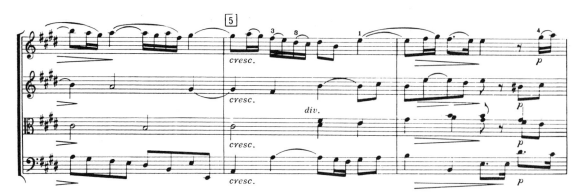

DIMINUTION

There are times in conducting when the reverse of augmentation is used to move the music at a quicker speed than is obvious from the indication of the signature. Metronomic markings may indicate such differences in the unit of beat, but the conductor always should be alert to the style of the music so that it may be correctly interpreted.

The music itself and the group's abilities should be the guide for the conductor. If the conductor patterns four when he should beat two, or patterns three when he should be in one, the music will be too heavy and tedious, the composition will seem overlong, and perhaps the brightness of spirit that it should possess will be missing. If the group is unable to perform the composition at a speed that imparts the desired effect, the conductor should examine whether the composition be programed or perhaps only a study number.

Other selections, though less obvious, consistently are performed with an abbreviated pulsation. Some music carries no marking of any kind to indicate that a diminutive approach should be used. The character of the music must be the guide.[1]

The most common use of diminution is the common "cut time" (alla breve) signature. Here the music would appear as if written in 4/4. With this signature (¢) it is intended to be performed in half the number of pulsations.

Another good example is the common 6/8 measure. Here the implication is that this meter would be conducted in six. We know that this is not the case, and in fact, most music that we will conduct in this meter will be in two pulsations to the measure. This is common for us, and we do not hesitate to think of it in

this way. Two less common signatures are the 9/8 and the 12/8 measures. Many times they will be performed and conducted in three and four respectively. If so, the common conducting patterns are used. Most groups that understand 9/8 and 12/8 meters will surely be able to understand either conducting procedure.

Because of tempo markings or the speed of an interpretation, it sometimes is necessary to conduct common signatures with a reduced pattern: the 4/4 measure may be conducted in two beats to the measure; the 3/4 measure may be conducted in one beat to the measure; the 2/4 and 2/8 measures may be conducted in one beat to the measure.

All these may need a faster tempo than is possible with the stick or hand moving to articulate the signature indicated, and fewer beats are used.

Patterns for the cut time measure or the 4/4 measure conducted in two are the same as if the music were written in a 2/4 signature.

The One-pulsation Patterns

The patterns for measures that are conducted in one pulsation to the measure are shown in Figures 18-16, 18-17, 18-18, and 18-19.

In conducting one to a measure, some directors begin with a pattern nearly like the one on page 261; however, before long they have permitted themselves to develop a pattern that looks like an ellipse. This is weak because it lessens the effectiveness of the downbeat itself as the arm and stick lose the beat point. Since the music is very rapid under these circumstances, if one loses the point of the downbeat, he is sure to have lost his authority.

Note: Practice this pattern so that the rebound is as inconspicuous as possible and not pronounced. Try also to alternate the rebound on each side of the downbeat stroke. If one does this, he is not apt to fall into the habit of conducting in an ellipse, but the alternation should be inconspicuous to the performer.

Figures 18-16 and 18-17 show patterns for one pul-

---

[1]One common use of a diminuted pattern occurs during the accompanying of a soloist who sings or plays a number of measures without accompaniment. Each measure may be indicated by a downward stroke of the baton on the first beat of each measure.

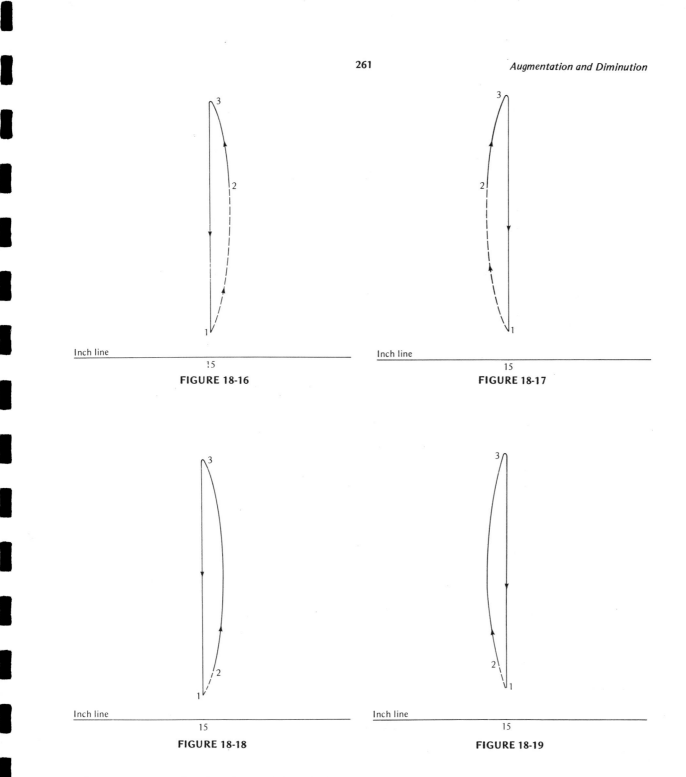

FIGURE 18-16   FIGURE 18-17

FIGURE 18-18   FIGURE 18-19

sation to a measure when the rebound is large. In fact, the rebound is almost the size of the complete down-beat motion. This rebound is executed quickly so that there is a short wait at the top of the pattern before the next downward movement. Figures 18-18 and 18-19 show patterns for one pulsation to a measure where the rebound is small in height. This type of pattern is generally used for slightly slower tempi than in patterns 18-16 and 18-17, especially if the music is more delicate or if the latter portions of a measure need some dynamic or accentual emphasis.

Deemphasis of Beat Two

At times, less emphasis on the second beat may be desired in the two-beat measures. This will cause the pattern to vary only slightly from the usual, but this variance should be obvious to the performers. There should be less emphasis upon the second beat of the measure and less obvious motion for the stick, an action achieved by concentration. The pattern, then, is usual except the manner in which the second beat is handled (see Figures 18-20 and 18-21).

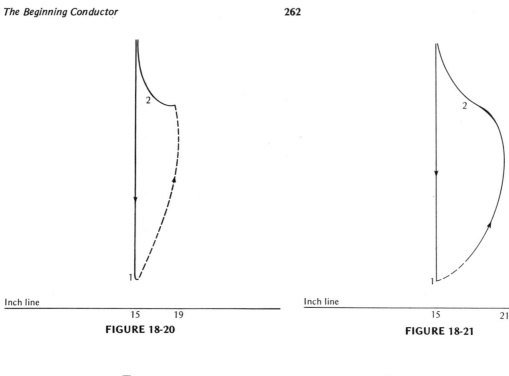

Inch line

FIGURE 18-20   FIGURE 18-21

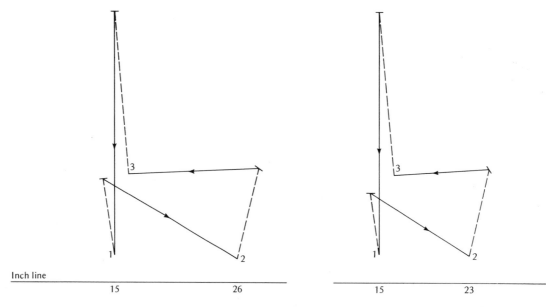

Inch line

FIGURE 18-22a

Alteration of Tempo

When the music moves from a slower tempo to a faster one, a conductor could desire to move from a four-pulsation measure to a two-pulsation measure. This could happen as a result of a decided change in the tempo as indicated by a double bar or as a result of a gradual acceleration in speed without a change in signature and note values. In the latter case the conductor should mark his score so that he is definite as to the exact measure that will carry the change in his pattern, rehearse it consistently with the performers, and be sure that the performance is as rehearsed. If the conducting is clear, precise, and consistent, the performers will understand what has been done without being told.

In a similar situation, it sometimes becomes necessary to move from a three-pulsation measure to a one-pulsation measure as a result of an accelerando. While conducting the accelerando, be sure that the second and third beats of each measure are increasingly small as you approach the pattern for one pulsation to the measure; mark the score where the accelerando will take place and where the music will be conducted in one pulsation to the measure, being sure to follow this at each rehearsal and again at the performance (see Figure 18-22).

For some reason the pattern of one pulsation to the measure often seems more difficult to master than other patterns. It is easy to alter to a two-beat pattern. If this occurs, move immediately into the correct pattern, but do not become mentally involved in wondering how this could happen or where it did happen. If the two-beat pattern is small, it is likely that the performers did not notice that you had slipped into the wrong pattern. However, if you continue this for long, it will control the general effect of the music by placing an accent on every other measure rather than a primary accent on every measure.

The pulsation pattern that makes use of the wrist alone places much too little significance upon the measure and also runs the risk of losing aesthetic control of the group. A general rule could be stated as follows: When the music is slow, the conductor may need to increase the number of beats for clarity and ensemble; as the music becomes faster, he may need to decrease the number of beats per measure in order to convey the overall structure of the work.

PRACTICE EXERCISES

1. Practice the patterns for one beat to the measure. Be sure that the pattern is quick and precise, light and not heavy. Try working at two metronomic indications: M.M. 72 and 90 = $\downarrow$.

2. Review "Take-Off," page 182, conducting with a one-pulsation pattern.

3. Practice the exercises in Figures 18-23, 18-24, and 18-25.

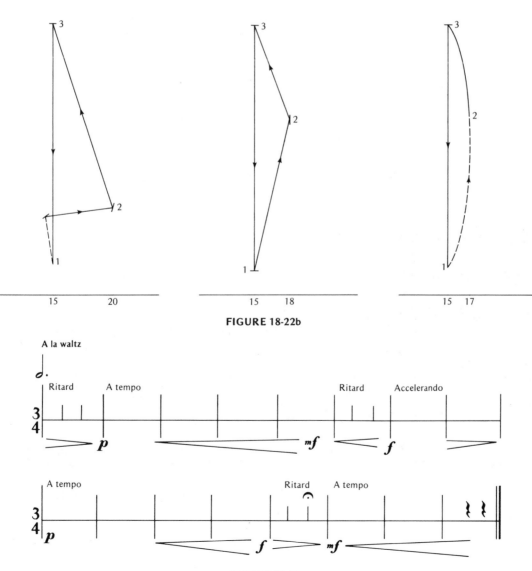

FIGURE 18-22b

FIGURE 18-23

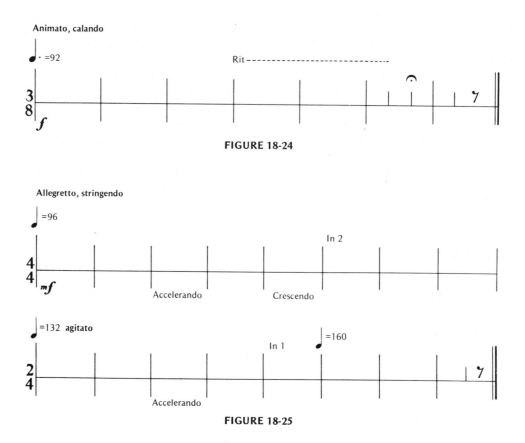

FIGURE 18-24

FIGURE 18-25

4. Practice the following musical examples.

№ 25. TO FORMER JOY.

※ *The original edition has G in the repeat, Altus part.*

The original edition has black notation in all parts until ¢

William Holborne's Canzonets
TO
Three Voices.
(1597)

Edited by EDMUND H. FELLOWES.
Revised by Thurston Dart and Philip Brett.

№ 1. CHANGE THEN FOR LO SHE CHANGETH.

* In the repeat the second set of words are to be sung.

19

Conducting Patterns: Fives and Sevens

Slowly the five- and seven-beat measures have been leaving the works of the one-time avant-garde composer and creeping into those works for amateurs. Not too long ago, compositions played or sung by high school students contained only the most common signatures. However, one may now frequently find more unusual signatures. In fact, this happens so often that one should not infer that these signatures have a special significance or status.

THE FIVE-BEAT MEASURE

Figures 19-1 and 19-2 are patterns for the five-beat measure; both are equally acceptable. The determinate is the music itself and the way the subsidiary accent falls in the measure. In certain cases a conduc-

tor may have a choice, since a measure may not carry any specific accentual indication. An example of this might be five unaccented quarter notes in a measure.

Most music carrying a five-beat signature will be divided rhythmically so that the conductor may choose the pattern most suitable to the measure. This means that one may find one measure using the pattern in Figure 19-1 followed immediately by a measure that would call for the pattern in Figure 19-2.

This alternation may not be consistent, and the beginning conductor may wish to mark his score to indicate those measures that call for each pattern. To reemphasize what we have said earlier, this only underlines the need for the conducting hand to feel at ease with the pattern and to be completely automatic in response.

The patterns in Figures 19-1 and 19-2 may be used for a five-beat measure of slow or moderate tempo.

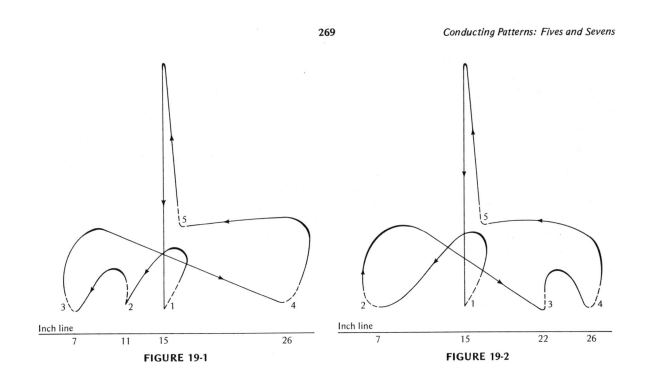

FIGURE 19-1   FIGURE 19-2

PRACTICE EXERCISE

Conduct the exercises in Figures 19-3, 19-4, and 19-5.

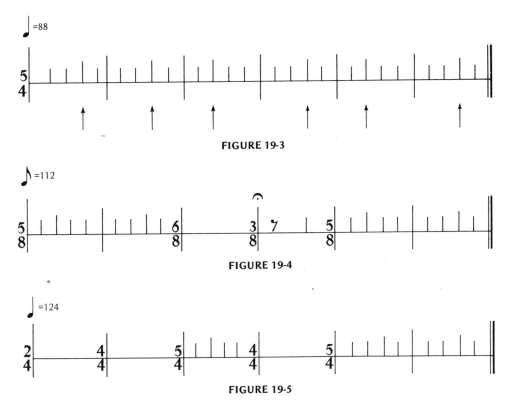

FIGURE 19-3

FIGURE 19-4

FIGURE 19-5

THE FAST FIVE (Irregular Two)

There may be times when the tempo is rapid and when a five-beat measure cannot be easily conducted with the patterns indicated above. This might be a 5/8 measure tucked between some measures where the quarter note is obviously the unit, or it might be a rapid 5/4 or 5/8 passage where the quarter or eighth note is the unit respectively. When this occurs, the conductor should be prepared to conduct in a two-point pattern that takes on an irregular pulsation.

For example, if the measure of 5/4 is divided two plus three, then the pattern will be as in Figures 19-6 and 19-7. To place the five beats, the conductor will reach the beat point for one on the downbeat,

for two at the top of the rebound, and for three at a beat point again near the downbeat line, while four and five will be performed during that rebound. Since there are two-fifths of the measure on the first beat and three-fifths during the second beat, or pulsation, this measure takes on an irregular aspect that must show in the conducting. The latter half of the pattern will take a longer time to execute than the first half. (The word "half" in this case refers to the distance covered and not to the time taken for the movement.) On the other hand, if the measure is divided in a reverse fashion, then the pattern should indicate this division by taking longer to execute during the first half. This is indicated by Figure 19-8.

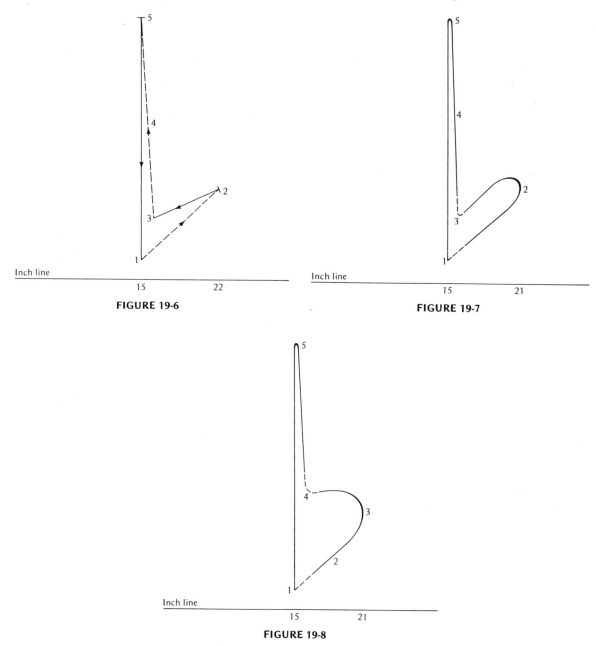

FIGURE 19-6

FIGURE 19-7

FIGURE 19-8

PRACTICE EXERCISES

1. Set the metronome at M.M. 132 for the quarter note. Conduct both patterns at this tempo, considering the quarter note as the unit. You will need five units for each measure and each pattern. Do not count aloud or form the beats with the lips.

2. Set the metronome at M.M. 176. Conduct both patterns at this tempo, using the eighth note as the unit.
   Note: Do not stop the baton at any place along the pattern, but learn to control the baton when it moves slightly slower for the three-beat portion of the pattern.

3. Conduct the exercises in Figures 19-9, 19-10, and 19-11.

FIGURE 19-9

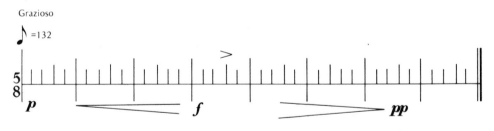

FIGURE 19-10

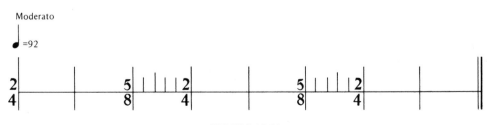

FIGURE 19-11

Conduct Figure 19-12 as indicated and in diminution.

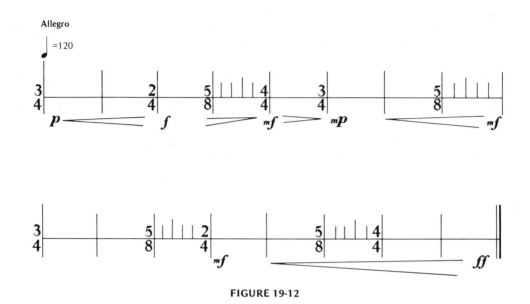

FIGURE 19-12

THE SEVEN-BEAT MEASURE

Although it is one of the lesser-used patterns, the seven-beat meter still warrants our attention. The same principle used in the five-pulsation unit is employed here; the measure is subdivided irregularly. Almost always it divides itself into three + four or four + three. Occasionally measures appear to follow a two + two + two + one division. The patterns shown below fit these demands.

The patterns in Figures 19-13, 19-14, and 19-15 may be used for a seven-beat measure of slow or moderate tempos.

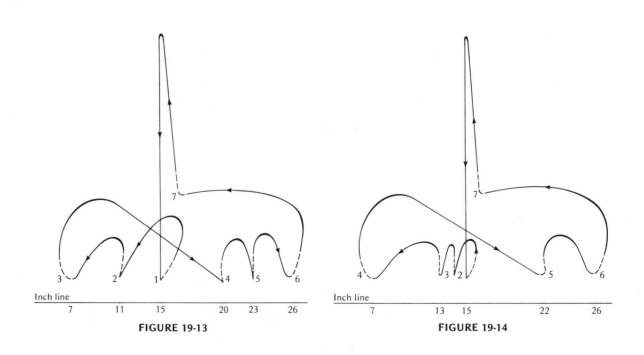

FIGURE 19-13   **FIGURE 19-14**

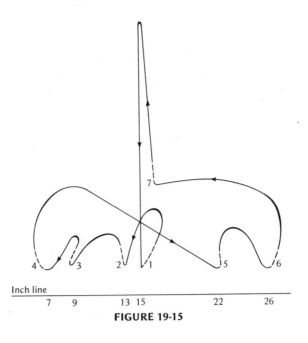

FIGURE 19-15

PRACTICE EXERCISE

Conduct the exercises in Figures 19-16 and 19-17.

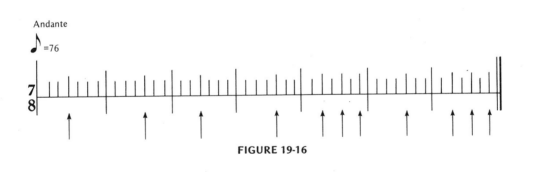

FIGURE 19-16

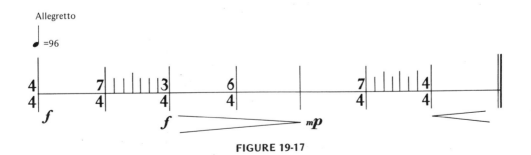

FIGURE 19-17

THE FAST SEVEN (Irregular Three)

When the tempo is rapid and a seven-beat measure cannot be easily conducted with the patterns indicated above, an irregular three is advised. This situation is most likely to occur when the signatures change from the quarter-note unit to the eighth-note unit. When this is the case, the pattern will carry some unevenness on one of the beat points and rebounds. Exercises with this in mind are shown in Figures 19-18, 19-19, and 19-20.

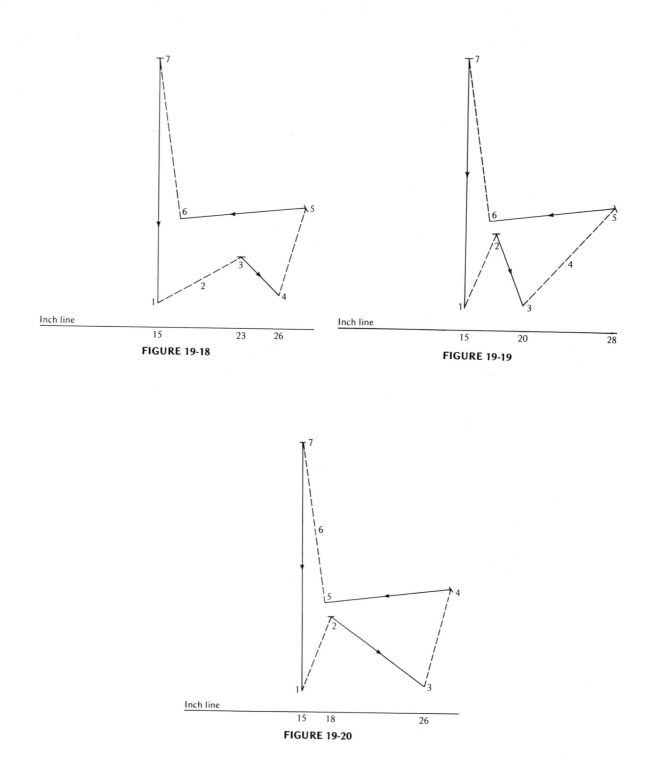

FIGURE 19-18

FIGURE 19-19

FIGURE 19-20

PRACTICE EXERCISES

1. Practice the patterns above making use of the metronome as needed to assist in evenness.

2. Conduct the exercises in Figures 19-21, 19-22, and 19-23.

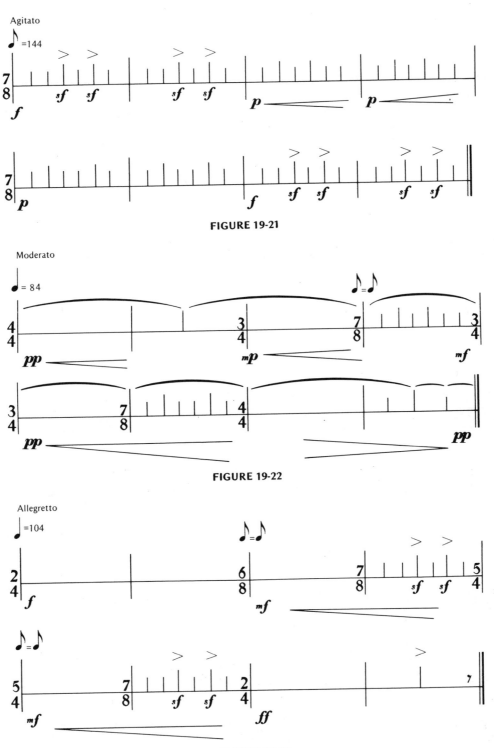

FIGURE 19-21

FIGURE 19-22

FIGURE 19-23

3. Practice your irregular three by having the class chant or compose melodies for the following:

    a.   Sing - a - song   all to-   geth - er
           1   2   3,   4 5,   6   7

    b.   Sing a   short song on   Mon - day
           1 2,   3   4 5,   6   7

    c.   Play a   tune in   sev - en   four
           1 2,   3 4,   5 6   7

4. Conduct selected portions of "Jesus Christ Superstar" for practice of fives and sevens.

5. Conduct the following musical excerpts using the material practiced beforehand in this chapter. Although marked "moderato" in the score, conduct the Heiden in a diminution of two and irregular two at half note = 66 in addition to conducting the quarter note at 96.

Divine Poems

For Mixed Chorus a cappella

John Donne (1573-1631)   Bernhard Heiden

(I)

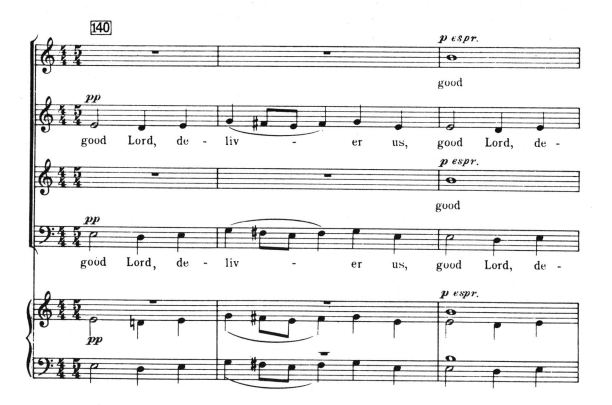

SYMPHONIC DANCE No. 3
"FIESTA"

Full Score

Duration: 6 min., 21 sec.

CLIFTON WILLIAMS

20

More About Style

Two words denoting style have been consistently used throughout the text: "legato" and "marcato." Although some would deny that these are directly opposite, they should in some way represent to you a kind of opposites in conducting technique.

Some selections will be mainly in one style. This is more often true of short compositions and compositions for young performers; sometimes, it is even true of entire movements. Such selections are most easily conducted, at least from one standpoint, since the style of conducting need be changed little from beginning to end. This should not mean that you move the baton in a set pattern and set size. Some conducting motions are dependent upon dynamics, entrances, and other aspects of a composition.

A good example of a single-style composition is the usual street march, often played for concert and even by orchestras. The introduction could be of a particular dynamic and instrumentation; the first strain might be of another; the second strain usually has something in common with the first; and the trio often changes in dynamic and instrumentation. But throughout the entire composition a similar style pos-

sibility exists, and something in the style is common in all sections. Another example might be a chorale-like vocal composition. The baton or hand may need a number of techniques to conduct this short composition well, but the overall style will be consistent.

Of a somewhat more intricate makeup is the composition that changes style more than once. An example of this kind of composition for the young performer is the sectional overture. It is common for these selections to have a portion of about thirty-two measures of one style, move to another style, and finish with a third or fourth style. One reason that these compositions prove difficult to perform well at the student level is that the rapid change of style cannot be captured by the performers. Also, the conductor probably has made little effort through his technique to assist the performers in changing style.

Even in a short composition the conductor may need to conduct a legato style for some measures, a marcato style for others, and a staccato style for still others. There are other possible styles. The violinist has a complete repertoire of bowing styles. These tell us something of the feasible styles in music.

These are explained in Appendix 5: "Bowings." As a conductor, you should be familiar with these to aid the string section and for use as conducting aids. A good exercise is to practice your technique to develop these conducting styles into observable differences in handling your baton.

Probably the choral conductor works much too little on style differences. This may account for his belief that the baton-free hand is more expressive, when in reality the fault is a developmental one. The instrumental conductor is forced to make a few differences in his conducting style, since he has no text to assist him and he wishes the music to change character in some way.

Willi Apel mentions several different uses for the word "style" in his *Harvard Dictionary of Music*.[1] Let us examine these noting how they may apply to conducting.

STYLE OF A SINGLE WORK

. This is an area that we have considered while preparing different conducting techniques. A few terms that one finds at the beginning of musical selections may give some indication of the style of a composition. Obvious terms that come to mind are:

alla marcia— in the style of a march
arioso— in the style between aria and recitative
cantabile— singing style
maestoso— majestic, stately

These terms suggest style rather than tempo. The terms for tempo, however, invariably give some feeling for style also, since a fast tempo will not often be associated with a soft, tender musical composition.

The style of a single work may or may not be singular throughout. The conductor must study the composition and ascertain if the style differs enough to demand that the technique change. Three examples come to mind. Consider the style of the early and later sections of "The Star-spangled Banner" as compared to the middle portion. What conducting differences, if any, do you foresee? Can you execute them? Consider the chorale "A Mighty Fortress Is Our God." What conducting differences do you foresee? Can you execute them? Does the Brahms' "Lullaby" contain any style changes that the conductor should consider in his technique?

[1] Willi Apel, *Harvard Dictionary of Music*, Cambridge, Mass. Harvard University Press, 1946, p. 714.

STYLE OF COMPOSERS

Some professional conductors are recognized as authorities in the works of certain composers; certain artists are known to be sympathetic to a particular composer. This means that concentrated study of the works of this composer has brought certain realizations that might not be apparent to the average musician. Many times the factors involved are not specific, such as a tempo interpretation or a rubato at a certain place in the music. Rather, they may involve a special feeling for the music, an approach to the meaning of the music that can at times be conveyed to others through words, but more often by a performance or a baton technique at a particular moment in the concert. These values may not be verbalized at rehearsals, but often the method of conducting during the performance adds this quality to the meaning of the work.

If you wish to conduct a composition properly, then, study the composition to know it and bring to it a kind of meaning that casual contact will not impart.

STYLE OF COMPOSITION TYPES

From your contact with music, you know that certain compositions are religious in nature, some are taken from operatic works, some are arrangements or movements of symphonic works, and some are from the Broadway stage. All these suggest a certain style. If a conductor is to know a composition and work within its style, he must know its source. For example, it is not enough to know you are conducting an overture to an opera. If you knew the background and story of the opera, you would probably understand how to conduct the overture with much more comprehensiveness of meaning and style. Some historical works—for example, the madrigal—indicate a particular compositional style. If you understand what the madrigal means historically, even though it might at times be performed by a choir, then you can conduct and insist on response in certain characteristic ways. This means that you as a conductor must understand a work in light of a particular compositional type, and in doing so, will be aided in conducting.

STYLE OF MEDIA

The style of the medium for which it was written often means much to a composition. We in music education or who work with amateurs find that we must conduct a composition for a different medium than for which it was originally composed. For example, band directors conduct compositions that were originally composed for orchestra or the piano, and some that are transcriptions of solo literature. This may be true also in the vocal organization. A few compositions may have been composed for the oratorio or cantata that are sung out of context; some are solo literature arranged for the choir. If we understand the medium for which the composition was originally composed, we can conduct it more authentically.

STYLE OF COMPOSITION

Contrapuntal and homophonic styles continue to involve us whether we are working with vocal or instrumental compositions. A good conductor will try to understand an obvious difference in the styles, style his conducting accordingly, and assist even young performers in an understanding of the composition.

STYLE OF NATIONALISM

In music literature classes one learns of the style of the German composer as compared with the style of the French composer. The name of the composer and his nationality should bring an additional dimension for the conducting style. For example, the vocal music of Russia should immediately bring to mind a definite choral concept. These previously learned concepts should not be forgotten when conducting.

STYLE OF PERIODS

Familiar to most of us are the names of the historical music periods. Less familiar are tonal and style differences that grew out of these particular periods of history. Artistic periods have brought special meaning and special sounds to musical compositions that need to be interpreted with understanding. When this is accomplished, the style of the composition unfolds, and the listener finds the composition more meaningful. The young conductor should make every effort to digest these styles so that he can convey the needed period characteristics.

Some of the seven style definitions mentioned above may overlap. Some compositions may be associated with two or three of the above categories. This does not negate any of its compositional style, but only secures it as an individual composition all the more. To reiterate, a good conductor needs to understand not only the background of a particular composition but also the background of many compositions in order to interpret properly the particular niche held by those musical selections that he wishes to conduct. Conductors who have difficulty in style probably have not been trained well enough in artistic historical concepts.

This means that you should study well everything that is presented to you in the area of music literature. As a band conductor, one needs to know the contemporary period extremely well, but other periods should not be neglected. Choral conductors need to know well all music's historical aspects, early to present. Choral literature from all periods is being performed continually. In fact, the choral field represents music literature more generally than other performance media. The orchestra director needs to be conversant with the characteristics of the baroque, classical, romantic, and contemporary periods. This is quite a task.

The amateur conductor's lack of training in music literature is evident on the podium more than most realize. Perhaps, as an amateur, you have been hoping for technique or rules to help you in the area of style. Other than the general characteristics of the selection, the background of the period, and the type of composition, there is little that can be said. There are no rules for holding or moving the baton a certain way that will transmit these characteristics to the performers. Nevertheless, they are transmitted. The performers know, even when they themselves are amateurs and have no knowledge of music history, periods, or types, when you have an understanding of a composition. Know your work, and your aesthetic sense will assist your technique in describing the interpretation you seek. The amateur conductor can be taught to move his hands correctly for the patterns; he can master the staccato beat patterns, the marcato, the legato; but unless he knows the composition and its place in the entire fabric of composer, country, period, compositional type, and medium, he will not conduct as well as he could, and the style of the composition could evade him.

21

The Rehearsal

The very personality of the conductor permits the rehearsal to operate at varying degrees of intensity and discipline. Almost any degree of intensity is correct as long as the conductor is able to assist the group effectively, to make music, to instruct, and to carry out the various items that are characteristic of a good conductor. Nevertheless, for every person who operates a good rehearsal, there must be two conductors who operate a rehearsal that is only partly as good as it could be.

Most amateur conductors do not have long rehearsal times and should use every minute at their disposal to assist the performers musically. Train your personnel to come to rehearsals with correct music, correct equipment, and correct attitudes as to talking and performance, ready to practice and learn. Any conductor can and should train his group to act responsibly at a rehearsal.

THE BEGINNING

Some conductors begin conducting on the podium as soon as fifteen or twenty students are seated and ready to play or sing. The remainder of the group come into rehearsal, find their instrument, place, and music, and join in. Other conductors wait until the full group is ready before they begin. No one method is correct for all conductors, but the conductor who begins on time usually will have the respect of the group, even the person who finds it impossible to be on time.

THE WARM-UP

Some conductors will not begin a rehearsal with an amateur group without proper warm-ups. This is indeed commendable. These warm-ups often give the performer his only professional approach to his instrument or voice during the day or week. The kind of material used for warm-up will depend to a great extent upon the kind of material the conductor experienced as a student performer.

Some choirs use material from the vocal studio, and the instrumentalist will generally use a chorale or chorale-type arrangement, some scales, or a rhythmic study. Some choir directors like to use physical exercises as a warm-up for a vocal organization. Under certain circumstances this kind of material has advantages. It is difficult to use physical exercises with adult or church choirs, however. With the church choir a good choice would be responses that are sung with some regularity and that need attention from the standpoint of intonation or memorization or hymns that need rehearsing for the coming service.

In the case of instrumental groups, conductors seem to prefer a chordal number to aid intonation or a unison scale to aid performers in reading literature that will be used later in the rehearsal. At times rhythmic studies should be chosen.

To conclude, no one type of warm-up is advisable at all times; no one type should be used by all conductors; no one type should be used for all groups. The warm-up should be a studied item for most amateur groups, since they depend upon the director to help them become professional in their approach to the rehearsal and since they come into the rehearsal room with the instrument or voice not ready to approach a difficult work.

PROCEDURES AND SUGGESTIONS

The advisability of turning to a difficult work almost immediately is questionable. Some texts advise that the most difficult work should be approached early in the rehearsal, since the group at that time is eager and attentive. I would agree, with minor but important reservations. After a short warm-up the amateur group is not quite ready to consider the most difficult item of the rehearsal. Rather, the conductor should approach literature with the same caution used in approaching the warm-up. He should plan a portion that is probably not too difficult as to technique or too demanding upon the voice, but which still might offer problems in rhythm, balance, or intonation. The more demanding problems will follow.

To be specific, use a warm-up, followed by a portion of literature that is similar in character to the warm-up. Follow this with a selection that needs intense work which would take up the majority of the rehearsal time. Near the end of the rehearsal, move to a selection or portion of a composition that is lighter, brighter, or that brings the group particular pleasure in rehearsing. This might be something that is full, melodically or rhythmically attractive, or somewhat easier than the more difficult material previously rehearsed.

Each conductor will know his group and will understand approximately how much attention they can give to some technical or reading problem. In fact,

at the high school level, rehearsals often depend upon the day of the week, the time of the year, and the time of the day. The director who is rehearsing late in the afternoon will surely have more problems than the person who is conducting a rehearsal early or later in the morning.

The mechanics of the rehearsal space are obvious. To remind one that he should plan on proper ventilation and light seems almost too elementary. Yet a number of rehearsal rooms are far from ideal, with the temperature often varying greatly throughout the rehearsal period. Also, acoustics are often a major concern for the amateur group. Many music ensembles rehearse in spaces that have been built for smaller groups or for other purposes and have been reassigned as a rehearsal room. The conductor should give immediate attention to the rehearsal space and its acoustics. If necessary, he should experiment with some of the more easily obtainable acoustic materials. Even new structures that look modern and attractive often have serious acoustical drawbacks. On numerous occasions I have been called to offer advice to a musical conductor about the problem that he faces in his few-weeks-old rehearsal space. New or old, a poor room can mean a poor rehearsal if the conductor cannot hear well.

Some rehearsal suggestions might be helpful to the amateur conductor.

1. Avoid sarcastic remarks, particularly from the podium. Some conductors believe that a sarcastic remark is a good discipline, but the persons being conducted do not agree. Some adults refuse to accept sarcasm, and others resent it. Students should not be subjected to it even if they cannot do much about it. You only weaken your own image as a conductor in using it.

2. Tapping the music stand with the baton, whether to gain the attention of the group or to stop the group during the rehearsal, can become a bad habit. Although you may not notice it, it only adds to the general noise of the rehearsal and can be an irritant.

3. Do not begin talking to the group until all the playing or singing has ceased. One student teacher had a habit of beginning his remarks almost the moment that he had raised his hand to ask for quiet. The result was as expected: Most of the group did not stop talking immediately, and so he had to repeat his statements. This, in turn, led the students to play longer, realizing that he would repeat anyway, until a problem resulted.

4. When you stop a rehearsal, review your own conducting to ascertain if a small change in the technique would assist the situation. If you are convinced that your technique is as you wish it, then ask the group to observe your technique more carefully. You may wish to have them observe the technique without performing. Only rarely should it become necessary to explain your techniques.

5. If you have erred in conducting, do not hesitate to admit it. Having observed you for some time, your group will recognize your baton technique and any small problem that might have occurred. Admitting your mistakes will place the rehearsal at ease, and the group will return to work much more quickly if they realize that you can comment at times on your problem as well as theirs. Some self-conscious new conductors overdo this to the point where the group has no confidence in him because he has disparaged himself so many times.

6. Do not be a run-through conductor. Too many amateur conductors fail to conduct and instruct, and merely run through a composition to hear it again or to have the group keep rehearsing. This is a waste of time for the conductor and the ensemble. It might be somewhat pleasing to the performers in that they may enjoy performing and not object as long as they are playing. The conductor who states that he has little or no time for sight-reading usually is the one who will run through several numbers at a rehearsal without truly working on them. A good rehearsal conductor soon earns the respect of his group, and they will learn more as a result of his rehearsal procedure.

7. Talking can be a problem. Try to say the things that need be said with the conducting technique. If it fails, perhaps you need to practice these areas when you study the score away from the group.

8. Do not try to explain too often in philosophical or aesthetic terms what you are trying to obtain in the music. Think about the techniques that will obtain the effect that you want and explain these to your group in musical ways, saving the aesthetic effect for yourself and the performers to hear and appreciate in the music itself.

9. Some conductors become overemotional during a rehearsal. If you have the personal technique to portray the feeling of the music, the performers will probably understand the emotions of the music and respond to both the technique and the emotion of the music without excessive energy on your part. Save some of your feelings for a performance. During a rehearsal, understand that the performers probably can fathom most of the meaning of the phrases, and rely upon this meaning to bring the final emotions to the fore at the time of performance. A constant rehearsal of high emotion usually brings a dry performance. One choral conductor insists that each phrase carry the exact performance emotion each time it is rehearsed or be repeated until such is the case. The result is a dry, unimpressive performance at which the participants are completely tired of and bored with the emotions conveyed by the music.

10. The conductor should have a mental image of what he expects of his group and should not wait until a rehearsal to decide upon interpretive effects. Changing musical detail constantly at a rehearsal is time-consuming and annoying, and eventually the performers will not attempt to respond to requests until they have heard the direction at least several times.

11. Try to rehearse as much as possible at regular tempo. At times there are advantages in performing certain passages or phrases at a slower tempo, but the group that is given a steady diet of slow tempi will expect these and not be able to rehearse well at a regular tempo. You will do your musicians a favor in the long run by expecting them to work almost at tempo most the time. When this is done, the conductor can best respond to the music heard and can be of most assistance to the group.

12. Choral conductors should aim to free their groups from the accompanying instrument as much as possible. Too many choirs use the piano or organ as a crutch in finding the pitch rather than as an accompaniment. During every rehearsal, each vocal organization should sight-read something without the use of an accompaniment prior to adding it. The accompaniment should come after the pitches have been heard and the phrasing has been secured. Then and only then will the vocal groups feel so free from the accompaniment that independence will result. When a reading or pitch problem occurs, try rehearsing without the accompaniment. After a while the choir will relish the challenge of solving their own problems without the hammering of the piano.

13. Avoid singing rhythms to your group from the podium. By pushing for a performance, we sink into the habit of rote teaching. This kind of teaching is necessary for the child in first grade as he builds a musical vocabulary. It should not occur at the adult level, even with the amateur group. If your group needs this kind of assistance, plan on being a teacher for part of the rehearsal and work with persons who have a problem. Usually they are most receptive and appreciative.

14. Amateur conductors often ask for a repeat of a passage without advising the performers why the repeat is requested and what they can do to make the passage more in keeping with his expectations. With school performers it sometimes is not enough to stop the group, explain a point to a tuba section, and then go back to a certain rehearsal number. True, in going back you are repeating so that the tuba section may correct their problem, but unless you have stated the reason, this often is not clear to the tuba section or to the entire group. Individuals of a choir section may get into the habit of thinking that they are not to blame and that they can continue in performing as before. A statement such as "Most of the sopranos had a problem in this measure" will tend to alert more of the group than a general statement.

One item cannot be overstressed. The conductor should come to the rehearsal well-prepared to conduct it. Scores should have been studied, and new music should not be sight-read by the conductor. Study the score beforehand and mark the score where you anticipate problems. Make a list of these problem spots and rehearse some of the material when you come to them before any extensive work is done on the number. Many times first impressions are lasting, and if sections are learned well in the beginning, they will remain well performed. If the problems are confronted early, the performers are more apt to remember your approach to them.

Spot rehearsing should be planned to make logical and musical sense, with little concern for performance order. For example, a conductor may begin with a passage in the basses near the end of the number that had proved troublesome at the preceding rehearsal. It might be necessary to spend several minutes on this passage, insisting that the performers consider the rhythm, the enunciation, the intonation, and the phrasing. The next spot for a rehearsal might be near the beginning of the composition where the entire

choir is performing a very loud passage. The conductor may choose these to offer contrast to the rehearsal, to offer contrast to the sections of the choir, to offer contrast in problems, and to offer contrast in loudness of performance for the rehearsal. The fact that they are not immediately adjoining in the music should be no consideration. The same kind of example could be given for the instrumental conductor. Later in the rehearsal the conductor may wish to conduct through these passages to hear how his rehearsing benefited and to show the performers how the music and the demands fit together.

Most amateur conductors eagerly anticipate the opportunity to attend a rehearsal by a well-known clinician-conductor. The observation soon grows wearisome, however, for one discovers that a well-known conductor has similar problems as those of any conductor and approaches them with no magic techniques or words. Rehearsals often do not give the clue to the success of a person that some amateurs think that it should, since the rehearsal is a matter-of-fact, hardworking situation. Professional conductors often are faced with problems similar to the amateur's, the difference being in degree. In his writings,[1] Richard Wagner listed several items that he thought were not properly executed by most conductors of his day.

1. *Incorrect choice of tempo.*

   Many compositions have no metronomic markings, and yet the young conductor should not hesitate to set a tempo based on his interpretive skills and the clues in the music. Too many public school conductors rely upon clinic sessions by college groups to assist them with tempo and/or interpretation of their concert and contest material. Nothing could be worse, since it eliminates creative thinking.

2. *Too-rigid adherence to choice of tempo once chosen.*

   This immediately brings to mind those conductors whose technique is so limited that some deviation seems a real effort for them. A too-strict interpretation also is evident in the school contest situation where the conductor knowing that he will be judged meticulously, is so very fearful of deviations which do not appear in the printed score that he sublimates what feelings he might have regarding the music. Many a school conductor has overdisciplined his group for the festivals so that a metronomic alteration is adhered to so mechanically as to be unfitting for the music and the caliber of student that he conducts.

On a similar point, for fear of being criticized by a judge, many conductors have taken too literally the exact location of a ritard or accelerando marking when they should have listened to the music and permitted the musical phrase to guide them with the change of tempo. If they had, they may have conducted a slightly different tempo on the day of the contest than the day before in rehearsal. We should never become so technical or so unmusical that we are overdisciplined by the score.

3. *Beating a solid four in the bar where alla breve was indicated.*

I have not seen this problem from any amateur conductor. But I have seen conductors fail to subdivide or abbreviate the conducting pattern because the score they were conducting did not call for it specifically. Failure to do so will give an amateurish and incorrect feel to the music. For a better discussion of this point see Chapter 18.

4. *Failure to establish where the melody lies in a given portion of the music.*

Many a composition has an obvious melody, and in numbers such as these almost all conductors will permit the melodic section to be heard. What Wagner meant I am sure was the less obvious places in a musical selection where no real tune as such is evident to guide us, but a musical phrase is important because it comes from the main theme or is a fragment of a rhythm that has taken on thematic significance. These are not always in obvious voices, and the conductor must seek to find what is important at all times, explain the structure of the music to his group so that they will understand what is expected of them musically, and, it is hoped, make it become obvious to the listener.

5. *No true piano or true forte.*

Most choirs can find these two volume ranges more quickly than most bands. The orchestra is usually at a midpoint between these two and has the added advantage of having most music written in such a way that it aids in the dynamics. The band and the band director probably errs more on this point because he knows that with the amateur player a piano with good tone is difficult. A conductor who works on these points will find that even the amateur group will respond with increasing finesse.

6. *Lack of control, resulting in uncalled-for accents and uneven lines.*

The conductor should be aware that his style of conducting can have much to do with this. Some conducting continually offers a wrong psychological accent to the performers to which they respond on a particular beat or place in the pattern. If this is the case, the conductor has only himself to blame for this lack of legato.

7. *Failing to put life and soul in the music.*

In this statement Wagner is criticizing the conductor who just conducts without trying to interpret the music as he feels and understands it. The right arm is in motion, but no difference exists in the style of the music, the size of pattern, or in other techniques; the left hand is only a beater of time or an imitator of the right. Music can only be meaningful when the conductor has a good technique at his disposal and is willing to study the score and use his technique completely.

We in music have a habit of looking up to the conductor who has a professional group and who might be conducting in a large town with many musical advantages. This does not mean, though, that he is a better conductor. Many of our professional people, such as doctors and teachers, are considered by many of us in smaller towns to be as competent as many a specialist in a large community. Strive to be as competent as possible, willing to assist those with whom you work since those who are working with you deserve your best and since you may be the only conductor they may ever know personally.

22

Final Words

After all the words, after all the exercises and the conducting in and out of class, there is still much to do. It takes many years to become a good conductor, but do not despair. If you have diligently applied yourself to the exercises and the suggestions in this text, you have made a good beginning and probably have come a long way.

This text assumed that you had almost no background in conducting. Had you conducted before, it could have been some assistance if you did not rely too heavily upon that experience. The text was conceived to work from the very simple to the more difficult. The order of development was that which had proved beneficial to many students studying before you. In fact, it was students who helped develop the order and the exercises.

Each semester at the completion of our conducting course, I advised students that they had made only a beginning. Now what they needed most of all was to go out from the classroom and conduct. You need the same advice.

Some of you will be taking positions in the public schools and will be conducting regularly. Even if you

are working in the elementary classrooms with very young children, much that you have learned is appropriate. Even the young child should see good conducting, just as he hears good grammar or learns a good vocabulary at a simple level. You can make a most important impression and at the same time practice your own skills.

If you are entering the instrumental field, you need not stop developing your skills. Discuss your conducting with other directors in nearby communities. Do not hesitate to ask them to observe you from the position of the audience and the ensemble and make comments. This can be helpful. A school closed-circuit video recorder can be invaluable in helping you with your own development.

Probably most helpful would be an additional course in conducting at an advanced level. However, at least a year's experience in conducting is advised before such a course is taken. Then it will be of much more value to you.

If you are interested in becoming a good conductor, obtain as much conducting experience as possible. In addition to regular employment, I suggest a church

294

choir, since this ensemble must perform publicly at least once a week. If you conduct a church choir, assume that it always should have your very best conducting procedures. Apparently many of us decide that the amateur need not observe us at our best. Poor conducting habits result. It is not common practice, but do not hesitate to use a baton at least part of the time. The singers will benefit, and you will develop an important part of your technique.

Over the next few years, take every opportunity to observe at first hand some professional conductors. When visiting in a large city where a symphony orchestra performs regularly, or when a touring group may come to your city or a neighboring one, enjoy not only the finesse of a professional group but also observe carefully how the professional conductor works. Do not assume everything that he does is advisable or to be emulated. Most likely he will have some bad habits just as the amateur does. He may do some things poorly in the performance that you observe. Be critical of what you see in light of what you know.

There are many small points that I could not write in this book, since no book can be large enough to cover all the personal needs of each student conductor. A few final items come to mind.

1. Perform with as many organizations during college days and afterward as possible. You will learn much by performing. By participating in different kinds of groups, you gain an understanding for the problems of the ensemble. A good conductor understands the media so that he can be aware of the problems of the performers. If you cannot conduct, then sing or play.

2. Do not hesitate to take additional courses in music literature. This may not have been your strongest class in college. Many young people do not appreciate the value of music literature study while in college. If this is not possible while on the job, try to study music literature yourself in small ways. When studying a score, refer regularly to source books that give background and better understanding to a work. One invaluable text is the unabridged *Harvard Dictionary of Music* by Willi Apel.

3. Have much patience. You do not prove much on the podium by becoming angry or failing to understand that most amateurs are trying to do their best for you. If things are not as you wish them, be sure to question your own techniques of conducting and your explanations.

4. Enjoy conducting. If you do not, this will be evident to almost everyone you work with. If you like conducting, young people will enjoy the hard work that you are asking them to do.

5. Keep your sense of humor near the surface most of the time, but do not be a jokester. If the rehearsal erupts into a humorous situation, even if the joke might be at your expense, do not hesitate to laugh with the group.

6. Consider your organizational ability. Think over the problems that may have come from your lack of organization. A good conductor of amateurs must be more than a prima donna of the baton. A conductor usually takes care of literally hundreds of details that hover around conducting responsibilities. Directors who are successful usually have an organizational sense. Other things must also be present, but without this, not much will happen well. You can improve in this area, and all conductors should make every effort to do so.

7. Be confident in your ability. Do not be cocky, but know what you know; seek to learn conducting better, but be confident that you have a technique that will assist you with the music that you have to conduct. Many times the difference between an amateur conductor and an experienced one is the area of confidence. The seasoned conductor will step on the podium, raise his arms, give a downbeat, and things happen. The inexperienced conductor should have the same confidence in his technique, and he will find that much goes smoother.

8. Try to improve your auditory imagery. This text has offered helps for you. You need additional development here if you are an average music student. To aid in this, study your scores, always trying to hear how your group will sound performing this number.

In one of my classes I give the students large collections of musical works to be evaluated. Their assignment is to look through the selections and without the aid of any accompaniment, choose those items that would be good music for high school ensembles and those that would not be of value. When students ask to use the piano to "hear" the numbers, I refuse because I wish to assist them develop their auditory imagery. You must begin sometime. If you always rely on the piano or some instrument, no development will even begin.

9. Appear positive on the podium during a rehearsal and especially before a concert. During more than 30 years of conducting I have never had a personal concert mishap, never had one student leave the concert because of nervous tension, heat exhaustion, or other reasons. Rarely even have students even stated that they were nervous. I credit this to the fact that I have always appeared sure of myself, even though I sometimes was not, and I appeared reserved and calm. A conductor who flurries at every little detail before a concert or performance only adds his inner feelings to those of the performer. Remember, uneasiness equals problems.

10. In a rehearsal do not tap the stand to hold your group together in rhythm or in this manner request them to slow or speed toward a different tempo. The physical rhythmic energy they develop must be their own and cannot be something that the conductor superimposes onto them aurally. Your conducting rather than tapping should indicate the rhythmic flow of the composition.

11. Do not talk too much on the podium. You probably have much work to do with the group, and you cannot do it with much talking.
Remember: If you have a good technique, you will need to talk less. When students are playing or singing, they are probably doing what the group is intended to do.

12. Get in a habit of thanking performers for the rehearsal and for the performance. Even in a school situation this is a good idea. If you are working with adult amateurs, this is most important.

13. Do not overpraise when it is not warranted. It sounds too fake. If the concert did not come up to what you had thought possible from the rehearsal, do not praise the group on those items. There must be many things that could be said that would still be an honest evaluation without getting involved in artificial situations.

14. Do not get so carried away with the emotions of the music that you forget your technical training. This happens to many an amateur. Sometimes it is not the emotions of the music so much as the emotions of the particular concert, so that the conductor becomes nervous or loses musical perspective. When this happens, it means that you have not studied the score well enough to ingrain its musical intent into your consciousness.

15. Do not rigidly follow the rules. Remember that what we have stated here in the text was meant to be a guide until you have developed a personal style that will cover your conducting needs. The most important thing is the music itself. You must conduct the music not by a rule that is an average of many situations.

Finally, after you have conducted about a year, go back through the book and reread it. You will be surprised how many of the items seem new to you, how many seem to hit the point of problems that have confronted you during the last year. Many of the items that you will find in the text are the result of experience with amateurs. One cannot hope to absorb all of them on one reading. What you do in conducting the first year will imprint their value upon your mind, and you will find much material as fresh as the first time.

Appendixes

APPENDIX I: MUSICAL TERMS

The music terms listed below should be known to any amateur conductor. This is not an all-inclusive list, but rather a minimal grouping.

a cappella (aw-ka-pel′-a) without accompaniment
accelerando (a-chel-er-awn′-doe) becoming faster
accent (ak′-sent) stress
adagio (a-dawj′-ee-o) slow; faster than largo
a deux (a-dyu′) for two; both
agitato (a-dji-taw′-to) excited
alla breve (awl-a-brev′) quick duple time; (¢)
allargando (al-lar-gone′-doe) slowing and louder
alla marcia (awl-a-mar′-sha) style of a march
allegretto (ala-gret′-o) slower than allegro
allegro (al-a′-gro) quick tempo
andante (on-dawn′-ta) moderate tempo
andantino (on-don-teen′-o) slightly quicker than andante
animato (on-ee-maw′-to) lively
arco (ar′-ko) bowed
arioso (ar-ee-o′-so) in style between aria and recitative
arpa (ar′-pa) harp

assai (a-sigh′) very
a tempo (aw-tem′-po) return to original tempo
a tempo primo (aw-tem-po-pree′-mo) return to first tempo
attacca (aw-taw′-ka) attached; without pause
basso continuo (baw-so-kon-tin′-u-o) thorough bass
basso ripieno (baw-so-rip-ee-a′-no) tutti group
bis (beez) should be repeated
b moll (bee-mowl)Bb minor
bouche (boo′-sh) stopped horn
bratsche (braw′-she) viola
brio (bree′-o) vigor
caesura (kay-soo′-ra) sign indicating a break in the music
caisse (kay′-sa) drum
campana (kam-pan′-a) bell
calando (kal-on′-do) softer and slower
cantabile (kon-tawb′-illy) singing style

297

cassa (kaw'-sa) drum
chiuso (chew'-so) stopped; for horn
clarone (kl-air-one') bass clarinet
col legno (kol-egg'-no) wood of bow on strings
con (kawn) with
concertino (kawn-sir-teen'-o) soloist group
corno (kor'-no) horn
corno Inglese (kor-no-ing-lay') English horn
coulisse (koo-lees') slide of trombone
crescendo (kray-shen'-do) increasing volume
cuivre (kwee'-vra) brassy horn sound
dampfer (dawm'-fer) mute
D.C. (Dee'-see') repeat from beginning; Da Capo (daw-kap-o)
descrescendo (day-kre-shen'-do) decreasing in volume
diminuendo (dim-in-you-end'-o) decreasing in volume
divisi (di-vee'-see) divides into two groups
dolce (dole'-chay) sweet and soft
doppio (dawp'-ee-o) double (example, double flat or double the speed)
double stop (dub'-ble-stawp') two or more simultaneous pitches on string instruments
down-bow (dow'-n-bo) bow pulled to the right
D.S. (dee'-ess') repeat from a sign; dal segno (dal-seg-no)
due (doo') same tone on two strings for greater volume
dur (doo'-er) German term for major
durezza (doo-ret'-za) play with hardness
eilend (eye'-lend) hurrying
fermata (fer-maw'-ta) pause; normally with a "birds eye"
fine (fee'-nay) end
forte (for'-tay) loud; f
fortissimo (for-tis'-ee-mo) very loud; ff
forzando (fort-zawn'-do) forced; fz
frog (frawg') end of bow nearest hand
fuoco (few-o'-ko) with fire; with spirit
gedampft (gee-dawm'-pft) muted
geige (gi'-ga) violin
gestopft (gee-stawpft') stopped; for horn
giocoso (gee-o-ko'-so) playful
glissando (glis-awn'-do) sliding scales; different from portamento
G.P. (gee'-pee') general pause; not grand pause.
grave (graw'-vee) slow and solemn
grazioso (grawt-zee-o'-so) graceful
groppo (gro'-po) trill
gruppo (grew'-po) trill
gruppetto (grew-pet'-o) trill

giusto (jew-ee'-sto) exact; strict rhythm
hastig (haw'-steeg) hasty
hautbois (hote'-bwaw) oboe
incalzando (in-cal-zawn'-do) pressing forward
langsam (long'-some) slow
largando (lar-gan'-do) slowing and louder
largemente (lar-ga-men'-tay) with breadth
larghetto (lar-get'-o) less slow than largo
largo (lar'-go) very slow
lebhaft (leb'-haw-ft) lively
legato (leg-aw'-to) smooth
leggiero (lay-zhair'-o) non-legato and light
leise (lice') soft
lento (len'-to) slow
l'istesso tempo (lis-tess'-o-tem'-po) same tempo
loco (lo'-ko) in this place or pitch; not an octave higher or lower
lunga (loo'-ga) long
maestoso (mi-sto'-so) majestic, stately
mancante (man-kawn'-tay) dying away
ma non troppo (ma-non-tro'-po) but not too much
marcato (mar-kaw'-to) marked; emphasized
massig (maw'-seeg) moderate
meno (may'-no) less
meno mosso (may-no-mo'-so) less quickly
mezzo (met'-zo) half
moderato (mawd-er-aw'-to) moderate speed
moll (mole') minor in German
molto (mole'-to) very
mordent (more'-dent) ornament; the note, note below, and the note
morendo (mor-en'-do) dying away
moto (mo'-to) motion
muta (mew'-ta) change of tuning; especially timpani or horns
non troppo (non-tro'-po) not too much
nut (nut) end of bow nearest hand
ossia (o-see'-a) alternative version
otez (o'-tay) take off
pauke (pow'-ka) drum; usually timpani
perdendo (per-den'-do) gradually dying away
pesante (pay-zahn'-tay) heavy
piano (pe-on'-o) soft; p
pianissimo (pe-on-is'-ee-mo) very soft; pp
pieno (pee-aye'-no) full
piston (pis'-ton) valves
piu (pee-oo'-ee) more
piu mosso (pee-oo'-ee-mo'-so) more quickly
pizzicato (pit-ze-kaw'-to) string plucked with finger
poco (po'-ko) little
poi (poy') afterwards; afterwards the coda

point (poy'-nt) upper end of violin bow
portamento (por-ta-men'-to) moving from one
    pitch to another with all intermedi-
    ate sounds included
portato (por-taw'-to) semi-staccato
posaune (po-sawn'-a) trombone
prestissimo (pres-tee'-see-mo) quickest of speeds
presto (press'-to) very quick
rallentando (rawl-en-tawn'-do) gradually slower
rattenando (raw-ten-awn'-do) hold back
ripieno (rip-ee-ay'-no) full orchestra
ritardando (rit-tar-dawn'-do) gradually slower
ritenuto (rit-en-oo'-to) immediately slower
rubato (rew-bah'-to) to rob; flexibility of tempo
scherzando (scaret-zawn'-do) playful
schnell (shn-ell') quick
scordatura (skor-da-tew'-ra) abnormal tuning of
    string instruments
secco (say'-ko) dry; a type of tone quality
segue (sayg'-way) immediately; page turn or
    section
sehr (say'-er) very
sempre (sem'-pray) always or continuous
senza (sen'-za) without
senza ripieno (sen'-za-rip-ee-ay'-no) soloists only
    or concertino
sforzando (sfort-zawn'-do) strong accent; sf
smorzando (smort-zawn'-do) dying away
sons bouche (sones-boo-shay') hand sounds,
    stopped notes

sordino (sore-dee'-no) mute
sostenuto (sauce-ten-oo'-to) sustained and some-
    times slowing the tempo
sotto (saw'-to) half or subdued tone
sourdine (sore-deen') mute
spiritoso (spear-ee-to'-so) spirited
stretto (stre'-to) concluding section of compo-
    sition usually at a quicker tempo
stringendo (strin-gen'-do) quickening; acceler-
    ando
subito (soo'-bee-to) suddenly
sul (sul') on; play on a particular string
tacet (ta'set) silent; no part
talon (ta'-lon) nut of bow
tanto (tawn'-to) much; non tanto: not too much
tenuto (ten-yew'-to) held; sustained
timpani (tim'-pan-ee) kettledrums
tremolo (trem'-o-lo) quick repeat of same pitch
tromba (trom'-ba) trumpet
troppo (tro'-po) too much
tutta (too'-ta) all
tutti (too'-tee) all
tutto (too'-to) all
upbeat (up' beet) note or notes before first
    measure line
up-bow (up'-bo) bow pushed to left
vibrato (vi-braw'-to) slight deviation of pitch
vivace (vee-vaw'-chee) lively
vivo (vee'-vo) fast
volante (vo-lawn'-tee) swiftly

APPENDIX 2: PERCUSSION TERMINOLOGY

Following is a list of percussion instruments found in musical scores. Many scores have an instrument list that is easily understood except for the names of percussion needed. It is advisable to have such a list of percussion available as below so that requirements may be checked. Notice that many of these names are for the same instrument, but different scores use different names for the same common instrument.

anvil small steel bars, struck with hard mallets
bacchetta drum stick
bacchetti di spugna drum stick with soft head
baguette drum stick .
bass drum Large drum of various sizes, no snares,
    played with soft headed stick
becken cymbals
caisse drum
campana bell
campanetta orchestra bells
carillon orchestra bells
cassa drum

castanets clappers, in the shape of a shell, made
    of wood
celeste steel bar keyboard instrument played
    with hammers, plays one octave above
    written pitch
chimes set of chromatic metal tubes; struck by
    hand held hammer
cinelli cymbals
claquebois xylophone
cowbells bell shaped in metal played with snare
    drum stick
crecelle rattle

crotales   castanets

cymbals   large metal discs played by hitting together, with snare stick or soft timpani
stick

echelette   xylophone

gigelira   xylophone

glockenspiel   orchestra bells; in the band these
are arranged for carrying on a lyre
shaped frame; sometimes called
bell lyra

glocke   bell

gong   large metal disk, played with soft mallet
in hanging position

gran cassa   bass drum

gran tabura   bass drum

grosse caisse   bass drum

grosse trommel   bass drum

guiro   gourd scraped with stick

jeu de timbres   orchestra bells

kleine trommel   snare drum

knarre   rattle

maracas   gourd filled with dry seeds

marimba   wooden bar keyboard with metal tube
resonators played with 2, 3, or 4
mallets

orchestra bells   rectangular steel plates arranged
in the manner of a piano key-
board. Played with mallets.
Sounds two octaves above where
it is written.

pauke   timpani

piatti   cymbals

petite caisse   snare drum

ratsche   rattle

rattle   wooden cog wheel revolved against a
wooden slat

scampanio   chimes

schnarre   rattle

schnarrtrommel   snare drum

tabor   tambourine

tabourin   tambourine

tambour   drum

tamburo   drum

tamburo militare   snare drum

tamburo grosse   bass drum

tampon   two headed drumstick for roll on bass
drum

tam tam   gong

tenor drum   a little larger than a snare drum;
played in the same manner

thunder machine   large drum with balls inside
to simulate thunder

timbale   kettle drum

tom tom   drum with no snares and special hol-
low quality

triangle   bar of steel bent in shape of triangle;
played with metal pin

trommel   drum

xylophone   wooden bar keyboard type instrument; played with mallets. Sounds
at actual pitch

APPENDIX 3: NOTE STYLES

Not many music teachers and students of conducting make discernable differences in the length of notes as they discuss their desirable interpretation with those they are conducting. Part of the problem in explanation and discussion from the podium is in the fact that the amateur conductor and the amateur performer are not acquainted with the following four terms. The words legato and staccato are common enough. The two between, which help indicate an obvious and real difference, are seldom used and taught.

Learn these differences and teach them to your students.

Legato

FIGURE A-3a

No perceptible break between notes; slur bowing

Leggiero

FIGURE A-3b

Regular smooth tonguing or detache bowing

Portato

FIGURE A-3c

Semistaccato; semidetached—not short; loure bowing

Staccato

FIGURE A-3d

Staccato; detached, not necessarily short; detache, sautille, or martele depending upon tempo of notes.

If the conductor will have clearly in mind exactly the differences in sound that these four degrees may mean, he will have much less difficulty in discussing his desires with those who are performing. The fact that we have named what we hear will not of itself eliminate the problems, but sharing the concept of the conductor with his performers will lead to an understanding of agreement and obtaining of accurate response.

APPENDIX 4: INSTRUMENTAL TERMINOLOGY

Sooner or later the amateur conductor will be faced with the reading of a score that makes use of foreign terms for some or all instruments. These terms may be found in orchestral scores and in foreign publications of band scores. At one time the directions in music for performer and conductor were written entirely in Italian. More recently scores have tended to make more use of musical or general terms from the language of the composer. If this tendency grows, the performer and conductor will need to become familiar with a larger body of foreign terms and instrumental names.

Listed below are the common terms for musical instruments that one may find on a standard or contemporary score. Some of these will become obvious through use while others will only be used occasionally.

English	*French*	*German*	*Italian*
piccolo	petite flute	Kleine flote	flauto piccolo
flute	flute	Flote	flauto
oboe	hautbois	Oboe	oboe
English horn	cor anglais	Englisch Horn	corno enghlese
clarinet	clarinette	Klarinette	clarinetto
saxophone	saxophone	Saxophone	saxophone
bassoon	basson	Fagott	fagotto
trumpet	trompette	Trompete	tromba
cornet	cornet à pistons	Kornett	cornetta
French horn	cor-à-pistons	Ventilhorn	corno ventile
trombone	trombone	Posaune	tromboni
baritone	bugle tenor	Tenor Horn	flicorno tenore
euphonium	basse à pistons	Baryton	eufonio
tuba	tuba	Basstuba	tuba
kettle drums	timbales	Pauken	timpani
snare drum	petite caisse	Kleine Trommel	tamburo militaire
bass drum	grosse caisse	grosse Trommel	gran cassa
violin	violin	Geige or Violine	violino
viola	alto	Bratsche	viola
cello	celle	Violoncello	violoncello
bass viol	contrebass	Kontrabass	contrabasso
harp	harpe	Harfe	arpa

APPENDIX 5: BOWINGS

String players make use of a large number of different bowings. However, for the amateur conductor a few of these should be sufficient. He should be familiar with their names, how they are played, and how to instruct his group in the proper execution of them. The group and conductor that can meet on a common ground of understanding of bowings will find the music more intelligible to all.

1. **Common bowings**

    a. **Down-bow**   symbol: ⊓ — bow moving from frog toward the tip or away from the body. Most musical compositions that do not begin on a pick-up will begin with a down-bow. Special accented notes often receive a down-bow, and several especially accented notes consecutively placed are played with consecutive down-bows. Most down-bows are considered to have a bit more weight or a bit more accent and are usually assigned to the antecedent portion of a musical phrase or the beginnings of the antecedent phrase.

    b. **Up-bow**   symbol: V — bow moving from tip to frog or in toward the body. Most musical compositions that do not begin on the first beat of the measure will be played with an up-bow. Special phrases that lead directly to important accented notes will be played with the up-bow so that the down-bow will come naturally in correct places. Up-bows will be used for most unaccented or unobstrusive notes, many times for several notes in succession. Notes preceding a pizzicato will be played up-bow so that the fingers will be near the strings. Most consequence portions of a phrase will be played up bow.

    c. **Slur**   The grouping of several notes on a single bow usually indicated by a curved line over the notes. Careful markings for string players by this symbol will keep all members of a section or of the entire string family bowing together. It is assumed by string players that if no slurring line is present, the notes are played one to the bow. A conductor will carefully mark all parts before the first rehearsal so that bowings will be accurate and correct from the initial run-through.

2. **Detache**   symbol: No markings — here the bow takes each note singularly or a separate bow for each note. The bow is moved quickly from one end of the bow to the other, and there is a slight pause between each note while the arm and wrist change motion. This gives a slight emphasis to the notes. This is not a difficult bowing for the amateur and is needed in music performed by the amateur conductor from time to time.

3. **Sautille**   symbol: . . . . . — This stroke should be taught by more conductors of amateur groups. Although not simple to execute, yet it is not so difficult that young students of three or four years experience cannot be expected to perform it. This is an essential bowing for accompanying figures and for clean performance of the staccato figure at some speed. In this bowing the bow is lightly tossed at the strings so that it bounces as it is pulled either to the right or left. It is almost always played in the center of the bow and can be executed either softly or loudly, although it is more often required at a modest to soft volume. It often is called by its Italian name of spiccato.

4. **Loure**   symbol: ‗‗‗ — In this bowing the notes of a group are played on one bow, and yet the bow is stopped between each note so that they have a certain separateness. This bowing is especially useful during accompanying figures and at modest to soft volumes. It is possible to give each of the notes of the grouping a separate volume so that a different grouping by volume can be made for notes of the same rhythm and pitch. It is simple but effective bowing.

5. **Martele**   symbol: ▼▼▼▼ — Despite the symbol this bowing is often used by the amateur for staccato notes. Here the bow is used in short strokes with strong pulls in opposite directions and usually at the tip. Since it cannot be executed at a great speed, it does suffice for slower staccato notes and has the added advantage of carrying enough weight in each stroke to have sufficient volume for many passages.

6. **Tremolo**   symbol: ♯ ♯ — This symbol should not be confused with the often-used abbreviations for repeated notes in rhythm. A similar symbol ♯ ♯ is often used in string parts to indicate that quarter notes should be played as sixteenths and sometimes to be played as eighths ♩ ♩ . In the tremolo three lines are placed through the stem indicating that only a very fast undulation of the bow should be used on the same pitch. This is a very popular string effect and can be easily executed by the amateur.

7. **Col legno**   There is no symbol for this bowing, but the words are placed in the music over the notes. The Italian words mean with the wood, and the player turns the bow over and plays with the wood on the strings. This is a special effect but in more demand in recent and special effect literature.

   String instruments may be requested to perform several special effects. The amateur conductor may need to use a musical dictionary to assist his performers in their meaning or a description of their execution.

APPENDIX 6: TEMPO INDICATIONS

Most musical compositions use terminology to give the performer and conductor some concepts of the tempo desired. Only a few of the compositions rely upon a definite statement as indicated by the metronome. In books on music and sometimes on the metronome itself you will find a chart that will aid you in taking the terminology and relating it to metronome indications. Usually these are in a range, since the terminology means slightly different things to different persons, and because one composition marked Allegro, for example, might be somewhat faster or slower than a second composition marked the same.

   For the most part I have found that charts in other sources have been too fast for any but the most professional musicians, and if one were to listen carefully to some of the world's finest conductors, he would find that they did not follow these indications either. Below you will find my suggestions for the tempo indication terminology.

Largo	40–58
Larghetto	50–64
Lento	60–72
Adagio	68–78
Andante	72–88
Andantino	84–92
Moderato	80–96
Allegretto	92–112
Allegro	100–128
Vivace	120–138
Presto	132–150
Prestissimo	148–160

APPENDIX 7: PITCH NAMES

All of us in music are quite familiar with the letter names of notes. Much less familiar is the exact letter name for the notes of the musical scale. Students are quick to make use of these correct names if the teacher will use this name regularly with them. How much more convenient this would be for all concerned, especially during rehearsals, if the conductor would refer to pitch names by the correct octave terminology, rather than try to explain his statement by using such descriptive terms as "high or low or middle." Amateur conductors are too prone to such questions as: "Trumpets, which part has the g in the last measure before rehearsal B?" To which the students will very often reply: "Which g do you mean?" The teacher will respond: "I mean the low g in the chord, which is your middle g on your horn."

Several systems of pitch names have been used over the past number of years. The following is quite simple and easy to use:

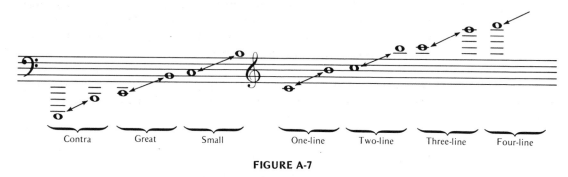

FIGURE A-7

Any pitch within the ranges of the above sevenths will take the name of the interval. For example: in the g clef a flatted note on the second space will be called "a-flat one." It would be correctly written: a^{b1}. A note on the bottom line of the f clef would be called "great G." It would be written as a capital letter "G." All other pitches would be similarly called and named.

Indexes

Composer and Music
Index

The abbreviation "arr." indicates arranger.

Subject Index

A cappella, 291
Accelerando, 36, 71, 81, 262, 293
Accents, 18, 46, 80, 249–251, 293
  on the half beat, 251
    conducting unnecessary, 251
  increase intensity with, 249
  larger rebound, 249
  to the left, 249–250
  left-hand, 66–67, 249–251
    on the half beat, 251
    large emphasis, 251
    to the right, 250
    for a section, 251
    on the upbeat, 251
  with rebounds, 46
  right-hand, 249
  and strings, 149
  uncalled for, 293
Accompaniment during
  rehearsal, 291
Accompanying, 3, 79, 291
Acoustics, 290
  of band, 7
  materials for, 290
  for rehearsal, 7
  of rehearsal room, 290
  of wind ensemble, 7

Aesthetic aspects, 288, 291
Afterbeat, preparatory for, 238,
  241
  (*See also* Half beat)
Allargando, 36, 106
Amateur performer, 4
Anacrusis, 42
"And beat" (*see* After beat; Half
  beat)
Apel, W., 287
Appearance, 5
Arm motions, 12, 14, 17–21, 26,
  28, 30
  fatigue during, 14, 26
  forearm rebound, 17–21
  and preparatory, 42
  (*See also* Cuing; Left hand;
    Patterns; Releases)
Attacks:
  delayed, 40
  florid, 40
  poor, 40
  (*See also* Preparatory)
Auditory imagery, 291, 295
Augmentation, 254–257
  to assist with clarity, 255
  to assist with ritard, 254

Augmentation:
  to assist with slow tempo, 254–
    255
  for four, 255
  signature guides, 254
  for three, 255
  for two, 255

Bach, J. S., 1, 2
Balance, 78, 80
Band, 161, 178
  assignment of parts, 178
    brass, 178
    woodwinds, 161
Baritones, 173, 178
  in f clef, 173, 178
  in g clef, 173, 178
Bass viol, 145
Bassoons, 156, 161, 163
Baton, 2, 5, 11–16, 28, 40, 234,
  290, 295
  without baton, 39, 40, 43, 230
  with church choirs, 295
  drills, 13–14
  early use, 2
  extension of arm, 12

311